Education and Immigration

Immigration and Society series

Grace Kao, Elizabeth Vaquera, and Kimberly Goyette, *Education and Immigration*

Thomas Faist, Margit Fauser, and Eveline Reisenauer, *Transnational Migration*

Christian Joppke, *Citizenship and Immigration*

Ronald L. Mize and Grace Peña Delgado, *Latino Immigrants in the United States*

Philip Q. Yang, *Asian Immigration to the United States*

Education and Immigration

Grace Kao, Elizabeth Vaquera, and Kimberly Goyette

polity

First published in 2013 by Polity Press

Polity Press
65 Bridge Street
Cambridge CB2 1UR, UK

Polity Press
350 Main Street
Malden, MA 02148, USA

ISBN-13: 978-0-7456-4831-6
ISBN-13: 978-0-7456-4832-3(pb)

A catalogue record for this book is available from the British Library.

Typeset in 11 on 13 pt Sabon
by Servis Filmsetting Ltd, Stockport, Cheshire
Printed and bound in Great Britain by the MPG Books Group

For further information on Polity, visit our website: www.politybooks.com

Contents

1   Education and the American Dream   1

2   Becoming American (or Not): Paths to Assimilation   25

3   Historical Overview of Immigration   51

4   Educational Attainment and Socioeconomic Status of Immigrant Adults   76

5   Educational Achievement and Outcomes of Children in Immigrant Families   106

6   Language and Educational Success   140

7   Conclusion   170

References   189
Index   210

To our husbands, Jeff, Steve, and Michael, for their
love and support

and

To our families for their sacrifices that made it possible for each
of us to experience our own immigrant families

1

Education and the American Dream

Picture the following family:
It is 1989; Juanjo is a 14-year-old boy. He is the son of a Mayan family from Guatemala, who fled the country trying to escape the civil war. They first moved to Mexico, but due to the lack of economic opportunities, they continued their migration north. The family recently arrived to the US, and upon their arrival, they applied for asylum, but the US denies their petition. They cannot return to their home country, so Juanjo's parents decide to stay in the US – undocumented. After they contact an acquaintance who migrated to the US a few years earlier, they are able to find an affordable apartment in a poor neighborhood in the town of Jupiter, Florida. First because of the war in Guatemala and then because of the constant moving, Juanjo has not attended school regularly since he was nine. He is now in the US and about to start classes in his local school half-way through the school year. Neither he nor his parents speak English.

Now imagine this other family:
In the year 2000, Hyunsuk's parents leave South Korea and establish their residence in Torrance, California. They migrate to the US because her father, who has a degree in management and finance, was offered an upper management position. They buy a house in an upper-middle-class suburban neighborhood, afforded by her father's high-paying job. Her mom also has a Bachelor's degree, but for now she will stay home taking care of her daughter, who is only two, until it is time to start primary school. Having learned English in school back in South Korea, Hyunsuk's parents can speak some English and they decide they will only speak to their daughter in English since they are now not just Korean, but Korean American.

Introduction

The United States is a country of immigrants. Immigration is a key part of why America is considered the land of opportunity. But what does it mean to be an immigrant in America? In this "land of opportunity," anyone could come to the US and expect to be treated just like anyone else. In the idealized vision of America, immigrants from all walks of life can live and flourish in a country where one's race, ethnicity, religion, or class background does not matter. A person could arrive to America without a dime in his or her pocket and without being able to speak a word of English, could "make it" after working hard because America offers freedom and equal opportunity for all.

The crux of the aspirations of the average immigrant (and arguably the average American) is motivated by the notion that one can achieve the American Dream through hard work and perseverance, and, ultimately, hard work and perseverance are rewarded by upward mobility via their children's educational achievement. For both the native-born and immigrants alike, education is seen as the best way to achieve upward socioeconomic mobility. Almost universally, parents want their children to do well in school and to go to college, so that they may one day have a "'good' job," a house, a family, and make a comfortable living. Immigrant adults may be willing to suffer as newcomers in a strange, unfamiliar land because of the belief that their (American-born or American-raised) children will learn to speak accent-less English, go to college, and obtain a secure, well-paying job (Zhou 1997).

Education – and in particular achievement and attainment – is an important way to judge how well immigrants "fit in" or assimilate into the US. Educational attainment usually refers to the number of years of schooling one receives, or the degrees one earns (such as a Bachelor's degree, Master's degree, etc.). Educational achievement refers to the grades, test scores, or other indicators that measure performance in school (such as your grade point average (GPA) or SAT score). Of course, achievement and attainment are not completely different from each other, but researchers often study these outcomes separately from one another. Arguably, there is no better single indicator of success for individuals and families than their educational attainment, or the number of years they attend school. Parents and children would no doubt view themselves or others with a Master's degree as more successful than those who dropped out of high school. However, opportunities to succeed in the US, whether in education or any other realm of life, are not the same for all individuals. Race, ethnicity, gender, national origin, and the ability to speak English fluently are important in shaping the very different lives experienced by immigrants.

Stories about immigrants in books and popular movies often portray those who arrive to the US as foreigners and aliens at first, but they eventually "learn the ropes," or assimilate, and then become "true" Americans. What does it mean to become an assimilated American? The ideal immigrant (as portrayed by Ben Franklin and Theodore Roosevelt, for example) quickly sheds his or her "foreign" ways and becomes an English-speaking American without a "hyphenated" identity – like Chinese American or Mexican American. He or she no longer identifies with his or her motherland, and later marries a native-born American and lives undetected among them. An indicator and result of successful assimilation is that an individual attains as much and as good an education as those who are not immigrants, as well as a similar type of job as another individual whose family has lived in the country over several generations.

Stories about assimilation often imply that immigrants are welcome when they become "American." However, not every immigrant has the chance to become "fully" American. Although the US presents itself as a "land of opportunity" that provides "equal chances" to everyone, a closer look through the past and present, as well as at personal and group experiences, tells a different story. Always implied, and often explicit through US immigration and citizenship laws, as well as popular attitudes towards racial, ethnic, and national-origin groups, is the reality that only individuals of certain racial, ethnic, and national origins have the potential to assimilate into (white) America. Hence, some immigrants were seen as "unassimilable" – that is, they would

3

never become wholly American. Interestingly, the category of people who do not "fit in" has evolved over time – this group has included African Americans, Irish, Italians, Poles, Jews, Chinese, Japanese, Asian Indians, Mexicans, and arguably all immigrants who are not seen as "white."

Those immigrants who do "fit in" are perceived to bring ideas and skills that allow America to thrive and become great. Indeed, many of our greatest statesmen, scientists, artists, and so forth were immigrants themselves (think of scientists such as Enrico Fermi and Albert Einstein, or inventor Alexander Graham Bell, or architects such as Ludwig Mies van der Rohe, Hideyo Noguchi, and I.M. Pei, or politicians such as Henry Kissinger, or naturalist John Muir). Because America is seen as the "land of opportunity," it attracts "the best and the brightest" from all over the world and can draw workers with specific skills that are in short supply in the US.

On the other hand, immigrants who do not "belong" or assimi-late are often portrayed as "cheap laborers" who unfairly compete with "real" (white and sometimes black) American workers. The perception is that these foreign-born workers are willing to do the same jobs for less money, which drives down wages and increases unemployment among native-born Americans. Outspoken oppo-nents of immigration argue that the foreign-born, particularly those who migrate illegally, drain the resources of our schools, hospitals, and other public services. They portray this group as not wanting to assimilate by learning English, or adopting "American" customs, which they believe further weakens the social fabric of America. These immigrants have been typically caricatured as uneducated, lazy, prone to crime, and simply inferior to (white) Americans.

In this book, we explore theories of how immigrants come to be assimilated into US society – whether the process approximates a "straight line," with immigrants becoming more culturally and socially similar to the native-born over generations, or whether the process is not straightforward, with some immigrants assimilating into the native-born middle class, while others join the ranks of the urban poor. We review theories that suggest that retaining parts of one's culture prior to immigration is helpful for some immigrants' achievement and attainment in the US. We also discuss the belief that immigrants hold advantages in educational achievement and attainment, especially over native-born minorities, because they compare themselves favorably to their peers who did not immigrate and are therefore optimistic about their chances of educational success in the US.

Throughout the book, we ask our readers to keep in mind some questions to help them assess which of the possible descriptions of immigrants' assimilation fits best. First, how does the way in which an immigrant comes to the US in the first place matter? Second, how does the reception of the group by the US matter for whether immigrants become "fully American?" Do US laws and policies shape the ability to become assimilated? Third, does it matter what types of jobs are available, where you live, and whether you have a community of co-ethnic peers if you are a recent immigrant? Does an immigrant's ability to speak English and/or the language of his or her parents affect socioeconomic outcomes? Finally, how do race, ethnicity, gender, and national origin shape all of the above? Does it matter for an immigrant's path to assimilation if he is Hispanic from Mexico, or if she is Asian from India? Throughout the book, we encourage readers to think about how race, ethnicity, and national origin of contemporary immigrants are central in thinking about their educational outcomes. Immigrants in the US not only arrive from an increasingly diverse set of countries, but also from a wide variety of racial and ethnic groups.

Throughout the book, we encourage our readers to think about both race and ethnicity as analytically, although not always practically, distinct (Hartmann and Cornell 2007). Ethnicity refers to identities that are chosen or assumed. Often, an individual can decide to adopt his or her ethnic identity. Race is typically assigned. People are placed in racial categories and judged according to that classification, whether or not they want to be. Race may be considered (we argue incorrectly) more "natural" or biologically determined or physiologically based than ethnicity, which is more often related to a place or social group from which a person came.

Racial classifications are systematically related to how power and resources in a country are distributed. Ethnicity may also be related to power and resource distributions in a society, but it is often less strongly so. In this chapter, we assert that it is important to understand the ways in which race, ethnicity, and immigrant status overlap when we think about the educational outcomes of these newcomers. In the next section we present a brief overview of the basic socio-demographic characteristics of the immigrants who currently reside in the US.

Today's Immigrant Population

Currently, over 38 million immigrants live in the United States (Gryn and Larsen 2010). This represents about 13% of the US population. Immigrants arrive to the US from all over the world, but, unlike immigrants who arrived during the 1800s and early 1900s, most of the immigrants today do not come from Europe. Among the foreign-born population in 1960, 75% had European origins (Grieco 2010). In contrast, by 2007, only 13.1% had European origins. In 1960, those from Latin America accounted for only 9.4% of the foreign-born population. By 2007, this number was 53.6%. Similarly, in 1960, only 5.1% of the foreign-born hailed from Asia; but by 2007, Asians accounted for 26.8% of the foreign-born population (Grieco 2010). Together, approximately three-quarters of the foreign-born population in 2009 came from Latin America and Asia. In 2009, Mexico alone accounted for 30% of the foreign-born population (Passel and Cohn 2009).

There is also a growing number of immigrants who come from Africa – although they still account for a minority of all immigrants in the US, adding about 4% of the foreign-born population (Grieco and Trevelyan 2010). The increase of immigration from Africa started in the 1960s with the end of European colonialism and the creation of many independent nation-states in sub-Saharan Africa. Many (mostly white) immigrants decided to migrate given the turmoil of these geopolitical changes, but migration of black Africans followed shortly thereafter. While many of these immigrants chose Europe as their destination, the numbers of those who migrated to the US started increasing during the 1980s as the European economies began to weaken. In the ten years between 1980 and 1989, 129,000 immigrants arrived from Africa to the US. In the six years between 2000 and 2005, the number of immigrants arriving from Africa to the US had increased to 353,000 (Kent 2007).

The majority of the newer immigrants (those who have arrived since 1965) are not white and their prospects for assimilation and equal outcomes in school and elsewhere remain uncertain. Further, understandings about race and ethnicity vary across different regional and national contexts, so immigrants can be somewhat surprised when they are classified by a distinctly American racial system different from one with which they are familiar. For example, individuals from Spain may be surprised to find themselves grouped together with other "Hispanics" rather than with "(white) Europeans." People from China may not expect to be grouped with "Asians" that include Cambodians or South Asians.

Immigrant Status of Youth

Because this book focuses on education, we will spend much time discussing school-aged immigrants, that is, children and youth. In the US, children in immigrant families account for almost one in four school-aged children in the US and this figure is expected to increase to two in five by 2020 (O'Hare 2004). Thus, immigrant children form a sizeable portion of the student population and are an integral part of the social fabric of the US. Their socioeconomic advancement in the country largely depends on their educational success.

Immigrants and their children are often referred to by their generational status. Throughout this book, we use the phrase *first generation* to refer to individuals who were born outside the United States and usually arrived to this country as adults. The *second generation* are individuals who were born in the US but have at least one immigrant parent. Finally, the *third and beyond generation* (which we will primarily refer to as *third generation*) are individuals who were born in the United States to native-born parents. We collapse the third and beyond generation for two reasons. First, as we focus on post-1965 immigration, there are virtually no fourth generation individuals who hail from that period. Second, their grandparents' birthplace is usually unknown from survey data with nationally representative samples. Thus, most social science studies usually cannot differentiate individuals who are third generation (native-born individuals with native-born parents but with foreign-born grandparents) from their fourth, fifth, etc. generation counterparts.

In this book, we often group children of the first and second immigrant generation using the term *children from immigrant families*. These children may themselves be US-born or foreign-born, but have immigrant parents. It is important to keep in mind that nativity, citizenship, and legal US residence are individual characteristics, and any "immigrant" family (in which, for example, the parents are foreign-born) may have children who were only born in a foreign country, only born in the US, or both US-born and native-born. These households may include those who are US citizens, legal permanent residents, or undocumented immigrants.

As you read through the chapters of the book, it is important to keep in mind that *children from immigrant families* are a very heterogeneous group. They range from children who were born and went to school in the US with well-educated, foreign-born parents who speak perfect English and may also have experienced all of their schooling in the US, to immigrant youth who arrived at age 17 with no knowledge of English and whose parents have very little education and who do not speak English.

In order to capture the importance of age of arrival for those who migrated before adulthood, Rumbaut (2004) proposed a specific terminology to differentiate among immigrant children according to their developmental stage and their age upon arrival to the US. He coined the term "decimal" generations, which, while they complicate the study of immigrants and immigration, are useful in understanding the diverse experiences of immigrants both in school and in their later integration into the labor market.

What are the "decimal generations" and what is their relationship to the educational outcomes of immigrants? The 1.25 generation typically refers to those who migrated as teenagers, that is, they spent their formative years in the country of origin. The 1.5 generation refers to those who arrived before adolescence, and who have experienced some education abroad and some in the US. Finally, the 1.75 generation is composed of those who arrived as preschoolers and will only have experienced US educational institutions. Because they arrive to the US at different ages, there is great variation among these "decimal generations" in how well they adapt to American schools and how fast they learn English. For example, a child who arrives at age 2, when he or she is just starting to learn and develop language skills, will have a very different experience from a 12-year-old who has completed a number of years of education in his or her country of origin, has had time to develop friendships in that country and has a mastery of their non-English mother tongue. Most likely the discordant experiences of the latter example are not comparable to those of the former (Orellana 2008; Suárez-Orozco et al. 2008). For that reason, researchers are trying to be more meticulous with their classification of these youngest immigrants. The experiences of the 1.75 generation are expected to be closer to those of the second generation (children born in the US to immigrant parents) than to their 1.25 generation counterparts. Unfortunately, most available data sources do not provide enough information to differentiate immigrants into the decimal generations, and others have sample sizes that are not large enough to perform detailed analyses. Thus, often researchers cannot directly test the assumptions behind Rumbaut's finer categories. Throughout this book, we have highlighted research that discusses the decimal generations; however, you will notice that data analyzed for this volume did not provide such detail.

Racial and Ethnic Diversity among Immigrant and Native Youths

As we have already mentioned in this chapter, immigrants are very diverse in their countries of origin and racial and ethnic makeup.

In order to provide a more detailed account of this diversity, we illustrate it with some tables. Table 1.1 presents the generational status by the race/ethnicity of children aged 0–18 in 2007–8. This table presents the percentage of Asians, Hispanics, blacks, and whites who are first, second, or third and beyond generation. We add the first and second generations of children together as they both have immigrant parents. First, note that among children aged 0–18, 5.1% are Asians, 15.7% are black, 21.2% are Hispanic and 57.3% are white. In the overall population, the vast majority of individuals are third and beyond generation (74.8%), while 3.3% are first generation, 18.9% are second generation, and a total of 22.3% are first or second generation children with immigrant parents.

Each race/ethnic group has a very different profile by immigration status. Examine each of the row percentages in the table. For example, among Asian American children, approximately 13.9% are first generation, 64% are second generation, and 17.2% are third generation and beyond. Almost 78% live in an immigrant family. So, for almost all Asian Americans today, immigration is something they have experienced first-hand and that may continue to shape their opportunities and lives.

For Hispanics, about 8.3% are first generation, 50.4% are second generation, and 37.4% are third generation and beyond. About 58.8% of Hispanic youth live in an immigrant family. Despite the association between Hispanics and immigration in the US media, a sizeable group of Hispanic children (37.4%) are native-born with native-born parents. This is in part due to the history of Mexican incorporation in the US. A large portion of today's Western and Southwestern US was a part of Mexico prior to the 1848 Treaty of Guadalupe Hidalgo that marked the end of the Mexican-American War. This includes the entire modern state of Arizona, which recently passed restrictive anti-illegal immigration measures (S.B. 1070; Support Our Law Enforcement and Safe Neighborhood Act, 2010) in 2010. One of its statutes is that anyone can be asked to produce "papers" that document their legal status. In a state that is 30% Hispanic, one suspects that Hispanics, even those whose families have lived for many

Table 1.1 Generational Status by Race/Ethnicity: Children Ages 0–18: 2007–2008

	1st Generation	2nd Generation	1st + 2nd Generation	3rd + Generation		
	Foreign-born children of immigrants	Native-born children of immigrants	Children of immigrants	Native-born children of natives	% Total	Total N
Asian	13.9%	64.0%	77.9%	17.2%	5.1%	3,739,000
Black	1.8%	9.5%	11.4%	84.0%	15.7%	11,619,000
Hispanic	8.3%	50.4%	58.8%	37.4%	21.2%	15,667,000
White	1.0%	6.1%	7.1%	91.0%	57.3%	42,324,000
All	3.3%	18.9%	22.3%	74.8%		
Total N	2,455,000	14,000,000	16,455,000	55,293,000		73,902,000

Source: The Urban Institute Children of Immigrants Data Tool
Note: Totals do not add up to 100% due to missing data on generational status

generations as both Mexicans and Americans on this land, are more vulnerable than whites to increased surveillance that results from this law. Because of their ethnic classification, even those Hispanics who may not have direct experiences of immigration may be treated as though they are newcomers.

For black youths, only about 1.8% are first generation compared to 9.5% who are second generation, and 84% who are third generation and beyond. This implies that, for most African Americans in the US, immigration is not something that influences their daily family lives. This is even more the case for white youths, of whom only 1% are first generation compared to 6.1% who are second generation. The vast majority (91%) are third generation and beyond. Again, this means that for almost all white youths, immigration is something that their families did not recently experience.

What are some of the implications of these patterns? First, for most white and black youths, immigration is not something that affects them personally. For many Hispanics and Asians, however, it is an overarching aspect of their daily lives. Second, because the vast majority of today's immigrants come from Latin America and Asia, when we think about the experiences of immigrant youth, we are largely thinking about the experiences of Hispanics and Asian Americans. In a way, it is very difficult to separate how much being an "immigrant" or being "Asian" or "Hispanic" shapes the educational outcomes of the members of those groups.

The Educational Attainments of Immigrant Adults

How well children do in school, what schools they attend, or how far they go are shaped by the experiences of their parents. Thus, in order to understand the educational outcomes of youth, we also need to understand those of their parents, the adults in immigrant families. Important differences in educational outcomes might be expected from those who immigrate as adults compared to those who arrive as children, and those who are born in the US and live in immigrant families. This is even true for individuals whose families come from the same countries and have the same racial and ethnic backgrounds. In other words, the educational experiences of immigrant children, immigrant adults, and their native-born children need to be understood separately. While there are undoubtedly overlapping circumstances among all of them, there are important differences that mark their everyday lives such as English language proficiency, bilingual fluency, the observance of particular cultural traditions, or even the country they consider "home." It is important to account for age at immigration when looking at the educational outcomes of immigrant children and their parents. Immigrants who arrive as children may complete their education in the US in its totality or in several countries. Undoubtedly, their experiences are not comparable to those who arrive to the US as adults. Age at immigration typically determines how and how much education is completed in either country.

As schooling experiences differ amongst adult immigrants, so do their levels of educational attainment. Some immigrants have only completed a few years of primary school, while many others have MAs and PhDs from top national and international institutions. In the US, some immigrant adults may have attended poorer public schools, perhaps with minority and other immigrant children, which did not well prepare them for college in the US, while others went to the best private schools that enabled their enrollment at elite institutions. In other words, adult immigrants arrive to the US on very unequal playing fields, and often these inequalities are further reinforced or even exacerbated among their children after they settle in the US, due to their racial, ethnic, and socioeconomic positions within the country.

The educational trajectories of adult immigrants largely determine their opportunities in the US in terms of where they live, with whom they socialize, and to which jobs they aspire. Their educational level is primarily what determines how and where they are absorbed within the US labor market. Their position in the US economy is also likely to be determined by where they live, the levels of education they have, and whether they find jobs where they can use the skills they may have acquired in their country of origin. The US receives immigrants with various levels of education, from those with very few skills, to highly skilled individuals. As you can imagine, life in the US is very different for a Guatemalan immigrant who arrives to the US as an agricultural worker and who only completed primary school in Guatemala compared to the everyday experiences of an English scientist who graduated from the University of Cambridge and who is later hired as a professor by Harvard University. Their levels of schooling outside of the US largely determine the starting position of these immigrants to the US.

Where immigrants live and with whom they socialize and work further amplifies racial and ethnic differences among immigrant families. Individuals tend to spend time with friends who are most similar to them. So, for instance, a well-educated family from India will also know other well-educated Indian families. Children in these families benefit from their association with their parents' friends and the children in those other families. On the other hand, the average immigrant from Mexico has very low levels of education. Mexican immigrant families will most likely settle in neighborhoods with other Mexicans, most of whom also have low levels of education, and, consequently, lower earnings. Neighborhoods with high concentrations of such immigrants may be associated with lower-quality schools, due both to the relatively modest revenue generated by local property taxes and the lower average parental education of children at school. Moreover, race and ethnicity play an important role in determining the social status of immigrants – it is likely that a white immigrant from Canada or the UK will be treated very differently in the labor market compared to a Latino immigrant from Honduras, even if all of these immigrants had comparable educational credentials.

Further, the socioeconomic position of the immigrants who arrive as adults to the US cannot be thought of as an outcome solely determined by their educational backgrounds. Ample research demonstrates that some immigrants may not receive the same returns to education compared to native-born individuals as well as to each other (Gibson and Carrasco 2009; Kao 1995; 1999; Kao and Tienda 1995; Keller and Tillman 2008; Portes and

Rumbaut 2006; Zhou and Bankston 1994). Their educational backgrounds may produce differential patterns of integration for contemporary immigrants. Thus, the place of education or where immigrants complete their education – either in the United States or abroad – is important in determining the [income] returns to education. The devaluation of immigrants' educational attainment may produce a mismatch between immigrants' educational attainment and their occupation after arrival. This, in turn, may lead immigrants to be either over- or underqualified relative to their coworkers. For instance, someone who is a surgeon in Russia may work as a medical technician in the US, suggesting that some immigrants may find it difficult to be hired in jobs where they can use their educational credentials, but there are important differences by country of origin. Immigrants from Latin American and Eastern European countries are more likely to end up in unskilled jobs than immigrants from Asia and industrial countries (Mattoo et al. 2005). The next chapters will explore in detail why and how these unequal opportunities related to education and job opportunities take place in the US.

While the educational histories of immigrant families may be as numerous as the number of immigrants in the US, there are some general patterns of how their socio-demographic characteristics relate to their eventual educational outcomes. The countries they grew up in, whether or not they arrived to the US as children or adults, the kinds of neighborhoods they settle in, whether or not they are fluent in English, and what race or ethnicity they are classified as in the US may provide some of the explanations for why some immigrant groups have better educational outcomes than others. These and other factors help us to understand why some immigrants have been able to use education in pursuit of the "American Dream," while, for others, education has been less successful as a route to social mobility.

Education and the American Dream for Immigrant Families

Education provides numerous benefits to both immigrant and native-born individuals. These benefits range from higher social status, lower unemployment and poverty rates, higher earnings, greater likelihood of marriage, better physical and mental health, better educational outcomes for their children, and even lower rates of death (e.g. Behrman and Stacey 1997; Lleras-Muney 2005; Schnittker 2004; Stevens et al. 2008). Census reports on educational attainment highlight the importance of obtaining an education on earnings. According to 2006 data, adults 18 years and older with a Master's, professional, or doctoral degree had a median income of approximately $80,000, while those with less than a high-school diploma had a median income of about $20,000 (Current Population Survey 2009). Other studies demonstrate that the benefits of obtaining higher levels of education go beyond earnings. Highly educated immigrant and native-born individuals also have better health and report higher levels of happiness (Franzini and Fernandez-Esquer 2006; Hao and Johnson 2000; Zhang and Ta 2009). Education not only allows individuals access to better paying and more prestigious jobs, but it also gives individuals the tools to make better informed choices in everyday life. These can range from the skills to communicate with children's teachers, their own doctors or lawyers, or simply reading sales contracts.

Beyond the benefits of education on earnings and health, education has important implications for the children of immigrants. As we discussed earlier, education is, without a doubt, one of the primary mechanisms through which class advantage is transferred from one generation to the next. Status attainment scholars from The Wisconsin School of the 1960s and 1970s demonstrated how schooling is the key intermediary between family origins and future labor force outcomes (Jencks et al. 1983; Sewell et al. 1976). Schools are the institutions responsible for providing those resources to individuals, which are key to their future socioeconomic success. Arguably, schools may be even more important when these resources are not available at home. This is one of the reasons why schooling is especially important to immigrants and the children of immigrants. For immigrant parents with little formal schooling and those who do not speak English, the educational outcomes of their children may be the main avenue through which the family is able to improve its socioeconomic standing.

Education and the Americanization Dream for Immigrant Groups

The consequences of having an educated populace go well beyond the individual and the family. On a societal level, cities, states, and nations have a direct interest in the education of the whole population given the many benefits that come with successful educational outcomes. Better educated residents earn more money to spend and invest in the local or national economy. They help to attract industries that need more educated workers, which in turn provide more tax revenue to cities and nations. An educated citizenry attracts more highly educated residents who may work in high-status professional jobs. Cities and neighborhoods with these more advantaged residents tend to have better schools, parks, and other community services.

For immigrants, the promise of universal education in the United States offers the opportunity for their children to go to college and to fully live the "American Dream." Moreover, schooling provides one of the main tools with which immigrants can become acquainted with the social expectations and norms in the US. Having the knowledge of these norms and expectations is what the general public and social scientists think of when they talk about the assimilation of immigrants. Thus, while we can consider schooling and education in terms of the subjects that are taught within the classrooms such as history or mathematics, schools serve an extremely important purpose that extends well beyond the content of the subject areas. Schools are also one of the primary institutions of socialization to American life. This means that in addition to teaching reading, mathematics, or science, schools also socialize children to become successful, well-adapted, and productive citizens in society.

Our beliefs that the US is a democracy and a meritocracy depend on the availability of free schooling to all youths (Bowles and Gintis 1977; 1986). In a society where the state provides free education so that anyone can go to school, if each student's performance is gauged using universal and objective criteria, we as a society believe that a real meritocracy exists. If anyone can go to school and earn high marks, then anyone can get a good job and make a good living. This is, in essence, the American Dream, which relies on the ideal of equal opportunity for all. In other words, schools are supposed to "level the playing field" that results from inequalities in family resources. Much of the recent debate on school reform is informed by these beliefs (Gray et al. 1996). The American public believes that schools can and should fix any remaining race, ethnic, and class inequalities in educational outcomes.

What is most relevant for the adaptation of immigrant children is the role that schools have always played in "Americanizing" youth. Historian Michael Katz argues that the development of the state-sponsored public school in the mid-1800s had much to do with the assimilation of Irish immigrants to the US. The Irish (who were also predominantly Catholic) were seen as "alien, uncouth, and menacing" (Katz 1987: 18). Indeed, if the Irish were viewed in such a negative light, one can only imagine the level of hostility that would have existed towards other immigrant and racial minority groups, such as the Japanese. This "Americanization" continued to be a primary function of the public schools through the twentieth century when this institution was central to instilling "American" values into the children of recently arrived Southern and Eastern European immigrants (Bryk et al. 1993).

The development of the public school in the US was partially driven by the view that children of immigrants could still be saved from their parents' negative influences. If newly arrived immigrants came with such "undesirable" cultural traits, it was imperative that the socialization of their children had to occur outside the family. After all, children could still be given a moral education and they could learn to become good American citizens. As Katz writes:

> The massive task of assimilation required weakening the connection between the immigrant child and its family, which in turn called for the capture of the child by an outpost of native culture. In short, fears about cultural heterogeneity propelled the establishment of systems of public education; from the beginning, public schools were agents of cultural standardization. (Katz 1987: 18–19)

Although the "Americanization" of immigrants and their children was primarily carried out in schools, historians have noted that these efforts expanded even beyond the classroom (Ravitch 2000 [1974]). Government agencies and private ventures established school and urban playgrounds in the industrial cities of the time (mainly around the Northeast "American" middle class) with the intent that immigrant children would be instilled with values that were not offered in their homes (Chudacoff 2007; Olneck 2008).

For immigrants who arrived to the US during the late nineteenth and early twentieth centuries, the mission of schools was clearly beyond just providing an education in academic fields. In addition to socializing children as "Americans," schools were in charge of aiding immigrant populations with important social services. In many cities across the US, public schools provided medical services, dental care, and even classes for individuals with physical or mental disabilities (Ravitch 2000 [1974]). These services were needed and deeply appreciated by the "71.5% of children in the New York City public schools who had foreign-born fathers in 1908, as well as the 67.3% of the children in Chicago, 63.5% in Boston, 59.6% in Cleveland, 59% in Providence, 58.9% in Newark, and 57.8% in San Francisco" (Ravitch 2000 [1974]: 56).

For immigrant children, school can be an especially important institution that helps familiarize them to life in the United States. Other students and teachers provide important lessons about everyday life and they can make immigrant students aware of

American norms and customs. Because their immigrant parents (especially those who are recent arrivals) often cannot help their children navigate through life at school, their primary socialization may come from interactions with people at school. From their relationships with non-immigrant schoolmates and friends, immigrant youth may see many different varieties of parent–child relationships, which may result in greater conflict with their own parents (Portes and Stepick 1993; Waters 1994; Zhou 1997).

However, schools also serve as sites of contestation, where immigrants struggle to maintain their ethnic identities. Angela Valenzuela (1999) documents how Mexican American children feel devalued and marginalized as Mexicans through a process she calls "subtractive schooling." Lee (1996) questions whether the expectations of Asian Americans as "model minorities" in schools serve their interests well. In other work, Lee explores how maintaining a Hmong identity can cause conflict among youth trying to succeed in a US school (Lee 2005). Immigrant parents worry that their children may become too "Americanized," begin to question parental authority, and lose some of the valuable traditions that connect them to their past. Immigrant parents and their children struggle with how maintaining an ethnic, cultural identity influences educational success in the US, realizing that schools are the key institutions through which their children will gain the skills necessary for upward socioeconomic mobility.

Education among Immigrants Past and Present

Most of the discussion in this book will refer to immigrants who arrived after 1965. As we will review in chapter 3, the historic 1965 Immigration Act, also known as the Hart-Cellar Act, reopened the US to immigrants from all over the world. However, throughout the book, you will encounter references to immigrants who arrived in the 1800s and earlier in the 1900s in order to understand changes over time in the immigrant population and the US in general. These comparisons are also useful to challenge and often debunk many of the popular myths that are widely used to portray immigrants both from the past as well as more recent arrivals.

Current debates on the assimilation of immigrants focus on the low levels of education of many of the recent arrivals compared to the US population. Many immigrants and children of immigrants have lower educational achievement and attainment than non-immigrants, though many also do better than their native-born same-race peers. It is also true that the average socioeconomic status of immigrants is lower than the US-born population (Perlmann and Waldinger 1997). While some immigrant children fare poorly in our schools, their worse outcomes may not be due to their immigrant status necessarily, but rather because they come from disadvantaged socioeconomic backgrounds. Recent studies provide sound evidence that, under similar socioeconomic circumstances, immigrants fare much the same in their educational achievement and attainment as any non-immigrant student (White and Glick 2009). Race complicates the relationship between immigrant status and educational outcomes, though, especially for blacks and Hispanics, whose educational experiences are also marked by discrimination and racial disparities that other racial and ethnic groups do not seem to suffer from (Carter 2003; Jencks and Phillips 1998; White and Glick 2009).

These discussions also mention that current immigrants have lower levels of education when compared to immigrants from earlier waves of immigration. Whereas there is some truth to these statements, the reality is not as straightforward as it may seem. Contemporary immigrants to the US come with very diverse levels of education. There are large proportions of people who have either very low or very high levels of education, much like an hourglass. Using US Census data, Fix and Passel (1994) demonstrated that during the 1980s, as well as for previous decades, immigrant education increased rather than decreased among *legal* immigrants. Thus, in general, the average level of attainment (highest educational level) of immigrants increased when compared to immigrants of previous generations. However, because of the great diversity of origins and conditions of migration, one key to understanding the educational level of immigrants in the US takes into consideration whether immigrants are documented or not. If undocumented individuals are counted alongside legal immigrants, the portrait of the educational levels of today's immigrant population is very different than if we only examined the population of documented immigrants.

In contrast, the distribution of education of the US-born population varies from that of the immigrant population: among natives, relatively fewer people have very low or very high levels of education. A greater proportion of immigrants have very low or very high levels of education compared to native-born individuals.

Thus, while the overall education level of recent immigrants is higher than in previous decades, the average education level of natives is rising faster, widening the gap between natives and recent immigrants. This gap, however, is almost entirely attributable to undocumented immigrants and refugees, not legal immigrants (Fix and Passel 1994). In short, when we talk about immigrants it is important to consider where they came from and under which social and economic circumstances. That will help us better understand what their educational paths in the US will look like.

Let us think again of the immigrant stories of Juanjo and Hyunsuk presented at the beginning of the chapter. Although these are fictitious characters, they portray situations that are conceivable among immigrant families arriving to the US. In the next chapters we will visit in detail many of the difficulties, as well as advantages, that Juanjo's and Hyunsuk's families may face in the US. But after reading this introduction you may start to understand that, even before they set their residence in the US, these two children and their families already had different opportunities to succeed educationally or economically. Once in the US, some of these differences will be amplified by the neighborhoods in which they live and the schools the children attend, the languages they speak, the types of jobs their parents are able to secure in the US, among other factors, many of which are related to the established racial hierarchies of this country.

Outline of the Book

In this first chapter we presented a general overview of the importance of education for all Americans, but particularly for immigrant families. The availability of schooling to everyone and the belief that universalistic standards (test scores, grades, years of educational attainment) determine socioeconomic outcomes lead to the belief, whether it is true in practice or not, in meritocracy, equal opportunity for all, and, most importantly, the American Dream. Immigrants arrive to the US because they expect that, through hard work and perseverance, they will experience better lives than the ones they left behind in their home countries, and they believe that their children will have exactly the same opportunities for achievement as non-immigrants. If we could make a single generalization about all immigrants, it would have to be that, like the majority of Americans, they believe in the American Dream.

Here we assert the importance of education as an indicator of assimilation and a precursor to upward mobility for immigrant families. We also present a brief overview of some of the main obstacles contemporary immigrants encounter in the US that may make this advancement less than a perfect straight line, such as discrimination, language issues, poverty, etc. In chapter 2, we consider assimilation in greater detail, and we review the ways that social science researchers have portrayed this process. In chapter 3, we present a historical account of the immigration flow to the United States and how the educational, economic, racial, ethnic, and economic characteristics of the immigrant population have been shifting over the last 200 years of immigration to the US. We briefly present the main immigration laws passed by the US and discuss their pivotal role in determining the origin and socioeconomic characteristics of the immigrants arriving to the US. This sets the context for the educational attainment of adults and educational outcomes for youths in the following chapters.

Chapter 4 presents data on the educational attainment and socioeconomic status of immigrant adults in the US today. Using data from the American Community Survey, we demonstrate the relationship between how far immigrants go in school and how well they fare economically. We pay close attention to differences in attainment – or highest level of education – by racial and ethnic background, and we use some of the theoretical explanations provided by social scientists to understand these differences.

Chapter 5 follows the format of chapter 4, but it focuses on educational achievement – that is, on academic performance (i.e. grades, tests scores, etc.) – as well as the attainment of children in immigrant families, either those who immigrated themselves at young ages or who are the children of immigrants, who are in school. As in the previous chapter, race, ethnicity, and national origin are placed at the center of our discussions. We also touch upon gender differences in achievement among immigrant groups.

Chapter 6 turns to the importance of language. Becoming proficient in English is one of the main goals to which most new immigrants aspire, in order to become full participants in US society. As with earlier chapters, we present evidence by racial, ethnic, and national origin of immigrants to highlight the great variation in language proficiency among contemporary immigrants and discuss the implications on educational outcomes that come along with the lack of English proficiency. We also discuss bilingualism and its potential advantages for children in immigrant families.

Finally, in chapter 7, we return to the main themes discussed in the preceding chapters in order to understand what the future of contemporary immigrants looks like both at the individual level and in their position within society. We also propose areas for future research that will further our understanding of this very diverse group living in the US.

2

___

Becoming American (or Not): Paths to Assimilation

The American Dream, that has lured tens of millions of all nations to our shores in the past century has not been a dream of material plenty, though that has doubtlessly counted heavily. It has been a dream of being able to grow to fullest development as a man and woman, unhampered by the barriers which had slowly been erected in the older civilizations, unrepressed by social orders which had developed for the benefit of classes rather than for the simple human being of any and every class.

James Truslow Adams (Historian), *The Epic of America*, 1931

Few would argue that a key element of the American ethos is the notion that America is the "Land of Opportunity" that offers equal chances for success for all. We are attracted to stories of "self-made men." They capture our imagination. Wealthy individuals (men) who built their riches from almost nothing include John D. Rockefeller (Standard Oil), Andrew Carnegie (Carnegie Steel), Cornelius Vanderbilt (various shipping and railroad enterprises), Warren Buffet (Berkshire Hathaway), and Bill Gates (Microsoft). Bill Clinton came from an extremely modest social class background and eventually became president of the United States. Thurgood Marshall, despite being the son of a railroad porter and being denied entry to law school at the University of Maryland because he was African American, successfully won the 1954 *Brown vs. Board of Education of Topeka* decision, which decided that the racial segregation of public schools by law was unconstitutional. He became a Supreme Court Justice in 1967. The lesson learned from the lives of these men is that no matter how humble your beginnings, through hard work and perseverance, anyone can succeed.

The possibility of the "American Dream" also captures the imagination of would-be migrants and immigrants. In fact, this narrative bolsters the belief that is likely held by almost all new arrivals. No matter how modest one's background is or how little English one speaks when an individual first arrives, over time, anyone can succeed. Success may be measured through one's educational achievement and attainment, career, income, wealth, or fame. New immigrants are likely to believe that even if they are unable to achieve this dream in their lifetimes, certainly their children will be able to do so. All it takes is hard work.

As we discussed in chapter 1, achieving the "American Dream" is the ultimate goal of the assimilation of immigrant groups. Successfully assimilated immigrants are those who are able to work hard in schools and use their education to achieve stable careers with good incomes. According to straight-line assimilation theories, the educational assimilation of any particular immigrant group is measured by the extent to which they have reached parity with the educational attainment of the native-born population (and sometimes the native-born white population). If occupational assimilation has occurred for this group, their similar educational attainment should lead to the same opportunities for jobs as native-born whites. Following this narrative, over time, the social and family lives of those from immigrant families become intertwined with native-born whites, until eventually, they cannot be differentiated from them.

Stories found in American history books and in popular culture suggest that to achieve in school and work, though, immigrants have to adopt some American culture and values. If an individual wants to assimilate into the "melting pot" and be treated as a true American and not as a foreigner, then s/he has to be willing to shed some of his/her ethnic and cultural identity and learn English. The lesson of these stories is that if you are willing to become a true American, then you have the chance to assimilate into the mainstream of America (Alba et al. 2002; Bean and Stevens 2003; Waters and Jiménez 2005). In this chapter, we ask the reader to consider how immigrants from different groups best achieve educational success and attainment. Does educational success require immigrants to become more like native-born Americans? Is there any benefit to retaining one's ethnic identity or cultural values to their educational attainment?

Of course, the notion that assimilation is contingent on the willingness of immigrants to shed their "foreign" (and hence un-American) ways overlooks the profound distinctions between racial and, to a lesser extent, ethnic groups. Undoubtedly, the experience of a new arrival from Canada (who is white) is fundamentally different from that of an immigrant from China (who is Asian), both in terms of the proximity of cultural norms between their countries of origin and the US but also in terms of their perceived similarity to the white mainstream in the US. The white Canadian and Asian Chinese immigrants may not only perceive themselves as more or less similar to the white mainstream in the US, they may also be treated differently by native-born Americans. A Canadian who shares the same racial category as whites in the US may be (more often) afforded the same privileges as native-born white Americans, while a Chinese immigrant may be treated as suspicious or dangerous (as Chinese immigrants were in the 1800s) or as a super-achiever who is inherently different from white, native-born residents, as the more modern "model minority" stereotype suggests (Kao 1995). Despite these ways that race and national origin may limit possibilities to achieve the "American Dream," a common belief is that the "American Dream" is open to all individuals equally, and this belief (along with challenges to it) has shaped the ways that social researchers have portrayed the process of the assimilation of immigrants for almost a century now. Is educational success equally attainable, regardless of class background, race, ethnicity, and national origin? For whom can the "American Dream" become a reality?

Let us briefly summarize how the last century of social research has grappled with the presence of immigrants in the US, and

27

what theories researchers proposed about how immigrants would change as they and their children spent time in the US.

Along a Straight Line: The Chicago School and Traditional Theories of Assimilation

Sociologists generally agree that the Chicago School of Sociology produced many of the best-known theories about immigration and assimilation. It is not possible to overestimate the influence of The Chicago School and its assimilation theory – in fact, most of the outcomes researchers currently study with respect to race, ethnic, and immigrant groups can arguably be traced to their research and writing.

During the early twentieth century, Chicago was a dynamic city with a growing population of immigrants. It is important to keep in mind that while we think of the current period as one with large immigrant populations, only about 11% of the US population in 2000 was foreign-born (Gibson and Jung 2006) and currently this number hovers around 13% (US Census Bureau 2010). In 1910, this figure stood at about 32% (Hirschman 2005). Researchers Robert Park and Ernest Burgess likened the city to an ecological system, where immigrants were like a new species being introduced to an existent ecosystem. They carried the analogy further, suggesting that while there would be a period of unrest and conflict in this changing ecosystem, eventually the new species (that is, the new immigrant group) would be absorbed and a new equilibrium would emerge.

Park and Burgess introduced their theory of assimilation, known as the *Contact Hypothesis*, in their classic book *The Introduction to the Science of Sociology* (1921 and later republished in 1969 and 1970). Here, over four distinct chapters, they argued that all immigrants would eventually be absorbed into the American mainstream and become American. What this meant was that they would have a common social identity. They state:

> Assimilation is a process of interpenetration and fusion in which persons and groups acquire the memories, sentiments, and attitudes of

other persons or groups, and, by sharing their experience and history, are incorporated with them in a common cultural life. In so far as assimilation denotes this sharing of tradition, this intimate participation in common experiences, assimilation is central in the historical and cultural processes. (Park and Burgess 1969 [1921]: 735–7)

Key to the completion of the assimilation cycle was language homogeneity (that is, immigrants must speak English) and inter-marriage (that is, marrying non-immigrants and individuals of other racial and ethnic groups). In other words, according to these authors, assimilation was reached when certain groups were indistinguishable from "Americans."

Park and Burgess (1969 [1921]) argued that there were four stages of the Contact Hypothesis: *Contact, Conflict/Competition, Accommodation,* and *Assimilation.* Simply put, as new immigrant groups came into contact with the established native-born residents, there would be a period of neutrality. After then, due to unfamiliarity between the two groups, Park and Burgess (1969 [1921]) argued that there would be conflict. Eventually, this conflict would turn into competition for limited resources (most obviously jobs). Accommodation was reached when the new ethnic groups formed friendships and other casual contacts with Americans. Finally, over time, the new group would be absorbed into the American mainstream and essentially be considered "one of us" by the local residents. According to Park and Burgess, this progressive and irreversible cycle would lead ethnic differences to diminish over time.

While Park and Burgess (1969 [1921]) did not specify the length of time this process would take, they did note that it was not achievable by the first generation (foreign-born arrivals to the United States). Elsewhere, Park noted that Asian Americans (specifically Japanese Americans) would have greater difficulty in assimilation than European-origin groups (Park 1928), and have experiences that are more similar to African-origin groups on the basis of skin color (Park 1914). Although Park was sensitive to racial differences, scholars generally overlooked this part of the traditional assimilation paradigm, arguing instead that all groups followed the same process of assimilation, until they were indistinguishable from native-born Americans whose families had been in the US for several generations.

Park and Burgess' Cycle of Race Relations

Contact

When Park and Burgess (1969 [1921]) wrote about contact, they were considering contact between any individuals and groups, not specific contact across racial, ethnic, or immigrant groups. They identified three common types of contact. First is the type of contact that an individual experiences him or herself. This is when an individual actually interacts with a person of another race, or when one visits another country. Second is a form of contact that relies on indirect modes of communication. This would include, for example, learning about Mexico by reading newspaper articles or watching Rick Bayless's *One Plate at a Time*, a cooking show featuring Mexican cuisine, watching travel videos on YouTube, or watching a National Geographic documentary on Mexico. This is not the same as a "sensory" contact, but it is still a mode of interaction that is valuable. Finally, and most importantly, they envision a third form of contact as one that comes from the web of social interaction between people and places. This third form is what immigrants themselves experience when they move to the US by directly coming into contact with non-immigrants and people from other racial, ethnic, and cultural backgrounds.

Park and Burgess (1969 [1921]) believed that physical space plays an important role in distinguishing between types of contact. They thought about contact in terms of neighborhood segregation, for example. Residing in the same place made sensory contact, the most beneficial, more likely to occur. They also argued for the importance of primary contacts (between family members, friends, and intimate partners). These close relationships typically resulted from sensory contact.

Park and Burgess (1969 [1921]) also considered that how much control groups had over their individual members influenced the likelihood of contact with members of other groups. The less control, the more permeable the boundaries of that group were to other groups' influences. When thinking about ethnicity, for example, if being Italian only meant that you read news about Italy once in a while but did not eat Italian ethnic food or celebrate Italian holidays, then being Italian would have no real bearing on your everyday life. If this were true of a majority of Italian Americans, then the permeability between Italian Americans and native-born Americans would be very high. Under situations in which groups loosely control their members, the likelihood of contact with other groups is higher. Contact can also occur over time – through the transmission of stories between generations. For example, this can occur through stories parents tell their children.

Competition

After the *contact* stage of assimilation, Park and Burgess (1969 [1921]) argued that *competition* between groups would ensue. Again, it is important to note that they thought about competition in a very broad sense. Groups compete against groups for resources, just as individuals compete with one another. Park and Burgess (1969 [1921]) theorized that natives and immigrants, after coming into physical contact, would compete for limited resources. Jobs were one such resource. Newly arrived immigrants offered an additional source of labor for employers. As a result of increased competition with greater numbers of immigrants, Park and Burgess (1969 [1921]) argued that the fertility rates of natives would be lower. In other words, they believed that populations naturally adjusted themselves in light of limited resources. Native-born white fertility declines were "blamed" on increasing migration from abroad.

Accommodation

After some period of intensified *competition*, Park and Burgess (1969 [1921]) believed there would eventually be *accommodation* between groups. For Park and Burgess, *accommodation* is the peaceful outcome of multiple conflicts between individuals, groups, organizations, and even nations. Though arguments and conflicts arise in the labor market, cultural norms, or social behaviors, accommodation is the state of equilibrium that keeps these antagonisms in check. Treaties and resolutions between countries are also a manifestation of accommodation.

It is important to note that a state of accommodation is not always desirable for all parties. For example, Park and Burgess (1969 [1921]) argue that the system of slavery or castes (or any relationship of subordination) is also a type of accommodation. The other undercurrent of their discussion, which is almost never mentioned in modern sociological accounts of the Contact Hypothesis, is the notion that humans also acclimatize to their environment.

Assimilation

Finally, after *accommodation* between individuals or groups occurs, *assimilation* follows. Assimilation is the last step of this process. To describe assimilation, Park and Burgess (1969 [1921]) refer to Israel Zangwill's 1914 play *The Melting Pot*. In it, the main protagonist states:

> Understand that America is God's Crucible, the great Melting-Pot where all the races of Europe are melting and re-forming! Here you stand, good folk, think I, when I see them at Ellis Island, here you stand in your fifty groups, your fifty languages, and histories, and your fifty blood hatreds and rivalries. But you won't be long like that, brothers, for these are the fires of God you've come to – these are fires of God. A fig for your feuds and vendettas! Germans and Frenchmen, Irishmen and Englishmen, Jews and Russians – into the Crucible with you all! God is making the American. (Zangwill 1914: 33, as quoted in Hirschman 1983: 397)

However, even before this play, there are references to the idea that America is a place where multiple ethnic groups are melted together into one. One of the earliest mentions comes from J. Hector St John de Crevecœur (1782) in *Letters from an American Farmer*, where he states:

> He becomes an American by being received in the broad lap of our great *Alma Mater*. Here individuals of all nations are melted into a new race of men, whose labours and posterity will one day cause great changes in the world . . . The Americans were once scattered all over Europe; here they are incorporated into one of the finest systems of population which has ever appeared, and which will hereafter become distinct by the power of the different climates they inhabit. The American ought therefore to love this country much better than that wherein either he or his forefathers were born. (de Crevecœur 1904 [1782]: 55)

While the notion of assimilation resulting in a "melting pot" is not widely used to describe modern American race relations by sociologists, it still enjoys wide usage in the American lexicon. The notion also complements the idea that America welcomes immigrants, no matter their social position and (arguably) their national origin. While in its more modern usage the "melting pot" may be perceived to encompass everyone, many of these eighteenth-, nineteenth-, and early twentieth-century writers envisioned a melting pot for Europeans (and only Northern Europeans at first) into the American mainstream. Park and Burgess (1969 [1921]), though, seemed to have a broader notion of which groups could assimilate that more closely approximates the modern vision of a "melting pot." In Robert Park's 1928 essay on "Human Migration and the Marginal Man," he notes that assimilation will be more difficult for Japanese Americans and African Americans. He writes:

> As I have said elsewhere, the chief obstacle to the cultural assimilation of races is not their different mental, but rather their divergent physical traits. It is not because of the mentality of the Japanese that they do not so easily assimilate as do the Europeans. It is because the Japanese bears in his features a distinctive racial hallmark, that he

wears so to speak, a racial uniform which classified him. He cannot become a mere individual, indistinguishable in the cosmopolitan mass of the population, as is true, for example, of the Irish, and, to a lesser extent, of some of the other immigrant races. The Japanese, like the Negro, is condemned to remain among us an abstraction, a symbol – and a symbol not merely of his own race but of the Orient and of that vague, ill-defined menace we sometimes refer to as the "yellow peril." (Park 1928: 890–1)

Still, he notes that the assimilation of all groups of people and races that live together is inevitable. What he did not specify is how long it would take to get there.

Assimilation is a slow and gradual process that occurs naturally, according to Park and Burgess. At the final stage, assimilated individuals share the same language, social history, and American identity (though individuals may retain some signs of their ethnic identity, as well). Education plays an important role in assimilation because it is through American schools that children of immigrants learned to become Americans, and because it is here that they acquired the skills needed to gain high-status occupations (Warner and Srole 1945). And, once immigrants and children of immigrants were occupationally successful and saw themselves as "Americans," they met and married other "Americans." Even today, social scientists focus on education and intermarriage as two of the main measures of immigrant assimilation in the US.

The works of other theorists after Park and Burgess have added greater specificity to the assimilation model. Three of these most influential works are *The Ghetto* (1928) by Louis Wirth, *The Social Systems of American Ethnic Groups* (1945) by William Lloyd Warner and Leo Srole, and *The Urban Villagers: Groups and Class in the Life of Italian-Americans* (1962) by Herbert Gans. Using different immigrant and ethnic groups (i.e. Jewish, Northern European, and Italian), these authors argue, like Park and Burgess had previously suggested, that eventually all groups tend to assimilate into a common group with similar cultural traits. These studies, along with others published during the decades preceding 1965 (or those that studied the pre-1965 migrants), emphasized that differences among immigrants and natives will naturally disappear through personal contact among the groups.

Despite the abundance of research on immigration, by the mid-1950s, there was still a lot of confusion about definitions of assimilation and about when and how assimilation occurred for distinct ethnic groups. The diversity of groups and their experiences led to many different portrayals of how assimilation was accomplished. Milton Gordon in *Assimilation in American Life* (1964) provided an attempt to characterize assimilation as having different dimensions. He identified seven such dimensions. These included: (1) cultural; (2) structural, (3) marital; (4) identificational; (5) attitude receptional (absence of prejudice); (6) behavioral receptional (absence of discrimination); and (7) civic (absence of value and power conflict) (Gordon 1964; Hirschman 1983). According to Gordon, ethnic groups could be assimilated on some dimensions and not on others. The final stage of assimilation (as Park and others noted), complete assimilation, would occur only when all of these seven steps were completed. In other words, if ethnic group X were not distinguishable from the American mainstream on all of these dimensions, then that group would have successfully assimilated to the US mainstream. For example, one could argue that in 2013, there are no meaningful differences between third generation Americans of English origin versus those of French descent. If you examined their odds of interethnic marriage, you would find that the French American person would not prefer to marry another third generation French American over a third generation individual whose ancestors hailed from England.

An additional element in Gordon's (1964) theory, like his predecessors', is that assimilation follows a unidirectional path. Once one has assimilated on one dimension, one cannot become unassimilated again. That is, it is unlikely that over time French Americans will start favoring others of French descent once they have not expressed that preference for a while.

This lack of preference in marriage for one's same ethnic background highlights the idea that assimilated Americans from European descent can choose whether or not and when to identify with their ethnic origins, as their identities as "Americans" are not questioned and their ethnic background becomes a secondary trait that they choose when to bring to the forefront. In her landmark study of Irish and Italian Americans, Mary Waters referred to "ethnic options" (Waters 1990). However, this "option" only applied to the ethnic identities of white ethnics. In other words, someone who is Irish American can choose to celebrate St Patrick's Day by eating corned beef, however his/her Irish identity may have no bearing on his/her everyday life. Waters and sociologists like Richard Alba (1990) argue that for white ethnics, ethnicity is simply an "option" that they can choose to celebrate or acknowledge whenever it is convenient to do so.

Gordon (1964) is to be credited for his effort to provide an overarching work that highlighted the complexity of the process of assimilation. However, he was writing during a period in US history when immigration to this country was at one of its lowest points. Because of World War I, World War II, and the Korean War, as well as strict policies that limited immigration to the United States, the decades in the mid-twentieth century witnessed a virtual standstill in terms of new arrivals. Immigration did not peak again until after 1965. The second or third generation white Americans who were represented in the work of Mary Waters (1990) or Richard Alba (1990) were descendants of individuals who lived in the United States while there were relatively few new arrivals – and most of them ethnically white. Because of this, Gordon's theory may not well characterize the experiences of non-white groups during the time of expanding immigration post-1965.

Gordon's (1964) dimensions of assimilation may not be captured in the experiences of Asian or Hispanic immigrants, for example. Despite the fact that Chinese Americans first arrived to the United States in the mid-1800s, they are, as a group, seen as newcomers. This oversimplification makes some sense when we realize that the vast majority of Chinese Americans who live in the United States are foreign-born or a child of foreign-born parents. Mexicans are also perceived as recent arrivals to the US, even though many are native to states that used to make up a portion of Mexico (remember that Arizona, California, Nevada, New Mexico, Texas,

Utah, and parts of Colorado, Kansas, Oklahoma, and Wyoming belonged to Mexico until the 1830s–1850s). They are not foreign-born, yet because a large subset of Mexicans are relatively new arrivals, Mexicans (and Hispanics overall) are lumped into one large and undifferentiated group. Even those who have been born in the US, whose families have lived in the US for generations, are not completely seen as "assimilated" by virtue of being associated with others of that racial, ethnic, or national-origin group.

Accommodating or Assimilating: Multiculturalism or the Salad Bowl?

In the 1970s, some social scientists proposed that the United States is less like a melting pot than it is like a salad bowl. In other words, even though ethnic groups live together, they do not "blend together" to resemble each other; rather, each group maintains its distinctness. A tomato does not turn into romaine lettuce just by sharing the same bowl, although the flavors from both may affect one another. This analogy better fits our modern notion of "multiculturalism," and better represents how immigrants think of themselves. Immigrants feel their children need not abandon their ethnic identities, but rather can combine the "best of both worlds" – that of their parents' ethnic and cultural backgrounds and that of America. This has also been called "cultural hybridization" (Appadurai 1996; Sassen 1996; Soysal 1994). Multiculturalism indirectly challenges the premise of the simple assimilation paradigm. Newcomers are not simply stripped of their foreignness and native cultural norms – instead, they are integrated into US society in a way that allows them to maintain some of their distinct cultural traits while they also transform the American cultural landscape.

As an example of cultural hybridization, academic researchers have noted that children need not culturally assimilate in order to succeed in schools. Margaret Gibson coined the term "acculturation without assimilation" to describe how Punjabi Sikh children were incorporated into schools in California (Gibson 1988). These immigrant children retained their parents' cultural norms but also successfully adapted to life in the United States. For example, she argues that while Punjabi Sikh American parents insist on traditional norms of dating and marriage, they accommodate to American norms while their children are in school. They do this even when they believe their ways are superior to that of native-born Americans because they want their children to assimilate and to succeed.

According to this multicultural perspective, immigrants raise their children as part of this "salad bowl." Immigrant parents want to retain what is best from their countries of origin while also adapting to US cultural norms. They often wish their children would speak their native language, and sometimes enroll them in cultural classes or pageants to reinforce their cultural heritage. They also want their children to speak "accentless" English and succeed in US schools.

Despite its descriptive appeal, though, the "salad bowl" analogy is probably not the most sophisticated or analytically useful tool for thinking about the assimilation and acculturation of immigrants. If the salad bowl analogy were true, then immigrants of all groups could achieve educationally, without regard for racial, ethnic, cultural, or national-origin differences. Empirical evidence shows, though, that some groups experience greater obstacles to educational achievement and attainment than do others. Who holds power in a society may play an important role in which groups succeed educationally and which ones get left behind.

The Role of Power: Cultural Ecology

Not all racial and ethnic groups have equal power in the US. Power refers to the ability to convert one's desires to realities. It is the ability to get what one wants. Power comes, in part, from having economic and political resources, and it translates in one's social status in a particular society. In other words, those with higher social status typically have more power in society. This definition of power is what differentiates "majority" from "minority." A minority group is seen as a group who has less power than the majority group (which, in the case of the United States, is whites) and occupies a lower status in society. Note that how many people form the group (its size) does not define who the majority and the minority are, but their power does. Sometimes, economic and political resources are held by the racial, ethnic, or status group with the greatest numbers in a society (thus, the *majority* group). However, there are many examples of race relations where the group in power is in fact smaller than those who have less social standing. The most obvious case is South Africa, where whites have more socioeconomic power and, until recently, more land rights. Certainly, in the history of colonization of countries in Africa and Asia, the smaller ethnic group (the English, French, Spanish, or Portuguese, among others) dominated those who were native to the colonized countries.

Immigrant groups have economic and political resources from two main sources. They may bring them from home countries and/or build them when they arrive in the US. Traditional assimilation perspectives suggest that the ability to access these resources in the US occurs as immigrants adopt "American" cultural norms and values. The adoption of these norms and values, though, is the choice of the immigrant. Uneven assimilation results from individual choices. However, variation in assimilation outcomes like educational attainment and labor force position by racial and ethnic groups suggests that something more than individual choice is at work. Who has power in the host society and whether or not newcomers of all races and ethnicities can access the resources needed to gain power may influence how groups assimilate into US society.

Racial, ethnic, or national-origin groups may be blocked from accessing economic and political resources through direct discrimination. For example, Mexicans and Asians were prevented from attending schools with white students in different regions and at different points in US history (*Mendez v. Westminster* 1946; Wollenberg 1978), and Asian immigrants were barred from owning land (Aoki 1998) and could not become citizens or vote (Calavita 2000).

Direct discrimination can prevent immigrants from attaining power in the US. Further, some researchers argue that groups adjust their values and attitudes to adapt to powerlessness. These explanations for continued racial and ethnic disadvantage are called "cultural deprivation models." The best known example of this type of model is Oscar Lewis's theory of the "culture of poverty" that he generated in studying Puerto Ricans in Puerto Rico and New York (he would study Mexicans as well and claimed that the culture of poverty also applied to non-immigrant groups such as African Americans) (1966a; 1966b). He argued that the experience of poverty over many generations led to cultural values that made it possible for people to survive under conditions of disadvantage, but these values were not consistent with working towards upward mobility (Lewis 1966a; 1966b). Lewis also argues that the culture of poverty is not necessarily the result of discrimination, but the result of the individual character-istics, implying that stigmatization of certain groups is due to their own characteristics. He writes:

> The individual who grows up in this culture has a strong feeling of fatalism, helplessness, dependence and inferiority. These traits, so often remarked in the current literature as characteristic of the American Negro, I found equally strong in slum dwellers of Mexico City and San Juan, who are not segregated or discriminated against as a distinct ethnic or racial group. [. . .] Provincial and local in outlook, with little sense of history, these people know only their own neigh-borhood and their own way of life. Usually they do not have the knowledge, the vision or the ideology to see the similarities between their troubles and those of their counterparts elsewhere in the world. They are not class-conscious, although they are sensitive indeed to symbols of status. (Lewis 1966b: 23)

Anthropologist John Ogbu elaborated on these "cultural depri-vation models" by explicitly incorporating the treatment of racial and ethnic minorities by the host society into his theory (Ogbu 1978; 1991). He argued that different minority groups have different outcomes because of the way they arrived to, or were incorporated into, the United States. He theorized that "involuntary" immigrants had very different frames of reference compared to "voluntary" immigrants, which in turn shaped their attitudes towards education. Involuntary minorities include African Americans, Native Americans, and Mexican Americans, who were brought to the US against their will or who inhabited the US and whose land was taken forcibly by Anglos. Voluntary minorities (which he sometimes referred to as immigrant minorities) included migrants from Europe, Asia, and Latin America, who chose to come to the US to seek better economic opportunities or to flee war or persecution.

This division does not characterize the experiences of all the members of any single racial or ethnic group because reasons for migration and incorporation into the US vary historically, even for those within the same racial and ethnic categories. For example, a Filipino laborer who arrived to Louisiana in the 1760s after deserting forced service for Spain had very different migration experiences from a college-educated Filipina nurse who arrived after 1965. A Filipino migrant likely faced more discrimination in 1760 than the other who arrived as a skilled worker after 1965. Similarly, the migration experiences of a Mexican from Juarez in 2008 is not the same as a fifth generation Mexican whose family roots in California extend back to a time before 1848 (the date of the Treaty of Guadalupe Hidalgo) when California was part of Mexico.

Putting aside the complexities of vast differences in migration experiences (even within racial, ethnic, and national-origin groups), for Ogbu (1978; 1991), involuntary immigrants were different from voluntary minorities in several essential ways. First, they have different frames of reference for comparing their present situations and their future possibilities. The voluntary immigrant sees his/her current situation, no matter how bleak, as an improvement over his/her life in his/her country of origin. However, involuntary minorities (such as African Americans) compare their conditions to that of white Americans.

Second, these two groups have very different folk theories about getting ahead through education. Voluntary minorities believe that if their children obtain a good education, they will manage to have good jobs. Involuntary minorities, in contrast, feel that they do not have the same opportunities as whites, and that even if they obtain more education, it will not help them get ahead.

Third, they differ in how they shape their collective identities. For immigrant/voluntary minorities, their identities come from their country of origin. A Chinese American immigrant will identify with China (and his/her life prior to their arrival to the United States). Ogbu (1978; 1991) argues that involuntary minorities, like African Americans, have a collective identity that is shaped by their experiences of discrimination in the host (US) society.

Ogbu (1978; 1991) argues that because of their experiences with incorporation in the US, "involuntary" minorities develop an "oppositional" identity. They define themselves apart from the dominant group (whites) and avoid behaviors that are associated with this group. For example, a large research literature has focused on whether black students in the US avoid "acting white." Because African Americans perceive that doing well in school benefits whites, but not themselves, getting good grades and achieving high test scores is associated with "being white." Ogbu and his colleague, Fordham (1986), observed that African Americans who performed well in school feared being told that they were "acting white," and would often "underperform" or hide their high achievement through athletics or being the class clown. Fordham and Ogbu (1986) argue that this, in turn, causes them to be less invested in education.

Although "voluntary minorities" also perceive that they may not get equal returns to their educational investments and may also experience discrimination, their reaction is different. Instead of disinvesting in education, voluntary minorities "over-invest." Psychologists Stanley Sue and Sumie Okazaki (1990) argue that Asian Americans invest more in education because they believe that they will face discrimination. Thus it takes greater investment in education for Asian Americans to achieve upward socioeconomic mobility compared to whites.

Ogbu's theory has been criticized for "blaming the victim" by suggesting that if ethnic group members simply shifted their frame of reference, they might be able to experience upward mobility. In other words, African American children do not do well in school compared to whites because studying is seen as "acting white."

It is important to note that a large number of scholars using both quantitative and qualitative data argue strongly against Ogbu's theories. Actually, many scholars find that African American youth have extremely high educational aspirations. For example, Ainsworth-Darnell and Downey (1998) use nationally representative data to show that African American youth have high educational aspirations. Recent research by Tyson and her colleagues shows that African American students are most prone to accusing other high-achieving African American students of "acting white" when there are few African American students in advanced placement or other higher-track courses (Tyson et al. 2005). Mostly, though, Tyson and her colleagues (2005) find that the prevalence of this phenomenon has been exaggerated and that high-achieving students of all races and ethnic groups face taunts from fellow students.

Even more recently, Harris's study on the causes of the racial achievement gap in American education provides robust empirical evidence that fails to find support for the tenets proposed by Ogbu's oppositional culture (Harris 2011). According to Harris, black students achieve less in school, but they value schooling more than their white counterparts. Black students perform less well in high school not because of their lack of interest in success but rather because they enter without the necessary skills. Harris's findings support the idea that research has to refocus and study prior achievement, as he finds evidence that the achievement gap becomes significant during pre-adolescence. It is the accumulation of socioeconomic and health disadvantages that slows the skills development of students that are accompanied by lowered teacher expectations.

While cultural explanations, such as those provided by Ogbu, that seem to directly "blame the victim" have largely fallen out of favor in the social sciences, those that "celebrate the winner" are still popular. The characterization of Asian Americans as "model minorities" is a good example (Kao 1995). Although it appears to celebrate the achievements of Asian Americans, scholars see this characterization as overly simplistic. Further, they see it as a way to indirectly blame other minorities for their educational outcomes by suggesting that if other minorities had the same qualities as Asians, they would achieve more. That is why scholars often refer to it as the "model minority myth."

As early as the 1960s, Asian Americans' high educational achievement and attainment had been noticed. For example, a *New York Times Magazine* article written by William Petersen in 1966 noted that Japanese Americans, despite their internment just 20 years prior, had managed to enjoy relatively high levels of socioeconomic success. He argued that Japanese Americans were exceptional because they faced terrible discrimination during World War II. He states:

> The history of Japanese Americans, however, challenges every such generalization about ethnic minorities, and for this reason alone deserves far more attention than it has been given. Barely more than 20 years after the end of the wartime campus, this is a minority that has risen above even prejudiced criticism. By any criterion of good citizenship that we choose, the Japanese Americans are better than any other group in our society, including native-born whites. (Petersen 1966: 21)

Asian Americans have continued to enjoy the praise of other Americans in celebrating their perceived success. During the 1980s, Asian Americans were heralded by politicians such as President Ronald Reagan and media figures such as journalist Mike Wallace for their high academic outcomes. At a meeting with Asian and Pacific American leaders on February 23, 1984, President Reagan stated:

> Asian and Pacific Americans have helped preserve that dream by living up to the bedrock values that make us a good and a worthy people. I'm talking about principles that begin with the sacred worth of human life, religious faith, community spirit, and the responsibility of parents and schools to be teachers of tolerance, hard work, fiscal responsibility, cooperation, and love. It's no wonder that the median income of Asian and Pacific American families is much higher than

the total American average. After all, it is values, not programs and policies, that serve as our nation's compass. They hold us on course. They point the way to a promising future. (Reagan in Woolley and Peters 2010a)

Many Asian immigrants to the US after 1965 came as a result of preferences for skilled workers in US immigration policy as well as the end of the zero quotas for many Asian national-origin groups. Their relatively advantaged socioeconomic status gave their children a headstart in their likelihood of achieving educational success. The Vietnamese (and later the Laotians and Cambodians) were an exception to this general pattern, coming with lower levels of economic or human capital as refugees and war migrants. However, they were also celebrated as "model minorities." Vietnamese Americans were said to have cultural values that were aligned with American values. Vietnamese Americans' values fit well with the "Protestant Ethic" that Anglo Americans believed informed their educational and economic success in the US. The "Protestant Ethic" is based on the belief that hard work and delayed gratification bring educational and economic reward (see Caplan et al. 1992, for example).

After the rate and character of immigration to the US changed dramatically in 1965, it was clear that old assimilation theories could not account for the varying outcomes of immigrants of different racial, ethnic, and national-origin groups. While some theories suggested that the cultural values of these groups, and the "match" between those cultural values and those of dominant whites in the US, were the reasons for disparate outcomes across groups, other researchers were not satisfied that these theories accounted for ethnic group differences. Many scholars, in fact, believed that how groups were incorporated into life in the US and the treatment they received from the host society was an important part of the story of why some racial, ethnic, and national-origin groups achieved educational success and socioeconomic mobility more easily than did others. These scholars proposed a theory of "segmented" assimilation.

It is not a Straight Line: Contemporary Theories of (Segmented) Assimilation

Scholars studying assimilation in recent decades have made two very important observations. The first is that assimilation does not always lead to upward mobility. Recent immigrants can assimilate by adopting the qualities and characteristics of disadvantaged minorities in the US, rather than those of the dominant group, whites. The second observation is that there is not one single, "straight-line" path to upward mobility for immigrants. Immigrants need not adopt the cultural values of the native-born in the US, and, in some instances, retaining cultural values may be beneficial to upward mobility. Scholars Min Zhou and Alejandro Portes (among others) have revised traditional assimilation theories by arguing that there are many paths to assimilation, and most importantly, assimilation does not always equal upward mobility as researchers in prior decades have suggested (Portes and Zhou 1993). They argue that *segmented assimilation* more accurately describes the multiple pathways towards assimilation. For some groups, their mobility patterns will match the traditional narratives of assimilation, while for others, assimilation in the US will actually mean downward mobility.

The assimilation paths of immigrants are not solely determined by their cultural values, according to these theorists. Segmented assimilation proponents noticed that cultural explanations seem to neglect the wide range in structural circumstances faced by immigrants from such diverse racial, ethnic, and national-origin backgrounds. Certainly, the highly educated family who arrives to the United States with a job in hand and whose first home is in a comfortable middle-class suburb has very different experiences from a recent arrival who has only completed elementary school, has no job, and has to live in a cramped apartment with other immigrants. Where immigrants reside affects their everyday experiences, the quality of schools and teachers, the socioeconomic status of their neighbors, and their experiences with crime and of neighborhood disorganization, thereby largely determining their

46

prospects for mobility in the short- and long-term future for themselves and for their children.

In their seminal essay that laid the foundation of the theory of segmented assimilation, Portes and Zhou (1993) argued that the coming of age of the second generation (whose parents arrived after the landmark 1965 Hart-Cellar Act) provided empirical evidence of the multiple pathways to assimilation. They argue that the increasing body of empirical research on this new second generation clearly demonstrates the inadequacies of traditional assimilation paradigms that were built upon studies of the experiences of the second generation of children of European immigrants at the turn of the twentieth century. In fact, adopting American customs and norms, which was always the first step toward upward mobility, now possibly led to downward mobility because poorer immigrants settled in areas that were heavily populated by poor and disadvantaged minority youth. They argue that this is in contrast to immigrant youth who can maintain close ties to their immigrant parents' communities and essentially resist Americanization. In other words, the local context of where individuals settle is key.

They then spell out three key features of immigrant group experiences that determine these different pathways toward either downward mobility to the lower class (and presumably black) or upward mobility to the middle (and presumably white) class. These three characteristics are: (1) color; (2) location; and (3) absence of mobility ladders (Portes and Zhou 1993: 83).

Color refers to the race of immigrants. Most of today's immigrants come from Asia and Latin America and, according to the racial categories that exist in the United States today, most of them are not considered white. As such, some argue that new immigrants are non-white minorities and are likely viewed as less assimilable than the white European immigrants. However, most new immigrants are also not black (although about 10% of Hispanics in the United States identify as "black"). A growing number of researchers who write in this area argue that the distinction may be shifting from a white/non-white division to that of a black/non-black differentiation. If this is the case, then recent immigrants who are not defined as black may eventually see more upward mobility than native-born American blacks (Bean and Stevens 2003; Lee and Bean 2007).

The second characteristic that shapes paths to assimilation is location. This refers to the residential location of certain immigrant communities. Portes and Zhou (1993) argue that new immigrants who settle in the inner-city near less advantaged native-born minorities will be more likely to experience downward assimilation. There is a caveat, however. If immigrant communities instill a strong sense of ethnic identity in their members, they may be "protected" from downward assimilation. This is illustrated in another of Zhou's works, with her colleague Carl Bankston (1998). In their book on the Vietnamese American community in the New Orleans area (Zhou and Bankston 1998), they argue that the Vietnamese American youths who maintained close ties to the Vietnamese American community (and to their parents) were more likely to be high achievers in school. Those who were not closely tied to their parents or to their local communities and also associated with inner-city youths had lower levels of academic performance.

The third factor shaping trajectories of assimilation is the "absence of mobility ladders." Immigrants who settle in inner cities that provide limited occupational choices to individuals who are not highly educated have a far more difficult time achieving upward mobility. Sociologists, starting in the late 1970s, wrote about a decrease in manufacturing jobs, particularly those located in cities (Cooney 1979; Cooney and Warren 1979; Dunne et al. 1989; Ortiz 1986). These jobs provided some mobility in that employees could move up from a lower-level unskilled position to a supervising or management position. These jobs often provided a "middle-class" income. These ladders to mobility no longer exist in the inner cities to the same extent as they did in the 1960s and 1970s. These inner cities are often where new immigrants first settle (Rumbaut 1994).

While the notion of *segmented assimilation* is appealing because immigrant outcomes are so diverse, few scholars have actually tested its central tenets empirically. It is hard to disentangle the roles of individual characteristics and community support systems in shaping the upward mobility of the second generation. For example, let us compare two hypothetical Mexican American families. The Garcia family includes parents who have an elementary school education and work in a factory assembly line in Chicago. Because they have few economic resources, they have to live in an affordable neighborhood with relatively high poverty rates. Their child goes to a local public school with other less advantaged students, where dropout rates are high and few students go on to attend four-year colleges. The Rodriguezes, in contrast, are a household comprised of a primary breadwinner with a spouse and a child. The primary breadwinner is a college graduate and was recruited from Mexico to work as a software developer in the Chicago suburbs. They are able to purchase a comfortable house in the suburbs, where the median income is well above that of the neighborhood of the Garcias. Their child attends a local school, where most children have parents who are college-educated and where almost every student graduates. A majority of these students attend four-year universities immediately upon graduation. While it is not difficult to argue that the educational experiences of the Garcia and Rodriguez children are shaped by their parents' economic resources and human capital as well as their residential neighborhoods, it is harder to determine whether the neighborhood and school independently affect their outcomes, or which played a more important role in shaping their educational careers. Ricardo Stanton-Salazar argues, for instance, that it is the difference between the social networks of lower-class and middle-class US and Mexican American youth that can, in part, account for differences in their educational outcomes (Stanton-Salazar 2001).

The experiences of immigrant families today are complex, and social researchers seem to be unable to capture all of these complexities in comprehensive theories of educational achievement and of assimilation. Immigrant families may stay in host countries for a short period of time, and then return to their countries of origin, as part of a strategy to increase mobility in their countries of origin. Families may alternate between spending time in their countries of origin and new host countries, perhaps even splitting their year between these different places. Whether or not they reside in home countries for periods of time after immigration, technologies afforded by the internet such as *Skype* or *Facebook*, and the relative ease of travel for those who have legal status and who have financial resources may enable immigrants to more easily retain connections to their countries of origin. Immigrants may send remittances to family living in countries of origin. Assimilation theories do not adequately characterize the experiences of families who are highly mobile and never intend to become "American," but rather see themselves as part of a global labor market.

In this chapter, we have reviewed the ways that social researchers describe the incorporation of immigrant families into the US, and how this may affect their future educational and labor market successes in the US; in other words, how they "assimilate." In the next chapter, we begin to look in more detail at these immigrant groups and their specific historical experiences. Who immigrated to the US and under what circumstances? How did these experiences differ by race, ethnicity, and national origin? Once we have a picture of the different histories of immigrant groups in the US, we will have a context for understanding their very different educational outcomes.

3

Historical Overview of Immigration

The history of migration is as long as the history of humans. Scientists now believe that humans first migrated out of present-day Africa (Ethiopia) approximately 200,000 years ago (White et al. 2003). With respect to America, researchers argue that the first human beings arrived to America between 20,000 and 35,000 years ago, crossing the Bering Strait (Cross 1973). They came with hopes of improving their living conditions, in search of food and a better life (Wepman 2008). These were the first immigrants and the ancestors of the Native Americans. Throughout the history of the US, immigrants have followed in the footsteps of these first arrivals – coming to the US to have a better life.

Emma Lazarus' famous poem "The New Colossus" that is displayed at the foot of the Statue of Liberty represents the most idealistic sense of how America affords the opportunity to individuals with little or no resources to "make it" in the United States:

Not like the brazen giant of Greek fame,
With conquering limbs astride from land to land;
Here at our sea-washed, sunset gates shall stand
A mighty woman with a torch, whose flame
Is the imprisoned lightning, and her name
Mother of Exiles. From her beacon-hand
Glows world-wide welcome; her mild eyes command
The air-bridged harbor that twin cities frame.
"Keep, ancient lands, your storied pomp!" cries she
With silent lips. Give me your tired, your poor,

Your huddled masses yearning to breathe free,
The wretched refuse of your teeming shore.
Send these, the homeless, tempest-tost to me,
I lift my lamp beside the golden door! (Lazarus 1883, engraved in
     1903)

However, in reality, the United States has not favored the most
disadvantaged migrants from abroad. Certainly, the patterns have
been to exclude groups by national origin, race, political beliefs,
and criminal behavior and to favor those who are white, from
certain national-origin groups, the better educated, and, later,
those with family members who are already in the United States.

Currently, the United States does not welcome all potential
migrants with open arms. In order to talk about contemporary
immigrants, and to create a context in which to understand their
educational attainment and achievements, we will fast forward to
the nineteenth century, when the first restrictive policies were put
in place. For now, we present some of the key regulations that
affect the educational attainment of the foreign-born population.
This chapter serves as a brief introduction to the immigration patterns from the nineteenth century to the present.

Throughout the chapter, we underscore how changes in
immigration regulations are related to the characteristics of the
immigrants arriving to the US. We also describe how immigrant
groups were initially positioned within the socioeconomic, ethnic,
and racial hierarchy of the US, and how, for some groups, their
relative racial status has changed over time. The historical context
of immigration in the last 200 years underlies the theoretical shifts
among immigration scholars discussed in the previous chapter:
from traditional understandings of assimilation that assumed
unidirectional upward mobility, to more recent ideas that allow
room for downward socioeconomic mobility among immigrants.
Throughout the chapter, notice the opposition Americans have
had to immigration and their concerns about the "assimilability"
of the most recent arrivals time after time. The groups those feelings were directed toward and the regulations that were in place
to restrict or prevent their migration to the US have changed over

time, however. These shifts in how and which immigrants came to the US as well as the changing context of reception have affected their opportunities to obtain a good education and, consequently, their social mobility over time. We ask the reader to consider: How do US policies toward immigration influence whether immigrants become "American?" How might these policies affect the jobs they get and the places they live? In later chapters, we will ask the reader to consider how the policies that lead to these patterns may influence the educational achievement and attainment of both immigrant adults and the children in immigrant families.

The two centuries that are the focus of this chapter can be divided into several distinct eras of immigration. In part, we have characterized these periods by the national-origin and numbers of immigrants. Within these periods, notice the relationship between the racial and ethnic makeup of immigrants and changes in immigration restrictions that support differential treatment of certain immigrant groups. As you read the chapter, refer to figures 3.1 and 3.2 to identify the total number of legal immigrants arriving to the US in each decade as well as their regions of origin for each historical period.

Pre-1820 or the "Laissez-faire" Policies toward Immigration

Entries to the US were not recorded until 1820, when the first Immigration Act was enacted. However, many immigrants had made their way to the US for a number of centuries and many ports across the country kept records of their arrivals. These "passenger lists," although not exhaustive of all immigrants arriving to the country, provide hints regarding the origins of those early settlers. According to records from the 1600s through the early 1800s, most immigrants who arrived to the US were Protestants from England, though those of Dutch, German, Czechoslovakian, Irish, Italian, and Russian descent also contributed sizeable numbers to the population (Colletta 1989). In addition, Africans were brought to the US as slaves starting in the beginning of the

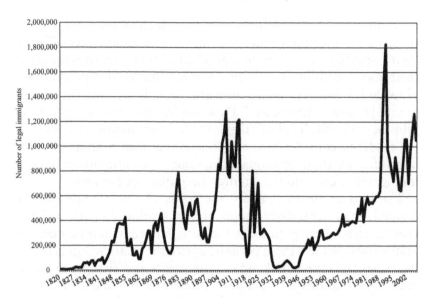
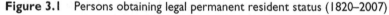

Figure 3.1   Persons obtaining legal permanent resident status (1820–2007)

Source: US Department of Homeland Security (2008)

1600s. (Because our book focuses on educational outcomes of immigrants, a discussion of slaves is beyond its scope. However, the privilege of the white population is built on the division of whites and non-whites, of which blacks represented the bottom of the hierarchy.) The overwhelming majority of these arrivals were not well-educated knights, gentlemen, or merchants. Most were farmers in search of "free land," laborers, or tradesmen. Some were vagrants, thieves, and other criminals (Wepman 2008).

The official discourse of the country at that time seemed to encourage an open door policy. President George Washington publicly shared that sentiment with a group of recent Irish immigrants:

The bosom of America is open to receive not only the Opulent and respectable Stranger, but the oppressed and persecuted of all Nations And Religions; whom we shall welcome to a participation of all our

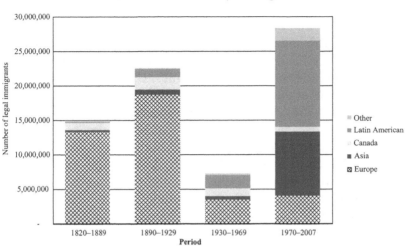

Figure 3.2 Region of origin among legal immigrants by immigration period (1820–2007)
Source: US Department of Homeland Security (2008)

rights and privileges, if by decency and propriety of conduct they appear to merit the enjoyment. (Washington 1938 [1783])

However, not everyone shared these generous feelings, and, by the late 1700s, some started to question the rights of the "newer" immigrants. Other early European settlers agreed with this sentiment, and eventually these feelings were codified in the Naturalization Act of 1790, approved by President George Washington. With this Act, for the first time in its history, the US set residency restrictions (two years) before allowing immigrants to naturalize. The Act also restricted naturalization to "free white persons" and their children and would set a precedent for limiting citizenship by race and ethnicity.

The Beginnings of Mass Migration: 1820–1880s

Millions of immigrants arrived to the US between 1820 and 1880, most of them from Northern and Western Europe. America received large numbers of people eager to join family members and friends who had migrated in previous years. Peasants and artisans who were displaced by the European Industrial Revolution were also looking for new opportunities. Up to the 1810s, it was estimated that about 6,000 immigrants were arriving per year (Hutchinson 1958). These numbers significantly rose starting in the following decade. Between 1820 and 1889, almost 15 million immigrants arrived to the US. Over 13 million of those were from Europe, though their origins had started to become more diverse than the settlers who had arrived in the previous centuries (US Department of Homeland Security 2008).

Between 1820 and 1880, Great Britain, Ireland, and Germany were the main sources of migrants to the US. Each country sent about 2 million immigrants during these six decades. Because many Irish immigrants were trying to escape the poverty and famine in their country during this time, the number of Catholics arriving to the US increased rapidly during this period. By 1850, Catholics represented the largest religious group, and some scholars estimate that they may have accounted for up to 40% of immigrants arriving during this time (Martin and Midgley 2003). In addition to the unprecedented number of Catholics among these new immigrants, with the 1848 Gold Rush, there was a visible increase in Chinese immigrants to the West Coast (Boswell 1986). Chinese immigrants sought jobs as laborers for the transcontinental railroad (Boswell 1986). By the 1870s, while immigrants from Great Britain and other Northern European countries continued to arrive in large numbers (Martin and Midgley 2003), the country was, for the first time, also witnessing the arrival of substantial numbers of Chinese (Boswell 1986) and Canadians (US Department of Homeland Security 2008; Vedder and Gallaway 1970).

By the end the 1880s, Germany and Great Britain were, in order, the leading sources of immigration to the US. In just the ten years between 1880 and 1889, Germany sent almost 1.5 million immigrants; the UK sent over 800,000, and Ireland another 700,000, together accounting for almost 3 million of the 5 million arrivals during this decade (US Department of Homeland Security 2008). Most of these immigrants arrived to the US after being "pushed" out by the demographic transitions in their countries (lower death rates) which overwhelmed the capacity of European labor markets to absorb the growth of the working-age population (Bergad and Klein 2010). The growth in unemployed working-age adults resulted in high levels of urban poverty and social conflict in Europe (Ueda 2007). In addition, the higher wages in the US relative to their countries of origin, the decrease in cost of travel, and the increasing economic opportunities in the US due to increasing industrial production, mining, and farming grains and cotton became "pull" factors, very attractive to the new immigrants.

At this time, the public was concerned with the assimilability of the new foreign-born individuals, especially particular national-origin groups. Starting in the 1870s, the US passed a large number of laws that redefined the rights of many immigrants, at the same time that they stripped legal immigrant status from others. For example, according to the Page Act of 1875, Section 5, no "obnoxious persons" were lawfully allowed. These included "persons who are undergoing a sentence for conviction in their own country of felonious crimes other than political or growing out of or the result of such political offenses, or whose sentence has been remitted on condition of their emigration, and women 'imported for the purposes of prostitution.'" In 1882, "mental defectives," "paupers," or "any person unable to take care of himself or herself without becoming a public charge" were also prohibited from immigrating to the country (Immigration Act of 1882).

While some laws restricted immigration for individuals who were deemed undesirable, others defined whole groups as such. For example, through the Act of 1893, the US began collecting data on whether new entrants could read or write, their marital and occupational status, and their physical and mental health. The Chinese were the first group to be explicitly limited from coming to the US by the Chinese Exclusion Act of 1882, signed by President Chester Arthur. The limitations were justified to the public because the Chinese were considered racially inferior. They had also become a scapegoat for high unemployment on the West

Coast. This Act prohibited Chinese from becoming US citizens for ten years, a limitation which was extended for another ten in 1892 (Geary Act), and made permanent in 1902 (Scott Act). These prohibitions against the Chinese were not repealed until 1943 when China and the US became allies against Japan (Magnuson Act). However, the 1943 Act was more symbolic than real, as it only allowed 105 Chinese to immigrate per year.

The First "New Immigrants": 1890–1920s

The last decade of the nineteenth and the early twentieth century witnessed an important peak in immigration. From 1905 until 1914, an average of more than a million immigrants entered the US yearly. In 1907 alone, a record of almost 1.3 million legal immigrants entered the US (US Department of Homeland Security 2007). In contrast to most of the immigrants who arrived in the earlier decades of the 1800s – predominantly from Northern and Western Europe – between 1890 and 1930, the majority of new arrivals were from Austria, Hungary, Italy, Britain, Canada, and Russia (the latter up until World War I), looking for economic opportunities not available in their own countries. The expansion of the railroad system, mining, manufacturing, and mechanical industries in the US provided employment for the immigrant population. Immigrants comprised the main portion of the workforce in many cities across the US. Immigrants increasingly became not only an important part of the labor supply, but also an important group of consumers in the US (Highman 2002 [1955]).

During this time, policies toward immigration remained relatively open; however, a number of steps were made to further regulate the immigration of "undesirable groups." For example, in 1892 the Office of Immigration, the precursor to the Immigration and Naturalization Services or INS (and what since 2001 became the USCIS – US Citizenship and Immigration Services), was created. In 1903, "polygamists" and "political radicals" were officially excluded from migration to the US (Immigration Act of 1903), and in 1907, because of tensions between the US and Japan, there were attempts to halt immigrants from Japan through the Gentlemen's Agreement of 1907. According to this Agreement, the US would not restrict Japanese immigration so long as Japan would not allow further emigration to the US. This Agreement reflected the growing tension between Asia and the US, which culminated in the California Alien Land Law of 1913. This Act made it illegal for non-US citizens to own land. This law was specifically targeted at Japanese and Chinese, as they were the only racial and ethnic groups prohibited by law from becoming citizens (see Farley and Haaga, 2000: 422).

A few years later, in 1917, the US Congress passed the Asiatic Barred Zone Act (also known as the Immigration Act of 1917), which further restricted immigrants from

> south of the twentieth parallel latitude north, west of the one hundred and sixtieth meridian of latitude south, or who are natives of any country, province, or dependency situate on the Continent of Asia, west of the one hundred and tenth meridian of longitude east from Greenwich and east of the fiftieth meridian of longitude east from Greenwich and south of the fiftieth parallel of latitude north, except that portion of said territory situated between the fiftieth and the sixty-fourth meridians of longitude east from Greenwich and the twenty-fourth and thirty-eighth parallels of latitude north, and no alien now in any way excluded from, or prevented from entering the United States shall be admitted to the United States. (Immigration Act of 1917)

In other words, this Act defined that individuals from an entire geographic region (Asia) were not allowed to enter the United States. It also reiterated the restriction on Chinese and Japanese immigrants. In other words, with this Act, the US excluded illiterate aliens from entry and restricted all Asians (those from the Asiatic Barred Zone, which includes the broadest definition of the countries we view as part of Asia today) from entry (Immigration Act of 1917). According to the National Archives, the barred zone included roughly "the East Indies, Western China, French Indochina, Siam, Burma, India, Bhutan, Nepal, Eastern Afghanistan, Turkestan, and the Kirghis Steppe and southeastern portion of the Arabian peninsula" (Smith 2002, footnote 29).

This law also restricted other immigrants, including prostitutes and:

> All idiots, imbeciles, feeble-minded persons, epileptics, insane persons; persons who have had one or more attacks of insanity at any time previously; persons of constitutional psychopathic inferiority; persons with chronic alcoholism; paupers; professional beggars; vagrants; persons afflicted with tuberculosis in any form or with a loathsome or dangerous contagious disease; . . . persons who have been convicted of or admit having committed a felony or other crime or misdemeanor involving moral turpitude. (Immigration Act of 1917)

Remarkably, all Asian immigrants are grouped with the above categories of people. In addition, these restrictions were not supposed to apply to those who were "government officers, ministers or religious teachers, missionaries, lawyers, physicians, chemists, etc."

As the substance of the laws enacted in this period suggests, ethnocentric biases regarding the newest immigrants were part of an accepted public discourse. In other words, the Asiatic Barred Zone helped to define the geographic boundaries of which modern nation-states were considered as Asian. Following this logic, individuals from these countries are now considered Asian American. In addition, some Asian groups are lumped together by others as well as by US immigration laws over the years by race – certainly, most non-Asian Americans would have trouble differentiating between Chinese, Japanese, and Korean individuals (and arguably even from Filipino, Vietnamese, and Thais). South Asians are lumped together as well. Because these groups are categorized as a single race in the US, but not necessarily in the other countries across the globe, first-generation immigrants from Asia may not self-identify as Asian or Asian American. This may only happen in second and later generations of immigrants from Asian countries.

This discourse targeted not only Asians but also those arriving from countries in Europe that had not sent the bulk of immigrants during previous decades. Unlike earlier historical periods, the majority of the new "stock" of immigrants was no longer from

Northern Europe; instead they were increasingly from Southern and Eastern Europe. These "new" immigrants were the target of xenophobia and fears that they would not be assimilable (Alba and Nee 2003; Highman 2002 [1955]).

In fact, there were active efforts to reduce immigration originating from Southern and Eastern Europe, though these were less harsh than those directed at Asians. One of these efforts was the implementation of a "literacy test" for new arrivals. This was the first immigration restriction directly based on "educational" skills. Because literacy among recent immigrants was lower than among immigrants who arrived in previous decades, it was thought that a literacy exam would deter them from migrating to the US (Alba and Nee 2003). Congress passed this legislation in 1897, stipulating that only those who could read and write would be admitted as immigrants. Despite several vetoes, in 1917 it became a law, attached to the aforementioned Asiatic Barred Zone Act of 1917. It required that immigrants over age 16 take a test to demonstrate they could read and write in at least one language (Martin and Midgley 2003). However, despite its intent, the test did little to reduce immigration from these countries (Alba and Nee 2003).

Though restrictive immigration policies based on fears that these new immigrants would not assimilate burdened new arrivals, other policies had unintended benefits. Southern and Eastern European immigrants, with language and customs different from those of earlier settlers, arrived as the idea of the "common school" was being discussed and developed by progressive educators in the US. During the 1800s, public education was a main focus of reformers. Most notable is the work of Horace Mann (1796–1859) who, during the 1830s and 1840s, worked to prioritize the need to "Americanize" newcomers and other non-privileged groups. Mann worked to convince affluent Americans that educating the "lower" classes was in the best interest of the whole nation. The school was the best place to accomplish this and teachers were better equipped than families to mold character and train "children in basic skills and attitudes" (Kaestle 1978: 15). Tyack (1974) saw this movement as one toward conformity, standardization and professionalization. Education of students became less the purview of local communities and more the concern of a nation that needed to sort students into appropriate roles according to their talents. Immigrant children were judged according to these "objective" standards. Immigrant students who performed well could receive a "good" education and become part of the American economic and social fabric.

While "a good education for all" was the ideal espoused by many reformers, reality often fell far from this lofty goal. The Supreme Court of the US had decided, based on the Dred Scott case of 1857, that institutions that provided "separate but equal" facilities were legal (*Dred Scott v. Sanford*, 1857). Like African Americans in the US, at whom this decision was directed, immigrants, particularly those who were not considered white, were educated in schools of lower quality, in lower academic tracks, and/or in completely separate schools. At this time, there were no programs designed to meet the needs of specific immigrant groups. All immigrants were lumped together as "foreign-born" (Cordasco 1973). In addition, while schooling was mandated for all primary and some secondary school students at this time, exceptions to this policy were granted so frequently that many children of immigrants and working-class families left school early to join their parents at work (Ravitch 2000 [1974]; Stainback and Smith 2004).

These efforts to "Americanize" newcomers were not simply a reflection of resentment against immigrants, however. According to Highman (2002 [1955]), the drive to "Americanize" youngsters was also a product of growing unemployment, poverty, and crime within American society, which was attributed in part to the impression that the Anglo-Saxon "race" was no longer maintaining its superiority within society. Southern and Eastern European immigrants were not simply a problem because they were the newest arrivals, but rather the growth of non-Anglo-Saxon ethnic groups threatened the power and status of Anglo-Saxon whites. Xenophobia against the newest arrivals would not deter them from coming, however, and immigration from Southern and Eastern Europe continued to increase in the years to follow. Most of the regulations passed during the early twentieth century tried to limit immigration to the US, especially from Southern and Eastern Europe. These policies were concerned with the "quality" of the new immigrants, as well as the prospects that they would "assimilate." Policy-makers assumed that the national origins of immigrants were the main indicators of the "quality" and "assimilability" of new immigrants.

The most important restrictions on immigration at this time were passed in the 1921 Emergency Quota and 1924 Immigration Acts. These measures both quantitatively and qualitatively restricted the entrance to the US of less "desirable" (European) immigrants by regulating immigration from Europe through quotas based on national origins. These quotas favored nationalities that were previously well represented in the US based on earlier census counts. For example, the 1921 Emergency Quota Act allowed 3% of the foreign-born population by national origin currently in the US to immigrate. The current population in the US was determined by the 1910 Census. This effectively limited the number of immigrants allowed in the country, while maintaining the existing racial/ethnic mix. This mix favored immigrants from Western and Northern Europe, as they were more numerous in the 1910 Census. The 1924 Immigration Act provided further advantage to these "white" immigrants from Western and Northern Europe by amending the quota system such that 2% of the total number by national origin as of the 1890 national census was allowed to immigrate. As planned, between the 1930s and 1950s, most of the immigrant visas were extended to new arrivals from Northern and Western Europe. About 14% went to Eastern and Southern Europeans and about 4% to other countries in the Eastern hemisphere (Martin and Midgley 2003).

It is important to note that immigration from Latin America was not a main source of concern during this time, thus most of the restrictions of this period did not apply to any Latin American country. However, some have noted that economic and political turmoil brought about by the Mexican Revolution (1910–29) pushed over one million Mexicans northward during this period. In cities like Los Angeles, the proportion of Mexicans (both immigrants and those who had resided there for generations) accounted for a sizeable portion of the population (Ruiz 2001). Mexicans were also present in the Great Lakes region as they were employed by the predominant industries of the region: steelwork, fishing, canning, and automobile (Gutierrez 1995). It is important to note, however, that the socioeconomic status of Mexican-origin communities during this time was characterized by segregation and poverty, as well as low-wage labor, and some considered Mexican immigrants more racially inferior than immigrants from Europe, and thus unassimilable (Galindo 2011).

The "New New Immigrants": 1930–1964

During this period, there was a significant shift in the origins of the groups immigrating to the US, which began to resemble those of contemporary immigrants. Europe (especially Britain, Germany, and Italy) and Canada were still the main regions sending most migrants during this time; however, Asia, Mexico, and the Caribbean became important sources of immigration, especially in the decade preceding 1965.

It is little known or publicly acknowledged that in the 1940s Latin American and Caribbean immigrants already accounted for one in three immigrants arriving to the US (Asia only accounted for 4% at this time). These proportions continued to rise in the following decades (US Department of Homeland Security 2008). Several economic and political changes in the US and around the world help explain this shift. Starting in the 1940s, increasing population pressure, urbanization, and unemployment in Mexico, improved communication between the US and Mexico, and demand for unskilled labor in the US at the beginning of World War II (which mobilized many young men into the military and many others into defense-related jobs) created the perfect conditions for a steady flow of migrants from Mexico to the US (Alba and Nee 2003; Bergad and Klein 2010; Massey et al. 2003b). Most of these immigrants were needed in agriculture, where it was the hardest to find native recruits. In order to fill these jobs and regularize the flow of immigrants from the southern border, the US and Mexican governments established what was known as the *Bracero Program*, which, while originally only conceived as a wartime need, lasted until 1964 and brought almost 5 million Mexican workers to the US (Garcia y Griego 1996). Although it was a program to "control" the flow of immigrants, many would have crossed the border before being recruited by growers (Massey et al. 2003b). These undocumented immigrants would be called "wetbacks," a derogatory term to designate Mexicans who crossed (presumably swimming – thus "wet") the Rio Grande to migrate to the US.

The shifts in racial/ethnic backgrounds and national origins of the immigrants arriving to the US at this time were impossible to ignore, and international pressures during the postwar period forced the US to take a stand regarding the treatment of racial minorities (Alba and Nee 2003). Several attempts were made in the following decades to craft more tolerant migration laws that would not discriminate against certain minorities. For example, the McCarran-Walter Act (also known as the 1952 Immigration and Nationality Act (INA)), passed after World War II, made all races who were already in the US eligible for naturalization, thus eliminating race as a barrier to immigration. It also eliminated discrimination by sex in immigration laws. This Act had a major impact on Asians who were now "eligible" for citizenship and, for the first time since the late 1800s, could be admitted under the quota system.

Despite these changes, the McCarran-Walter Act did maintain the quota system passed in 1924, and it also created a system of preferences that encouraged skilled laborers and families of US citizens, which still exists in contemporary immigration policy. It is important to note that presidents John F. Kennedy and Harry S. Truman were in favor of abolishing the preference system established by the 1924 quota systems, but they did not succeed and the INA was in place through the mid-1960s.

In addition to the usual migrants searching for better economic opportunities, the 1950s and 1960s also saw the arrival of large numbers of immigrants fleeing persecution. Over 200,000 immigrants escaping from Hungary arrived in the early 1950s. Following that, the Cuban Revolution of 1959 caused hundreds of thousands to flee Cuba for the US in the following years. Because there were no special provisions for refugees, or in other words, refugees were not different from other immigrants and thus they needed a sponsor, refugees were accepted in the country with temporary visas. It was not until a few decades later that the US passed the Refugee Act of 1980 in which persecuted individuals would fall into their own separate category of "refugee."

From Liberalization Back to Increased Restrictions: 1965–2000

For many immigrants today, their presence in the US was really made possible when the landmark Hart-Cellar Act (also called the 1965 Immigration and Naturalization Act) was approved. This law explicitly abandoned the national-origins quota system instituted earlier that restricted individuals on the basis of race, ethnicity, and/or nationality from immigrating to the US. It formed a seven-category preference system that focused (as did the 1952 McCarran-Walter Act) on family reunification and skilled workers. More importantly, while the Hart-Cellar Act maintained a quota system that divided the world into Western and Eastern hemispheres (where the quotas were 170,000 and 120,000, respectively), the number of migrants who entered under family reunification preferences was not limited by the quota. In other words, the total worldwide quota of 290,000 immigrants could be exceeded if, for example, one million individuals applied for entry based on family reunification.

The 1965 Hart-Cellar Act and the immigration acts that have followed it have attempted to shape the racial, ethnic, and educational levels of today's immigrant population, and they are still at the center of much scholarly research and political debate. However, given that the decades preceding 1965 had already witnessed the arrival of large numbers of immigrants from Mexico and Asia, some have argued that politicians and scholars may be overstating the effects of the Act on the flow of immigrants (Massey 1995).

In the four decades between 1960 and 2000, the US received over 24 million legal immigrants. The national origins of these immigrants dramatically differed from those who arrived in previous periods, and their differences continued to grow with the increasing immigrant population. In the decade between 1960 and 1970, Mexico already accounted for 13.7% of all legal immigrants, and Asia for another 11%. Three decades later, between 1990 and 2000, immigrants from Asia accounted for 29% of all legal immigrants, and a single country – Mexico – added to 28% (US Department of Homeland Security 2008). In the same decade, the Caribbean contributed over 1 million legal immigrants (or 10% of total legal immigrants). From 1990 to 2000, immigrants from Europe accounted for less than 14% of legal immigrants, whereas 100 years earlier they had been over 92% of all legal immigrants.

More specifically, two countries contributed over 1 million of their citizens to the migrant population to the US: Mexico (with 5 million) and the Philippines (with 1.5 million). Many other countries sent immigrants well in excess of half a million individuals such as (in order from more to fewer): Canada, the Dominican Republic, India, Korea, Cuba, the UK, Vietnam, China, Jamaica, and Russia. The diversity of these countries is remarkable, which reflected in the racial and ethnic backgrounds, English knowledge, and socioeconomic origins of these immigrants.

More than ever before in US history, immigrants increasingly comprised one of two major socioeconomic groups: human capital migrants (highly educated, white-collar and professional employees) and labor migrants (low-skilled and under-educated). This has created a bimodal distribution of immigrants by employment and education (Ueda 2007) – remember the hourglass figure discussed in chapter 1. Another unprecedented characteristic of immigration during this period is the rise of female migrants. Especially as a result of increasing family reunification and labor migration, female immigrants began to outnumber male immigrants in annual admissions totals, from the early 1980s on (Morawska 2009).

In addition to the Hart-Cellar Act of 1965, additional unprecedented changes to immigration legislation took place during this time. The US responded to the rise in forced migration, more specifically to petitions from refugees and asylum-seekers. Although the acceptance of refugees had started at the end of World War II, these were part of the normal immigration process, and types of immigrants were not distinguished from one another. However, in 1980, Congress permanently institutionalized a system for admitting refugees (Refugee Act of 1980). Through this Act, the US defined the term "refugee" to conform to the 1967 United Nations Protocol Relating to the Status of Refugees (2007) and made clear the distinction between refugee and asylee status. Essentially, refugees are groups that, by virtue of political or other persecution, are unable to live in their country of origin. States (governments) recognize certain groups as refugees. Asylum-seekers are individuals who request that they be admitted to their new host country based on their own circumstances. In other words, refugees are those who are recognized as such by other governments, while asylees are individuals (who may face the same type of persecution), but are not part of the group that is considered refugee.

This Act eliminated refugees as a category of the preference system and imposed a ceiling of 270,000 refugees. From the end of World War II to the turn of the twenty-first century, over 3.5 million refugees and asylum-seekers arrived to the US, making this country an international destination for the resettlement of forced migrants.

Although preoccupation with undocumented arrivals precedes the twentieth century, concern about the large flow of undocumented immigrants in the post-1965 era culminated in the November 1986 Immigration Reform and Control Act (IRCA). The main objectives of the provisions included in this law were: (1) to reduce the flow of illegal immigration by (a) imposing penalties on employers who hired undocumented immigrants; (b) increasing enforcement at the borders; and (2) to legalize those already in the US who had resided in the United States in an unlawful status since 1982. It also created a new classification of seasonal agricultural worker (SAW) and made provisions for the legalization of such workers. As a result of the IRCA, about 2.7 million unauthorized aliens became legal immigrants. However, some argue it also incentivized additional illegal immigration towards the country (Martin and Midgley 2003), especially from Mexico. Fraud through the SAW program as well as the lack of oversight of the employer sanctions prevented this new policy from effectively slowing down the arrival of undocumented immigrants (Martin 1994).

Although most immigration policies are designed to control the entrance of those coming from abroad, two federal initiatives from this time mark notable exceptions by directly targeting immigrant students already in the US. These policies reflected increasing awareness of the widespread presence of immigrants participating in US institutions. In 1974, the Supreme Court ruled that under Title VI of the Civil Rights Act, immigrant students who were not proficient speakers of English were entitled to special assistance that allowed them equal participation in school programs (*Lau v. Nichols* 1974; McDonnell and Hill 1993). A few years later, in 1982, the decision in *Plyler v. Doe* guaranteed that all children, regardless of their immigrant status or that of their families, had the right to public education. As a result, school districts were no longer allowed to inquire about the immigration status of parents or their children (Soltero 2006). However, it would not take long for political movements to seek to curtail these rights for immigrants.

The increasing presence of immigrants across the US and the large numbers of undocumented arrivals intensified the debate about immigration, and pressures to reform legislation mounted. Opponents of immigration argued that too many immigrants were using social services like hospitals, police, and schools, and that their use cost US-born, tax-paying citizens. Proposals to make undocumented aliens ineligible for some social services were put forward. Among these proposals were those that challenged whether the children of undocumented immigrants should be able to attend US schools, even when the children were born in the US and thus citizens by birthright (White and Glick 2009). The best known of these proposals is the California Proposition 187, which aimed to prohibit access of undocumented immigrants to a number of public services (including schools). Immigrants had been targeted as the scapegoat of California's economic recession by Governor Wilson, and his proposal to eliminate social services to undocumented immigrants was passed by California voters, though most of the provisions were later eliminated by counter challenges (Massey and Capoferro 2008).

In addition to the tensions regarding the use and charges of abuse of social services by undocumented immigrants, concerns about terrorism were also on the rise in the US by the end of the twentieth century, especially after the 1993 World Trade Center bombing attributed to seven individuals of Middle Eastern origin living in New Jersey. Several laws sought to address the main concerns that were debated during this time: welfare and terrorism. In 1996, three related immigration laws were approved: the Antiterrorism and Effective Death Penalty Act; the Personal Responsibility and Work Opportunity Reconciliation Act (PRWORA); and the Illegal Immigration Reform and Immigrant Responsibility Act (IIRIRA).

Through these Acts, the US expedited the procedure for removal of alien terrorists and changed the conditions of application for asylum-seekers. They made the detention and deportation of criminal immigrants easier and expedited the removal of individuals who requested asylum but could not support their claims of persecution. These acts made it more difficult for those who had been denied entry to reapply. It also increased border personnel, INS investigators, and surveillance equipment and technology. Eligibility for certain public benefits was reduced – even for legal immigrants – although later restored for legal immigrants (Zimmerman and Tumlin 1999). These laws even impacted the education of immigrant students. They made it impossible for undocumented students to be eligible for benefits such as financial aid or in-state tuition, if they were to continue their education after graduating from high school.

September 11, 2001–Present

The terrorist attacks of September 11, 2001 on the World Trade Towers in New York City increased focus on the protection of

US borders against foreign terrorism that was already stated in the 1996 Acts. Only one month after the 2001 attacks, the US passed the USA PATRIOT Act (its full name is the *Uniting and Strengthening America by Providing Appropriate Tools Required to Intercept and Obstruct Terrorism* Act). Among other things, the PATRIOT Act tripled the number of Border Patrol, Customs Service, and INS personnel at various points of entry and at the northern border. The law required the Attorney General and the Federal Bureau of Investigation (FBI) to provide the Department of State and INS with access to criminal history databases. It also mandated new technology to identify all visa and admissions applicants. It expanded the scope of aliens ineligible for admission or deportable due to terrorist activities and provided for mandatory detention until removal of any alien suspected terrorist. It also authorized longer detentions and made it more difficult to appeal decisions denying admission to the US. The viewpoint that control of immigrants was a national security issue was made clear with the dissolution of the Immigration and Naturalization Services (INS). Just a year after 2001, the INS was dissolved under the Homeland Security Act of 2002. All the functions of the INS were now the responsibility of the new Department of Homeland Security (DHS).

In 2005, two bills were proposed to deal with immigration reform: the Secure America and Orderly Immigration Act and the Comprehensive Enforcement and Immigration Reform Act. Both bills aimed for the legalization of immigrants who had resided in the US for a long time, and sought to establish guest worker programs, but neither was voted on in the Senate. More recently, the Comprehensive Immigration Reform Act of 2007 (CIRA) – a compromise from the failed attempts in the two previous years, also focused on unauthorized migration, but failed to pass the House. Its primary objectives were to further increase border security, create a guest worker program, provide a path to citizenship for undocumented workers, increase worksite enforcement, and add more criminal penalties for undocumented aliens. While the bill did not pass, the issues of terrorism, undocumented aliens, and border control remain at the forefront of the immigration debate.

Fears about immigration led to these more restrictive immigration policies. These policies limited the educational opportunities of undocumented immigrant students. Many policy-makers and law-makers were concerned that, as a result of these restrictions, many children of immigrants living and studying in the US may have their social and economic opportunities curtailed because of their lack of legal status. Starting in 2001 and reintroduced several times in the following years, Congress tried to address this issue with the "Development, Relief and Education for Alien Minors Act" (DREAM Act 2009), which aimed to provide *qualified* undocumented high-school students who wish to attend college or serve in the armed forces an opportunity to apply for legal status. The act would allow for in-state tuition without regard to immigrant status. The conditions to qualify under the DREAM Act were: (a) to have lived in the United States for at least 5 years and have been under the age of 16 at the time of entry; (b) to have graduated from high school or have been accepted to a college or institution of higher education; (c) be of good moral character; and (d) not be deportable on account of a criminal conviction, alien smuggling, or document fraud. It is estimated that 65,000 youth would be eligible every year (Passel 2003). In December 2010, a revised version of the DREAM Act was considered by Congress. In this iteration of the Act, some changes had been introduced to the bill; most importantly, provisions to provide in-state tuition had been stripped out in order to appease opponents. The proposal passed at the House, but failed in the Senate. While the DREAM Act is still an aspiration for many law-makers, there has been little attempt to revive it.

Settlement Patterns: Then and Now

Although immigrants have settled all across the country in urban, suburban, and rural areas, many new immigrants, particularly immigrants from Ireland, Italy, and Eastern Europe, who arrived at the turn of the twentieth century, settled in urban areas, where there was a need for low-wage labor. They often first settled in communities with co-ethnics, who were able to help house them and find them jobs initially. Asian immigrants to the US initially settled on the West Coast and in Hawaii, doing agricultural work, working in mines, or building railroads. Asian immigrants began to form ethnic enclaves, dominated by male laborers, in some places on the West Coast. Hispanics, many of whom were not immigrants per se, but lived on land annexed by the US, were initially concentrated in areas around the Mexican border, in the Southwest and in California, and African immigrants were mostly those involuntarily brought to the US to work on plantations, mostly in the Southern part of the US (Takaki 1993).

While these patterns still exist in some ways today, they are also changing. "Gateway" destinations are those places where immigrants first settle in the US, and the traditional "gateways" are typically large cities like New York, Chicago, San Francisco, and Boston. "Former gateway" cities like Cleveland, Buffalo, and Detroit, industrial, manufacturing towns with plentiful low-skilled job opportunities at one time, no longer see a high influx of new immigrants because they no longer are centers of manufacturing and industry. "Emerging gateways," such as Las Vegas, Seattle, the Twin Cities in Minnesota, Salt Lake City, and Raleigh-Durham, are seeing higher than average immigrant populations, largely due to the economic opportunities available for more highly skilled new immigrants in those places (Singer 2004).

So, while Asian immigrants are still concentrated on the West Coast, largely in urban areas, and ethnic enclaves exist in Los Angeles, San Francisco, and Orange County, California, they are also found in high rates in Portland and Seattle. New Orleans and Houston have large Vietnamese communities, as does Falls Church, Maryland. Hmong immigrants have large communities in Minneapolis and St Paul. Raleigh-Durham has seen large communities of Mexican immigrants arrive, and Hispanic, and particularly Mexican, immigrants are settling in communities in the Midwest where there have been few minorities in the past. African immigrants today settle mostly in the Washington, DC metropolitan area.

Immigrants today still disproportionately reside in cities, but compared to the past, immigrants are also more likely to be found in suburbs and in rural areas than ever before (Singer 2004). Some immigrants still settle in ethnic enclaves, typically in urban areas, and this has both advantages and disadvantages. Recent immigrants in ethnic enclaves often find it easier to find work. Immigrants who do not speak English proficiently are able to shop and get around these neighborhoods better because members of the community speak the same language. Immigrants who live in ethnic enclaves may benefit from the social capital of these tight-knit communities. However, ethnic enclaves are often located in or near less advantaged neighborhoods with worse schools and community services. Immigrants who locate in the suburbs often have better schools, better neighborhood services, and more educated neighbors. Children in immigrant families can also derive beneficial social capital to help them succeed in schools from these sources.

Conclusion: Immigrants, Old, New, and Forthcoming

The fear that new immigrants will not "fit in" to the US has been present for centuries. The laws and policies that were crafted in response to changing immigration rates and the shifting profile of the immigrant population reflected the fears that US-born residents had about immigrants. Many worried that new immigrants of that period were too different from US-born residents of the country and were therefore "unassimilable." Asians were seen as part of the "yellow peril" and viewed as racially inferior and unassimilable. Southern and Eastern Europeans were targeted as an unassimilable group at the turn of the twentieth century. Today, similar arguments are applied to Hispanic and arguably Asian immigrants. United States-born residents worry about competing for resources with race, ethnic, or national-origin groups that remain "separate" in US society.

Despite centuries of immigration to the US, and specific efforts to address the issue of undocumented children, there is still no national policy regarding how to best incorporate immigrant students (whether documented or undocumented) in the educational system (Suárez-Orozco et al. 2008). Schools differ according to how they incorporate and teach non-English speaking or Limited English Proficient (LEP) children. They also vary in the types of services they offer to newly immigrated families, and in whether or not they connect immigrants to other neighborhood social and community services. Some schools may accommodate students who must migrate with families to follow seasonal labor or return to their countries of origin for long periods to visit family or be cared for when the family is unable to work in the US, while others do not. Throughout US history, much legislation has been crafted which has limited potential migrants' access to the US. Immigration laws have made it easier for the US government to keep immigrants under surveillance, deport them, and restrict full use of US social services. Less immigration legislation has been devoted to opening opportunities for migrants to come and ensuring access to needed social services upon arrival, though certainly the DREAM Act and other legislation has tried to do just that.

These laws have shaped the immigrant population that currently resides in the US. Documented immigrant adults may arrive in the US as a result of preferences for skilled workers. These immigrants may be highly skilled, from places where the supply of educated individuals exceeds the demand for well-paid skilled employment. On the other hand, family members seeking to reunify, refugees, or undocumented immigrants may arrive with few educational qualifications, which may result in them occupying unskilled employment in the US. This chapter provided the context with which we can understand the very different educational profiles of adult immigrants that we describe in the next chapter. It is important to understand the educational differences among adults because these affect the types of educational opportunities available to their offspring – the children in immigrant families.

4

Educational Attainment and Socioeconomic Status of Immigrant Adults

Introduction

In Francis Ford Coppola's *The Godfather: Part II*, we see Vito Corleone (the main patriarch of the films *The Godfather* and *The Godfather: Part II*) arriving as a young boy on his own with absolutely no financial or family resources. Still, in this story, he becomes the "Godfather" and builds an extremely success-ful empire. Despite the success story portrayed in this movie, in reality, the United States has not consistently favored the most disadvantaged populations from abroad. Certainly, as we review elsewhere (see chapters 2 and 3), the patterns have been to exclude individuals by national origin, race, political beliefs, and criminal behavior and to favor those from other national-origin groups and the better educated and, later, those with family members who are already in the United States. In this chapter, we ask the reader to consider how these policies shaped the current population of adult immigrants. How might the characteristics of adult immigrants shape their children's educational achievement and attainment? We will provide evidence of how, in general, the stories that portray experiences from rags to riches are few and far between and more complicated than one may expect.

Earlier in this book, we showed that how migrants are *selected* for entry to the United States is the primary reason they are so different from the native-born population. It takes considerable resources for individuals and families to uproot and move to the United States. For example, no matter how much a typical rural family in China, like one whose household members have only completed primary school and whose household income is US$300 per month, would like to migrate to the US, that family simply cannot do so. Hence, what is absolutely certain is that immigrants are different from other individuals who remain in their country of origin. Immigrants are not a randomly selected group. Sometimes they are among the most advantaged subpopulation from a country. Sometimes they are slightly better educated than the average citizen of their country of origin. Either way, they are often different in many important respects from the overall population of the country from which they come. They do not represent the typical "Filipino" from the Philippines or "Mexican" from Mexico. From our experiences with immigrants from a particular race, ethnicity, or national origin, we cannot draw conclusions about typical cultural values or behaviors of others who share the same race, ethnic group, or nationality.

For example, immigrants typically have different levels of education from those who remain in their native countries. Feliciano (2005) demonstrates that there is educational selectivity for most immigrant groups; that is, immigrants tend to have more education than the population of non-immigrants from particular countries. More specifically, according to her analyses, out of the 32 immigrant groups she studied, 31 were positively selected on education (the exception was Puerto Ricans – though more recent data from Puerto Ricans in Florida also support the existence of positive selection among this group; Duany 2011). Despite the general pattern of educational selectivity of immigrants, though, Feliciano also shows that there is great "variation in the degree of educational selectivity depending on the country of origin and the timing of migration from a particular country" (Feliciano 2005: 147). More specifically, the farther the distance between countries, the more positively selected immigrants are. Following this argument, Asians and Africans are highly selected groups, and Mexicans are less so. According to Feliciano, immigrants from countries with high levels of schooling are also less positively selected compared to those countries with low levels of schooling.

In addition to being different from those they leave behind, immigrants are also unlikely to be comparable to individuals in their country of destination, in this case, the US. They differ from their non-migrant counterparts both in terms of measurable characteristics (such as age, education, income, and so forth) and also in terms of less tangible traits (perhaps aspirations for their children, optimism, willingness to take risks, ambition, etc.). In this chapter, we explore the differences in the educational attainment of foreign-born versus native-born adults in the United States. We pay particular attention to variation by race, ethnicity, and national origin. We also review the extent to which these differences parallel inequalities in family income and poverty levels of immigrant and native-born racial and ethnic groups. We end the chapter by linking the selection and composition of immigrant adults to our perceptions about which immigrant groups have "made it" and assimilated, and which are perceived to be unable to attain success in mainstream America.

Two Examples of a South Asian and a Mexican Family in Fiction: The Ganguli Family in The Namesake *and the Sanchez Family in* Mi Familia

Let us take for example two characters from two popular films (one of which was adapted from a bestselling novel) to illustrate the dramatic differences between the educational resources of immigrants. Jhumpa Lahiri's 2003 novel, *The Namesake* (which was adapted and made into a film in 2006 by Academy Award-winning Director Mira Nair), follows the trajectory of an immigrant family from India. The father, Ashoke Ganguli, is a Bengali student who, after a near-death experience, decides to attend the Massachusetts Institute of Technology in the United States to study for a PhD in Engineering. He and his wife eventually settle in the United States where he becomes a university professor. When his wife, Ashima, first arrives in the United States, she is surprised by the lack of familiar foods and the isolation faced by many new immigrants. For example, in the film version, she makes her own version of *chaat* (a common street food in India) by mixing Rice Krispies, peanuts, and some spices. She accidentally shrinks her husband's sweaters in the dryer as she had never used one in India.

However, the trajectory of their lives is one that is guided by their relative socioeconomic advantage. After all, Ashoke Ganguli will earn a PhD and become a college professor. Eventually, they move into a large house in the suburbs. Their son, Gogol/Nikhil Ganguli, graduates from Yale University with a degree in architecture, and later, in the novel and film versions of the story, he meets a Bengali woman who is finishing her PhD in French literature. While the emphasis of the novel is not about the educational attainment of these fictional characters, it paints a plausible portrait of a relatively privileged South Asian family who migrates to the US in the late 1960s. These characters are well educated and occupy high-status white-collar occupations, and they eventually settle in the suburbs. While they experience many of the common hardships that all immigrants face – for instance, the parents live in a basement apartment on a graduate student stipend and later their house is spray-painted with racist slurs – they also arrive to the United States with formidable educational resources despite their relatively modest financial assets.

In contrast, in *My Family* (or *Mi Familia*) (Nava 1995), a film about a Mexican American family that settles in East Los Angeles, California, the father, José Sanchez, is the first to migrate to the United States. This journey lasts one year and is made by foot. He marries a US-born woman who is later illegally deported to Mexico. The film jumps to many years later, when one of their sons accidentally kills an individual and later becomes a fugitive and is shot by the police. Though some of the Sanchez children are successful (they go to college and one even becomes a lawyer), one of their other sons eventually serves time in prison. In many ways, the movie portrays immigrant success, but also poverty and hardship (such as going to prison and deportation), through several generations. The family in *Mi Familia* portrays some of the elements of segmented assimilation that we have discussed in previous chapters. The contexts in which these individuals live in the US are important in understanding their experiences. In addition, not all children of immigrants end up doing better than their parents. Some of them may even end up in a worse (downward) individual situation than that of their parents (in other words, they experience downward assimilation).

While an argument can be made that these stories promote stereotypical examples of the trajectories of immigrant families from India and Mexico, they also highlight the difference in the average educational attainment of immigrants from these two respective countries of origin. What is notable about these two films is that the first person to migrate from both families is the father. This pattern of migration is a typical route taken by many migrant families. The Indian American father, Ashoke Ganguli, and the Mexican American father, José Sanchez, arrive in the United States with very different educational backgrounds and purposes. Both families begin with limited financial resources but they are armed with very different levels of education and their eventual trajectories and those of their children are quite different. While these are two fictional families, we will see later that their situations match well with the average educational attainments of Indian American and Mexican American immigrants. Using nationally representative data, we will review descriptive statistics (means and frequencies) of educational attainment of foreign-born adults by national origin, and we will see that Asian Indians are among the most well-educated immigrants, while the average level of education of foreign-born Mexicans is among the lowest of all national-origin groups.

While Indian Americans are among the most educated individuals in the United States, the average educational attainment of an adult in India is very low. However, as we have suggested above, these immigrants are not like average native-born Americans because they are selected on a number of traits, some of which are measurable (like education and income) while others are more difficult to quantify (their tolerance for risk-taking, optimism, etc.), nor will they be like the average Indian in India. They may be among the most advantaged individuals and families from their countries, like Indian Americans, or among the least educated, as in the case of Mexican Americans.

Differences by Race and Ethnicity

There is great diversity both across and within the immigrant population overall by race, ethnicity, and national origin, and also across and within any particular national-origin group. US policies, as well as conditions within the particular countries from which immigrants come, shape who is "selected" to migrate to the US and who remains in the countries of origin. When researchers talk about differences between immigrant populations and their counterparts who reside in their countries of origin, they use the term *selection* (e.g. Borjas 1987; Feliciano 2005; Jasso 1988; Rumbaut 1997a; 1997b). When researchers think about selection, they want to know how and which differences in education and occupational status are associated with the countries of origin of migrants.

Of course, social scientists disagree about the extent to which selection matters at all for how immigrants fare once they arrive in the US, and on whether migrants who are "selected" to come to the US are better off than those who choose to remain in their native countries. For instance, as we mentioned above, South Asian immigrants to the US have far higher average educational attainment than those who remain in their countries of origin. In particular, in India, data from 2006 indicate that only 63% of the population is literate (World Bank 2012) and only 40% of adolescents attend secondary school (World Bank 2011a). This is in stark contrast to the overwhelming majority of Asian Indian Americans, of whom 80% of those between 25 and 29 years of age have a Bachelor's degree (NCES 2005). In Pakistan, only 30% of all children receive secondary education and this number decreases to 19% when examining those who complete upper secondary education (World Bank 2011b). However, in countries like Mexico, a much higher proportion, approximately 70%, of youth attend secondary school (UNESCO 2011). Mexicans with high educational attainment who come to the US seem far less different from those who remain in Mexico because educational attainment in Mexico is higher, on average, than it is in India or Pakistan.

The difference between the average educational attainment of individuals remaining in the countries of origin and the average educational attainment of immigrants from that country gives us an idea of the extent to which they are "selected." Asian Indians, for example, are among the most educated immigrants to the US today, while Mexicans are among the least educated. This suggests that Asian Indians are far more *positively selected* in terms of education than are Mexicans who immigrate to the United States. One way to think of the idea of "positive selection" is that the average immigrant from India is far more educated compared to the average person in India, while this is not true of Mexicans. It is important to consider selection when we examine ethnic group differences in the educational attainment of adults in the US later in the chapter.

Immigrants not only differ in their degree of *selection* from their countries of origin, they also differ in their conditions of reception in the US (Borch and Corra 2010; McHugh et al. 1997; Portes and Bach 1985; Portes and Böröcz 1989; Portes and Rumbaut 2001; 2006). Life in a posh suburb is very different from life in a poor inner-city neighborhood in many ways, including the schools, the hospitals, and other services that are available to residents. It is also important to remember a point made in previous chapters: immigrants come from a wide range of racial backgrounds, and their place in the racial hierarchy of the United States also affects their experiences. A white immigrant from the United Kingdom will undoubtedly have a different life in the United States compared to a new arrival who is black from Haiti. Native-born US residents will tend to have very different stereotypes about how the white versus the black immigrant may perform in school, behave in his or her neighborhood, and more generally "fit in" to mainstream US society.

While sociologists compare the average outcomes of different immigrant and native-born racial and ethnic groups, one must keep in mind the considerable heterogeneity within each of the groups. However, despite the fact that group averages may hide the great diversity of backgrounds within immigrant groups, we demonstrate that there are vast differences in the patterns of educational backgrounds among national-origin groups. Differences in resources that may be a result of selection into the US or conditions of reception once living in the US may at least in part account for why some ethnic groups seem to be more successful than others. The resources that are available to groups because of how they immigrate and settle in the United States may help explain why our stereotypes of Asian Americans, for example, are so different from popular images of Hispanics. These resources are also key in explaining their assimilation trajectories in the US, from the types of neighborhoods in which they reside to the jobs they hold, and their experiences with discrimination.

Remember that individuals from different ethnic backgrounds not only come with very different levels of resources (such as education or monetary assets), but because friends and family members are likely to have the same racial and ethnic backgrounds, these differences can become magnified. In other words, these differences are exacerbated because immigrants are much more likely to be acquainted with co-ethnics than others (Light and Bonacich 1988; Nee et al. 1994; Perez 1992; Portes 1987; 1998; Portes and Stepick 1993; Zhou 1992). If an immigrant is Indian, then that individual is not only more likely to have higher levels of education but will also know more people who are well educated. Thus, it is reasonable to expect that a child of Indian immigrant parents (Indian American) will be likely to be surrounded by adults and children who are well educated or have high educational aspirations; hence, college attendance may be a given. For Mexicans, who have lower levels of education on average, association with people from the same ethnic background and with similar immigrant experiences leads to them being less likely to know people who have higher levels of education. This is very important because the ability to gain knowledge, information, and support from highly educated co-ethnic residents, which is called "social capital" by sociologists, is key for attaining socioeconomic mobility for immigrant adults and their children (Bankston 2004; Portes 1998). We discuss the importance of social capital next.

Social Capital among Immigrants

Social capital is an important concept that describes the resources that are embedded in relationships between people (Bourdieu 1980; Coleman 1988; Kao 2004; Portes 1998). This term is widely used to describe a variety of characteristics, but we will use it primarily with respect to the resources available to individuals that stem from their relationships with others. Children of well-educated and affluent parents enjoy both material resources and benefit from the expectations and norms of the upper class. This, in turn, provides children from these families with a much better chance to become highly educated and earn high levels of income when they become adults (Coleman 1988). Children who are closer to their parents presumably can enjoy a greater intensity of social capital than children who never spend any time with them. Clearly, children whose parents are less educated are disadvantaged in terms of their social capital. Parents with lower levels of education are often unable to assist children in planning and managing their education so as to achieve high educational attainment.

James Coleman, a highly influential sociologist, wrote an oft-cited essay that formally described three elements of social capital (Coleman 1988; Kao 2004). These are: (1) obligations and expectations; (2) information channels; and (3) social norms. Obligations and expectations refer to transactions and experiences between individuals or even between groups. For example, if John Doe agrees to lend Mary Smith $50, the expectation is that Mary Smith would reciprocate the favor if John Doe needed it. The availability of this resource (the ability to borrow $50) is a form of social capital.

Information channels refer to the fact that the more friends we have (and the more different they are from each other), the greater, and perhaps better quality of, information we are able to access. For example, a child who wants to apply to the University of Pennsylvania needs to acquire a lot of information about what classes to take in high school, the importance of extracurricular activities, letters of recommendation, SAT tests, and so forth. A student whose parents have PhDs, whose friends are also well educated, will have access to more information than someone whose parents only finished elementary school and whose friends also have not attended college. Classic examples also point to the experience of finding a job (Granovetter 1974). If referrals from friends are important, then having friends who are well-placed to help is crucial.

Finally, social norms are an important aspect of social capital. For example, let's say that John Doe, Mary Smith, Jane Lee, and Sandra Guerra are a tightly knit group of friends. The four of them regularly take turns hosting dinner parties, and exchange birthday presents. If Mary Smith suddenly stopped hosting a dinner party or buying presents for her friends, one could imagine that John, Jane, and Sandra would stop calling her and eventually drop her as a friend – these would be considered sanctions against violating the norm. Since John, Mary, Jane, and Sandra are all friends with each other, this configuration of relationships represents network closure. One can imagine that the norm of hosting dinner parties or exchanging birthday presents would be harder to enforce if John and Mary were friends, Mary and Jane were friends, Jane and Sandra were friends, but that John and Jane (or Sandra) were not friends, etc. In a closed network, obligations and expectations are more easily enforced.

Social capital is important because it influences how children in immigrant families achieve educational success. Social capital in the form of information and resources comes from communities which hold the right types of information. As in our previous examples, a South Indian family whose parents hold college or postgraduate degrees from the US, who live in a community in which many students' parents have gone to college, and who have highly educated friends will be able to provide information and resources relevant to going to highly selective universities, for instance. This suggests that these students will be able to achieve educational success in a pretty straightforward way – perhaps much like the straight-line assimilation theories that the Chicago School of Sociology proposed.

Social capital in the form of norms, obligations, and expectations may also be important. For groups without good information about higher education in the US, like the Vietnamese, responsibility to a tightly knit ethnic community may drive educational success. For those groups that have ethnic social capital – social capital that comes from obligations to and supervision from one's ethnic community – educational achievement can be due to the desire to please community members (Zhou and Bankston 1998). The operation of this type of social capital reflects the process of segmented assimilation, or accommodation without acculturation, more than straight-line assimilation (Gibson 1988). Children of immigrants maintain ethnic identities and this serves to enable educational success (Gibson 1988).

Social capital from parents may be the most useful for students' educational achievement and attainment. Parents who have higher education, particularly from a US institution, are able to help their children navigate the process of going to college by providing relevant information on high-school course-taking, application procedures, and possibly financial aid and other ways to pay for college.

We turn now to the educational attainment of adult immigrants, many of whom may be parents to children in immigrant families. It is important to note that some of these immigrant adults are those who immigrated as adults and others may have immigrated as small children. Though we do not separate them in the following tables, it is very likely that when someone immigrates (whether as an adult or a child) influences his or her knowledge of US education, which in turns affects the social capital that the adult can provide for his or her children.

Educational Attainment of Adult Immigrants

In this chapter and the previous one, we have discussed how the educational outcomes of adult immigrants are shaped by the immigration policies of the US, the motivations that immigrants have to leave their countries of origin, and the kinds of resources available to them once they settled in the US. We have also argued that the educational attainment of adult immigrants is important for their children's outcomes. Not only do more educated adult immigrants have better jobs and live in better neighborhoods, which leads to more resources for children, they also provide more social capital to children in their families and communities. In this section we introduce recent data on educational attainment among immigrants of diverse origins. The data discussed below will illustrate the differences across groups that we have suggested throughout this and previous chapters. As you read the following tables, think about how these differences reflect the theories of assimilation we have described earlier. Which immigrants are most likely to achieve educational success? Are these outcomes related to race, ethnicity, or national origin? Does this reflect a straight-line pattern or something more complicated?

Throughout the remainder of the chapter, refer to tables 4.1, 4.2, and 4.3. These tables present the percentages of the total US population by racial/ethnic groups, as well as specific breakdowns for each of the ethnic and immigrant populations reviewed in this book. More specifically, data on Asians are included in table 4.1, Hispanics in table 4.2 and Africans in table 4.3. Again, note that the tables include data for all ethnic groups and separately only for immigrants. In each of these tables the first two columns with numbers show percentages of adults 25 and older who have at least graduated from high school and at least completed a Bachelor's degree. The last three columns in each table show median household income, percentage in poverty, and the average household size for each of these populations. These figures come from the American Community Survey, 2008, a survey of a nationally representative sample of Americans. This survey is conducted annually by the US Census Bureau and has taken the place of the long form of the Census, which was used to collect more extensive data from a subgroup of individuals completing the decennial censuses.

First, please turn to table 4.1. The figures in the first row show that of the entire US population aged 25 and older, 85% have at least graduated from high school, and about 28% (or actually 27.7%) have at least graduated from college (American Community Survey 2008a). The median household income is

Table 4.1 Socioeconomic indicators among Asians in the US (ethnic groups and foreign-born)

	% at least HS graduate[c]	% at least college graduate[c]	Median household income	% below poverty	Average household size
US population (total)	85.0	27.7	$52,029	13.2	2.6
White non-Hispanic[a]	90.1	30.7	$56,826	9.3	2.5
Black non-Hispanic[a]	80.8	17.5	$35,435	24.1	2.7
Hispanic (any race)	60.8	12.9	$41,470	21.3	3.5
Asian ethnic groups	85.1	49.7	$70,219	10.5	3.0
Chinese[b]	80.2	52.1	$68,202	11.9	2.9
Filipino	91.6	48.0	$79,840	5.4	3.4
Asian Indian[a]	90.6	70.1	$90,528	7.8	3.0
Vietnamese	73.3	27.8	$55,667	12.9	3.3
Korean	89.7	49.8	$53,887	13.4	2.7
Japanese	93.5	46.3	$61,743	8.9	2.2
Cambodian	58.8	12.5	$44,198	20.1	3.8
Hmong	58.3	11.6	$42,199	26.2	4.9
Laotian	68.7	13.0	$57,420	11.1	3.6
Pakistani	86.1	54.3	$60,183	16.4	3.8
Thai	82.4	42.9	$47,626	15.8	2.6
Bangladeshi	83.0	49.5	$49,117	15.8	3.7
Foreign-born Asian groups	83.6	48.6	$76,404	11.7	3.1
China[b]	78.2	50.1	$63,511	13.1	2.9
Philippines	91.1	49.7	$81,099	4.7	3.5
India	91.2	74.1	$93,731	7.6	3.0
Vietnam	68.0	23.8	$56,524	11.9	3.5
Korea	90.6	50.9	$51,989	14.6	2.7
Japan	93.2	47.7	$57,031	11.5	2.1
Cambodia	56.7	14.1	$50,690	16.5	3.8
Laos	61.5	12.8	$56,128	12.6	4.4
Pakistan	85.4	52.7	$65,036	12.8	3.9
Thailand	80.7	38.6	$48,320	20.4	3.1
Bangladesh	85.3	49.2	$50,619	18.5	3.8
Indonesia	92.8	50.0	$58,689	12.8	2.7

Source: Adapted from American Community Survey 2008 (US Census Bureau 2009) (1-year estimates)
[a] Single racial identification
[b] Chinese includes Taiwan and Hong Kong
[c] As percent of US population 25 years and older

about $52,000, and 13.2% of the total US population lives in poverty. Finally, the average household size is 2.6 individuals. You can interpret the rest of this table the same way for each ethnic and/or immigrant group in the tables.

Let us interpret the first two columns of tables 4.1, 4.2, and 4.3 next. For white adults aged 25 and older, 90% have at least a high-school diploma, while approximately 31% have at least a Bachelor's degree (American Community Survey 2008b). For African Americans and Hispanics, approximately 81% and 61%, respectively, have at least graduated from high school, and approximately 18% and 13%, respectively, have graduated from college (American Community Survey 2008c; 2008d). In other words, African Americans and in particular Hispanics are much less likely to hold a Bachelor's degree compared to the white population.

In contrast, Asian Americans are far more educated, on average, than their white, black, and Hispanic counterparts (American Community Survey 2008e). As a whole, approximately 85% of Asian American adults aged 25 and older have at least a high-school diploma, while 50% have at least a Bachelor's degree. This pattern is consistent with general patterns of racial stratification (in terms of income, occupational status, etc.) in the United States. Asian Americans are approximately four times as likely as Hispanics, three times as likely as African Americans, and one and a half times as likely as whites to have at least graduated from college. However, there is a substantial range of educational outcomes among Asian American ethnic groups. In the middle part of table 4.1, we present these numbers for the largest Asian American ethnic groups. At one end of the spectrum, we can see that 70% of Asian Indians aged 25 and older have attained at least a Bachelor's degree, while 91% have at least graduated from high school. This is in contrast to other Asian ethnic groups, such as Hmong, Cambodian, and Laotian adults 25 and older, among whom only about 12% of each group have at least graduated from college. Similarly, only about 60–69% of them have a high-school diploma. These numbers are comparable to the overall educational levels of Hispanics.

Table 4.2 Socioeconomic indicators among Hispanics in the US (ethnic groups and foreign-born)

	% at least HS graduate[a]	% at least college graduate[a]	Median household income	% below poverty	Average household size
Hispanic ethnic groups	60.8	12.9	$41,470	21.3	3.5
Mexican	54.8	9.0	$40,647	22.9	3.7
Puerto Rican	72.9	15.8	$39,039	24.0	2.8
Cuban	76.0	25.4	$42,724	14.2	2.7
Dominican	63.2	15.5	$34,604	24.4	3.3
Costa Rican	76.9	26.1	$48,307	16.0	3.0
Guatemalan	45.9	8.9	$41,225	21.7	4.0
Honduran	49.5	10.3	$36,922	22.2	3.7
Nicaraguan	73.5	19.1	$48,945	14.0	3.5
Panamanian	89.1	30.2	$47,827	11.8	2.7
Salvadorean	47.2	8.3	$43,490	16.2	3.9
Argentinian	87.2	38.8	$54,163	11.3	2.7
Bolivian	88.9	34.8	$61,504	9.1	3.5
Chilean	89.7	36.1	$60,463	7.9	2.9
Colombian	84.3	30.9	$49,384	11.3	2.9
Ecuadorean	69.6	17.9	$50,665	13.3	3.5
Peruvian	88.6	30.0	$50,901	9.8	3.2
Venezuelan	91.0	51.3	$53,673	14.0	2.9
Spaniard	87.4	30.0	$54,526	11.5	2.6
All other Hispanic	75.8	16.5	$43,087	17.5	2.8
Foreign-born Hispanic groups	51.9	11.5	$39,871	20.1	3.8
Cuba	71.2	22.2	$37,758	16.4	2.7
Dominican Republic	59.6	14.1	$33,089	22.5	3.4
Mexico	38.5	5.2	$36,449	24.0	4.2
Costa Rica	70.9	21.7	$43,760	17.5	3.0
El Salvador	45.3	7.3	$43,519	14.8	3.9
Guatemala	43.6	8.1	$40,366	19.9	4.1
Honduras	47.7	9.4	$36,960	21.4	3.8
Nicaragua	70.4	16.5	$45,297	13.6	3.5
Panama	86.5	26.3	$41,337	11.7	2.7
Argentina	85.7	37.8	$53,930	10.4	2.7
Bolivia	87.0	31.5	$58,231	8.1	3.4
Brazil	85.3	33.5	$53,591	10.4	2.9

Table 4.2 (continued)

	% at least HS graduate[a]	% at least college graduate[a]	Median household income	% below poverty	Average household size
Chile	88.6	32.8	$53,939	9.3	2.8
Colombia	82.5	29.2	$47,251	11.4	2.9
Ecuador	67.4	16.0	$48,854	13.5	3.6
Peru	88.3	29.2	$49,527	9.7	3.2
Venezuela	91.7	51.4	$54,853	13.3	3.0

Source: Adapted from American Community Survey 2008 (US Census Bureau 2009) 1-year estimates
[a] As percent of US population 25 years and older

However, in general, Asian Americans are a well-educated group (NCES 2005). With the exception of the groups we mentioned above, most of the other groups enjoy median educational levels of about a Bachelor's degree. For example, 80.2% of Chinese adults aged 25 and older have at least graduated from high school. In addition, about half of Chinese adults aged 25 and older have at least a Bachelor's degree. Despite the heterogeneity of educational attainment levels within the broad pan-ethnic groups, the general educational advantage of Asian adults (with the exception of the Hmong, Cambodian, and Laotian ethnic groups) compared to Hispanic and African American adults is apparent.

The patterns described in the tables above do not completely address the issue of selection of Asian American immigrants. We cannot tell from these numbers alone which adults are foreign-born versus native-born. To explore this issue, refer to the bottom section of table 4.1 where we discuss the percentage of the population of each ethnic group who are foreign-born. Selection of Asian American immigrants may provide clues as to why Asian Americans have such high educational attainment compared to whites and non-Asian minorities. Keep in mind that ethnic groups are not exactly comparable to national-origin groups. Someone might identify as ethnically Chinese but actually have been born in Vietnam. In addition, there is a small fraction of migrants from

Table 4.3 Socioeconomic indicators among Africans in the US (ancestry groups and foreign-born)

	% at least HS graduate	% at least college graduate	Median household income	% below poverty	Average household size
Black, non-Hispanic[a]	80.8	17.5	$35,435	24.1	2.7
Ancestry groups[b]					
Cape Verdean	70.5	14.9	$45,466	19.0	3.1
Ethiopian	83.5	25.8	$41,382	20.5	2.9
Ghanaian	91.5	31.7	$51,934	11.0	3.0
Nigerian	95.6	60.5	$59,017	10.3	3.3
African	84.5	24.4	$38,772	22.5	2.7
Place of birth					
Foreign-born Africans	88.0	42.0	$50,424	16.9	3.1
Ethiopia	83.6	26.0	$41,846	19.4	2.9
Kenya	95.2	48.7	$51,770	20.7	2.7
Somalia	58.1	11.3	$19,977	50.1	3.7
Egypt	94.9	64.8	$58,302	15.0	3.1
South Africa	97.7	60.4	$88,518	6.9	2.6
Ghana	91.8	34.8	$52,832	8.3	3.1
Liberia	88.0	28.4	$42,455	16.2	3.4
Nigeria	95.3	60.5	$61,407	10.0	3.4
Other African Country	85.6	29.5	$38,749	23.9	3.1

Source: Adapted from American Community Survey 2008 (US Census Bureau 2009) (1-year estimates).
[a] Single racial identification
[b] Numbers obtained under "Ancestry Groups"

Africa who are white or Asian. There are ethnic Asians who were born in Latin America (think of the former President of Peru, Alberto Fujimori).

As a whole, with the exception of migrants from Latin America, foreign-born individuals are a well-educated group compared to the overall population. Specifically, approximately 42% of adults aged 25 and older who were born in Africa have at least a Bachelor's degree. For North Americans outside of the US (such as Canadians), this figure is almost identical at 41%. Similarly, 36% of adults born in Europe have at least a Bachelor's degree

(American Community Survey 2008a). Finally, approximately 49% of foreign-born adults from Asia aged 25 and older are college educated. This number is almost identical to what we found for Asian Americans overall. However, note that Africans, most of whom would be seen by others as racially indistinguishable from African Americans, have much higher levels of education compared to the overall population of African Americans. This difference between native-born African Americans and African-origin black immigrants complicates the relationships between these two groups.

The second way to present educational differences is by ethnic/national-origin groups. Asian Americans who were born in India have by far the highest level of education. Almost three-quarters of the adult population born in India have at least a college education. Again, at the other end of the spectrum, we find that 13% of adults aged 25 and older who were born in Laos and 14% of those born in Cambodia have at least a college education. These levels are comparable to both the overall Hispanic population as well as the Hispanic foreign-born population. With the exception of individuals born in India, Laos, Cambodia, and Vietnam, approximately 40–50% of the other Asian national-origin groups have at least a Bachelor's degree. Thus, the average Asian American child is far more likely to have college-educated parents than the average Hispanic child – hence it is no wonder that Asian American youth have high educational outcomes.

Table 4.2 presents the educational attainment levels of adults aged 25 and older from Hispanic ethnic and immigrant groups. Let us start with the ethnic groups: overall, approximately 61% of Hispanic adults have at least a high-school diploma and 13% of Hispanic adults have at least a Bachelor's degree. These levels are substantially lower than for the US population overall as well as for white non-Hispanics, black non-Hispanics, and Asian Americans. As evident with the Asian population, Hispanic ethnic groups also have heterogeneous educational profiles. At the highest end of the spectrum, over half of Venezuelan adults have at least a college degree. Comparably, about 40% of Argentinian, 36% of Chilean, and 35% of Bolivian adults have at least a college degree. These levels are similar to those for the overall Asian group as well as for many Asian American ethnic groups.

At the other end of the distribution, we find that approximately 9% of Mexican and Guatemalan, and 8% of Salvadorean, adults aged 25 and older have earned at least a college degree. The numbers for high-school graduates are even more sobering – approximately half of Mexicans, Guatemalans, Hondurans, and Salvadoreans have finished high school. However, given that Mexicans alone comprise approximately 40% of the Hispanic population, their educational attainment levels will affect the overall Hispanic figures far more than any other ethnic group. In other words, unlike the relationship between the outcomes of any particular Asian group and the overall average of educational attainment of Asian Americans, the overall mean of educational attainment of Hispanics is largely determined by the experiences of Mexican Americans.

As with Asian Americans, it is important to examine the extent to which foreign-born Hispanics differ from the overall Hispanic population. The bottom section of table 4.2 presents the educational attainment profiles of foreign-born Latin American national-origin adults. Similar to the comparison between the foreign-born and overall Asian American populations, the foreign-born Latin Americans are not all that different from the overall population in terms of educational attainment. However, foreign-born Hispanic adults are, in general, slightly less well educated than the overall population both among all groups and within-group comparisons. Specifically, approximately 13% of the overall Hispanic population has at least a Bachelor's degree compared to just over 11% of those who were born in Latin America. As an example of this, approximately 22% of Cubans who are foreign-born have a four-year college degree, while this figure is 26% for the general Cuban population. Similarly, approximately 5% of the foreign-born Mexican population is college-educated while 9% of the overall Mexican adult population has completed college.

Finally, we focus on African ancestry individuals and immigrants from sub-Saharan Africa in table 4.3. These numbers are not exactly comparable to those for Asian and Hispanic ethnic groups, because ACS did not ask African Americans for their ethnic group affiliation. Instead, these groups are identified from questions about ancestry. Note that this is an extremely well-educated population. Approximately 88% of adults who identify as coming from sub-Saharan Africa have at least graduated from high school, while 42% of adults have at least completed college.

However, there is considerable variation here as well. If we observe individuals of African ancestry, almost 96% of Nigerian adults aged 25 and older have at least a high-school diploma and more than 60% have at least a Bachelor's degree. In contrast, among those who identified as Cape Verdean, only about 70% have at least graduated from high school and 15% have a college diploma. Still, these figures are higher than for Hispanics overall. Adults from all of the African ancestry groups listed here, with the exception of Cape Verdeans, are more likely to have graduated from college than either African Americans or Hispanics. In fact, Nigerians are five times as likely to have a college diploma compared to the general black non-Hispanic population. This suggests there is a wide disparity in the educational backgrounds of immigrants from Africa versus black immigrants from other countries, and also compared to African Americans.

The bottom panel of table 4.3 presents the educational attainment profile for foreign-born Africans by country of origin. Again, we see that Nigerians, along with South Africans and Egyptians, are extremely well educated. For instance, almost 95% of adults born in Egypt have at least graduated from high school and almost two-thirds have at least graduated from college. This is comparable to the figures we saw for Indians. Similarly, more than 95% of adults born in Nigeria have at least a high-school diploma while almost 61% have at least a Bachelor's degree. At the other end of the spectrum, we can see that only 58% of adults born in Somalia have at least graduated from high school while 11% have at least a Bachelor's degree. Because most Somali immigrants arrived as refugees, similar to the Vietnamese, Cambodians, Laotians and the Hmong, their educational profiles are distinct from their counterparts who immigrated through traditional means.

We use national origin and not necessarily race or ethnic identity to organize our tables. As mentioned previously, it is possible that those who come from Vietnam could be ethnically Chinese. It is also likely that those who come from regions that we categorize as "Hispanic," like the Dominican Republic, may see themselves as racially black. Although we do not separate out Caribbean blacks in this table, in a recent report from the Population Reference Bureau (Kent 2007), the author finds that 88% of blacks born in the Caribbean or Latin America have a high-school education or more, and 20% have a Bachelor's degree or more. Blacks from the Caribbean tend to be less educationally selected than those from Africa.

Race and Ethnic Differences in Household Income

While educational attainment is the main focus of this volume, when thinking about how adult outcomes influence children's educational achievement and what obstacles ethnic and immigrant minorities may encounter in the US, we cannot ignore differences in household income. Families with more money can better afford educational resources (such as computers and books) at home, and even provide additional tutoring opportunities. In fact, one of the key advantages that some scholars have pointed to are the Asian-style cram schools (popularly known as *kumon, hakwon,* or *juku*) that many children of immigrants attend (Kim and Park 2010; Kwok 2004; Rosegaard 2006). These extracurricular courses provide children with additional exposure to mathematics and English. They are not geared towards providing remedial support to students, but they are designed to give all students *additional* academic support. The tuition charges are over $100 per month, so it is not affordable for all parents. In China, Japan, and Korea, such learning centers are common, and some people argue that they have given children from these countries an edge over the United States in standardized reading and mathematics scores.

The data on household income, percentage of individuals who live in poverty, and average household size appear on the right panels of tables 4.1–4.3. With respect to the information on income, it is important to note why we report medians, not means (or averages). The mean household income is a simple average, arrived at by adding all of the household incomes in the population and dividing that number by the number of cases. The median household income is the figure at which half of all cases are above that number and the other half fall below that number. Hence, a median household income of $50,000 would simply mean that one-half of all households earn less than $50,000 while one-half earn more. We use medians here rather than means because a mean value can be disproportionately affected by a single or a small group of very high or very low incomes. A small group of households who have very high incomes can make the mean much greater than the median, and mislead us when thinking about the typical household.

Like the information we presented for the educational attainment of adults, we also provide separate figures in the tables for only the foreign-born population. We examine household income, poverty levels, and average household size for ethnic and foreign-born Asian Americans (table 4.1), Hispanics (table 4.2), and Africans (table 4.3) respectively.

Poverty levels are determined by the US Census Bureau following the Office of Management and Budget's Statistical Policy Directive 14 (US Census Bureau 2011). For 2008, a family of four who has earned $22,025 or less was considered to be living in poverty. For a family of two, this figure was $14,051. Income that is used to compute one's poverty status includes all earnings as well as unemployment compensation, Social Security, investment income, alimony, child support, and so forth. Poverty is judged based on income *before* taxes, so the actual amount households have to spend may actually be less than their reported household income. Still, in absolute terms, these income levels are very modest. Hence, some social science researchers will actually use a cutoff point to determine economic hardship at 150% of the poverty cutoff (e.g. Burchinal et al. 2009; Duncan et al. 2010).

For the entire US population, the median household income was $52,029 while the poverty rate was 13.2%. However, this figure masks the extreme range of median household income by race and ethnic origin. Note that the median household income for whites in 2008 was $56,826, while it was $35,435 for blacks, $41,470 for Hispanics, and $70,219 for Asians. In other words, the median Asian household in the US earns an income that is roughly twice the median for African Americans and approximately 69% higher than that of Hispanics. This is probably not surprising given the substantial educational advantage of Asians over all of the other racial and ethnic groups. Similarly, 9.3% of white households live at or below the poverty line compared to 24.1% of blacks, 21.3% of Hispanics, and 10.5% of Asians. It is interesting to note that while Asian households have far higher median incomes, they are slightly more likely to live in poverty compared to whites. Among Asian Americans, there are greater proportions of poor people and wealthier individuals compared to whites. There are proportionately fewer Asian Americans than whites in the middle of the income distribution.

We find differences in the patterns of household income and poverty that are similar to what we found when we looked at educational differences by ethnic origins. The most striking pattern, however, is one that differs from the patterns in educational attainment. All Asian and Hispanic ethnic groups, with the exception of Dominicans, have household incomes higher than that of African Americans. Recall that at least several Asian ethnic groups (Laotians, Cambodians, and Hmong) had average educational attainment levels that were markedly lower than those of African Americans and Hispanics (particularly those from South America).

Next, we turn to income and poverty rates for Asian American ethnic groups. At the two ends of the spectrum, we find Asian Indians, with a median household income of $90,528, and Hmong households with a median income of just above $42,000. With the exception of Hmong, Cambodian, Thai, and Bangladeshi households, all other Asian American ethnic groups have median household incomes that are above the median income for the overall US population. In addition, the median household incomes for all Asian ethnic groups are higher than that of Hispanics or African Americans.

Specifically, Filipino families have a median household income of $79,840 compared to $68,202 for Chinese, $61,743 for Japanese, $60,183 for Pakistani, $57,420 for Laotian, $55,667 for Vietnamese, and $53,887 for Korean households. This may seem to result from the differences in education attainment across ethnic groups, as these patterns seem to match closely those found in educational attainment. These differences are also related to considerable racial and ethnic variation in average household size, which is apparent from the third column of the table. For example, Hmong households average five individuals compared to Japanese households, which include on average just over two people. It may be that the more members there are in a household, the more workers there are who can contribute to the overall household income. On the other hand, if these are children, instead of adults, the consequences of a larger family are different as they are less likely to contribute to the household income.

Next, we focus on column 4 in tables 4.1–4.3, which display poverty rates for racial and ethnic groups, as well as by specific Asian ethnic groups. As you can observe from the top of table 4.1, the poverty rate for the US population overall is 13.2%. It is 9.3% for whites, 24.1% for blacks, 21.3% for Hispanics, and 10.5% for Asians. Again, as with income, it is evident that there is considerable heterogeneity in poverty rates among Asian ethnic groups. Interestingly, just over 5% of Filipinos live in poverty compared to almost 8% of Asian Indians, despite the much higher median household incomes of Asian Indians compared to Filipinos or any other group. Like with Asians overall, this reflects the greater heterogeneity of incomes among Asian Indians. Relatively more Asian Indians are affluent as well as poor compared to Filipinos. On the other end of the distribution, an astounding 26% of Hmong Americans live in poverty – this number is not only two and a half times the poverty rate of Asians overall, but also slightly higher than the overall poverty rates for blacks or Hispanics in the US. Hmong households are much larger than the average Asian, white, black, or Hispanic household – hence their slightly higher household incomes relative to blacks and Hispanics overshadow their higher poverty rates. Other Asian American groups with poverty rates higher than those of the US population include Cambodians

(20.1%), Pakistanis (16.4%), and Thais and Bangladeshis (both at 15.8%). Groups whose poverty rates are similar to whites include Asian Indians and Japanese Americans.

Hispanic national-origin groups also have vastly different median household incomes (table 4.2). The incomes range from almost $62,000 for Bolivian households to approximately $35,000 for Dominican households. In general, Hispanics from South America and Spain are more affluent than their Central American or Mexican counterparts. In fact, Bolivian, Chilean, Argentinian, Venezuelan, and Spanish origin households have higher median incomes than the US population as a whole. These patterns are consistent with those presented in the tables regarding educational attainment.

Note that Peruvian, Ecuadorean, Colombian, Nicaraguan, Costa Rican, and Panamanian households have median incomes ranging from approximately $51,000 to just under $48,000. These figures are just below that of the general population but still well above the average household income of all Hispanics (at $41,470). Similarly, their poverty levels are also similar to the general population, and well below that of Hispanics overall.

Salvadorean, Cuban, Guatemalan, and Mexican households have median incomes ranging from $40,647 to $43,490, which is close to the overall Hispanic median household income, but well below that of the overall US population. These incomes are still well above the median household income of African Americans of $35,435. However, poverty rates of these four groups suggest that their similar incomes mask variation in their economic well-being. Specifically, Mexican and Guatemalan households have poverty rates that are over 20% – close to the overall level of Hispanics and blacks. On the other hand, the poverty rates of Cuban and Salvadorean individuals are much more modest.

Overall, the poverty rates for Hispanic national-origin groups range from about 8% for Chileans (which is lower than that of white non-Hispanics) to 24.4% for Dominicans, which is approximately the same as that of black non-Hispanics. Interestingly, despite the wide range of poverty rates, the overall Hispanic poverty rate is also close to that of Mexicans (and other Central

Americans), given that they comprise the majority of Hispanics in the US. Compared to Asian national-origin groups, the range of poverty rates among the Hispanic national groups is very similar. Specifically, the range of poverty rates among Asian national-origin groups is 5.4% (Filipinos) to 26.2% (Hmong), while the range among Hispanic national-origin groups is 7.9% (Chileans) to 24.4% (Dominicans). However, the household income range is much larger for Asians, ranging from just over $42,000 for Hmong to over $90,000 for Asian Indian households. Among Hispanic national-origin groups, the range in median household incomes is from approximately $35,000 for Dominicans to $61,500 for Bolivians.

The last indicator that we analyze in this chapter is average household size for all national-origin groups. As we suggested above, larger household sizes may lead to higher median household incomes (because there are more earners), but also higher levels of poverty (because there are more mouths to feed). For example, among the Asian ethnic groups, Hmong households have median household incomes of $42,199 (table 4.1) and have a poverty rate of 26.2%. Compare this to the figures for Cuban households (table 4.2), whose median household income is $42,724 but whose poverty rates are only 14.2%. Alternatively, note that Hmong households average 4.9 people while Cuban households have on average 2.7 individuals. More similar to Hmong households are Guatemalan households, whose median incomes are $41,225 with a poverty rate of 21.7%. The average household size of Guatemalan households is 4.0, which is still substantially lower than that of Hmong households but much higher than almost all other Hispanic national-origin groups. That is why it is important to consider household size when looking at the financial well-being of households.

When we focus on foreign-born individuals only, we can appreciate that foreign-born households earn slightly lower incomes when compared to the overall population of people in that same ethnic group. For example, the median household income of all Mexican households is $40,647 compared to $36,449 for foreign-born Mexican households (table 4.2). The only exceptions to this pattern are for Salvadoreans, Hondurans, and Argentinians, where the median household incomes of foreign-born households are almost identical to those of their entire populations in the US of the same ethnicity. For Venezuelans, foreign-born households ($54,853) actually earn more than for the entire US population of Venezuelans ($53,673) although this difference is substantively modest. When comparing poverty rates, the story is more complex. Overall, the poverty rates for foreign-born nationals are very similar to the figures we see for all of those in the US from their same ethnic groups.

Race and National Origin

Throughout this chapter we have aimed to demonstrate that large racial and pan-ethnic categories such as white, black, Hispanic, and Asian oversimplify the complexity and variation in education and other socioeconomic differences by ethnicity and national origin. Groups as different as Asian Indians and Hmong are both typically classified as Asian, yet Hmong individuals are five times as likely to live in poverty, and Hmong households have a median income that is less than half that of Asian Indian households. These differences are far greater than those between whites and blacks (or between any other large racial or pan-ethnic group). To some extent, this is also the case for Hispanic national-origin groups. Puerto Ricans have a poverty rate that is three times that of Chileans (24.0% versus 7.9%) – again a far greater difference than that between blacks and whites. In popular media, we have a sense of the great disparity in socioeconomic status between whites and African Americans, but not of the disparities between ethnic groups who are classified under the same categories such as Hispanic and Asian. This is partly due to the fact that racial differences are more apparent due to the historical legacy of how people are classified, and quite simply because it is easier for most Americans to keep track of four or five groups such as white, black, Hispanic, and Asian American (and sometimes Native Americans) than the multitude of ethnic and national-origin groups and their complex immigration histories comprising the US population.

However, with the exception of a few groups, almost all Asian Americans are advantaged compared to almost all African Americans and Hispanics. These advantages are especially apparent in terms of educational attainment. The relatively higher educational attainment of Asian American adults translates to higher household incomes, and both of these sources of advantage lead to more resources for their children's educational outcomes. As we will see in subsequent chapters, Asian American children have superior educational achievement and higher eventual educational attainment compared to their other minority (and in many cases white) counterparts. Hence, it is likely no accident that Asian Americans are often called the "model minority" (Kao 1995). Asian Americans are stereotyped to be far more successful than other minority groups (and sometimes even more than whites) – we can see that, to a great extent, these stereotypes do reflect their relatively advantaged positions.

It is easy for most people to believe that there are innate cultural differences among national-origin groups, and sometimes these cultural values are credited for their relative success and failure in the US. However, it is difficult to demonstrate with empirical data how cultural values may lead to educational success. We do know that most foreign-born Asian American groups have higher levels of education and consequently overall better socioeconomic resources, likely shaped by some combination of immigrant selection, incorporation, and cultural values. This, in turn, gives their children a great likelihood of achieving high levels of educational and eventual occupational attainment, and they may be considered "assimilated," at least in some ways. Hispanic children, particularly those of Mexican origin, are less likely to have these advantages.

In a way, our portrait of national origin and ethnic differences in socioeconomic attainment matches well the examples we used at the beginning of this chapter. Asian Indians, like Ashoke Ganguli in *The Namesake*, do have the highest levels of educational attainment. Because of their relatively high levels of education, they also have the highest levels of household income, and this affords their children greater educational resources and opportunities at home. In the novel and film, Ashoke's son Nikhil/Gogol was able to attend Yale and become an architect. He later marries Moushumi, another South Asian American who is completing her PhD in French literature at Columbia. These are not average profiles of any ethnic group in the United States, but they represent a less unique Asian Indian family in the United States compared to a typical Hmong or Mexican American family. Recall from table 4.1 that 70% of Asian Indians have at least a Bachelor's degree compared to 12% of Hmong and 9% of Mexican adults aged 25 and older.

If you recall the characters and experiences we presented earlier from the movies *Mi Familia* and *The Namesake*, you can now reflect upon and evaluate the complexity of how inequality takes place among immigrants and minorities in the US. You can also appreciate how some families are able to succeed while for others it may be harder. For example, the characters in *Mi Familia* not only live in the US with less social capital than the Gangulis from *The Namesake*, but they also have different language abilities. Whereas the families in both films suffer from racial and ethnic discrimination, the Ganguli family, particularly due to the educational attainment of the father, is able to move to a better-off neighborhood and send their children to good schools. On the other hand, the characters in *Mi Familia* live in a much poorer neighborhood and are exposed to violence, drugs, alcohol, and death from early in their lives. It is much harder to succeed in these conditions, and while some children are able to do so despite the challenges, others do not.

In the next chapter, we show the patterns of educational achievement among children in immigrant families. Like the previous chapters, this chapter provides a context in which to understand those differences. Immigrant families arrive in the US for different reasons and under a myriad of different circumstances, and they settle in varying communities. Adults in these families have educational and socioeconomic profiles ranging from the most advantaged Asian Indians to some of the least advantaged Hmong, Guatemalans, and Mexicans. The educational and financial resources and the social capital of these families most surely affect their children's outcomes. And, it is often by these outcomes that we judge whether or not children of immigrants are "assimilating" or fitting in to US society. It is to those outcomes that we turn in the next chapter.

5

Educational Achievement and Outcomes of Children in Immigrant Families

As you may recall, Ashoke Ganguli (the father in Jhumpa Lahiri's *The Namesake*) and José Sanchez (the father in the film *Mi Familia* or *My Family*) completed very different levels of education and obtained vastly different types of jobs. Ashoke Ganguli migrates to the US to pursue a PhD at the Massachusetts Institute of Technology (MIT) and later becomes a professor. In contrast, José Sanchez crosses the Mexico–US border on foot and works as a manual laborer in Los Angeles. Their reasons for migrating, their socioeconomic backgrounds in their countries of origin, and what they did upon arrival to the US were radically different. These differences affected their educational trajectories and work careers. How might their lives have affected the educational opportunities of their children?

In fact, Gogol Ganguli, Ashoke's son, goes to college and rebels against his father by going to Yale rather than MIT and eventually finishes a Master's degree in architecture at Columbia University. Although some of his children do complete college degrees and become successful, one of José's sons ends up going to prison. Another of his daughters becomes a nun and eventually leaves the Church and marries a former priest. But even within the Sanchez family there is variation in outcomes. While the narrator has both a college and law school education, other siblings are not so fortunate.

While these works of fiction are simply that, these families are believable because despite the idea that there is equal opportunity for all in America, intuitively and through social science research findings, we know that the child of an engineering professor and the child of an uneducated and unskilled migrant worker will, in all likelihood, not have the same socioeconomic outcomes, regardless of their shared identity as children of immigrants.

As we saw in chapter 4, Asian, Hispanic, and African-origin adults attain vastly different levels of educational attainment and household incomes. In general, with the exception of Cambodians and Laotians, Asian ethnic groups have higher educational attainment levels than Hispanic ethnic groups. There is some overlap between the most advantaged Hispanic ethnic groups (such as the Chileans, Argentinians, and Bolivians) with the mid-range Asian ethnic groups (such as the Chinese and Koreans). However, the average levels of education are much lower for Hispanics than Asians, largely because one of the most disadvantaged Hispanic groups (Mexicans) also comprises 40% of the total Hispanic population. There is no single Asian national-origin group that accounts for such a large proportion of the Asian population.

The majority of Asian national-origin groups and Hispanic national-origin groups (with the exception of Mexicans) exhibit educational differences between the foreign-born and native-born populations, and while there are overall differences between the educational outcomes of foreign-born adults relative to the entire population when we examine specific national-origin groups, the main story of vastly different educational resources across groups is more notable. The relative ranking of various Asian and Hispanic national-origin groups does not change. Despite the substantial range of educational experiences within the large pan-ethnic groups of Asian, Hispanic, and to some extent blacks, broadly speaking, Asian American national-origin groups occupy a more advantaged position in terms of education, income, and poverty status than their Hispanic counterparts. This suggests that racial differences still matter above and beyond national-origin differences.

In addition, most minorities, upon arrival to the US, are lumped into one of four or five larger pan-ethnic groups. Their membership in these groups (whether they are meaningful to individuals themselves) significantly affects their everyday lives. To clarify, a new Chinese immigrant may not identify with Filipinos or Koreans or with the label "Asian American," but because other people will classify the new immigrant as "Asian American," that racial designation will affect his/her everyday life. Independent of his/her individual family background, the images that are associated with his/her ethnic and even his/her pan-ethnic group affect daily experiences and likely influence his/her eventual socioeconomic outcomes as stereotypes and expectations for the pan-ethnic group are extrapolated to the individual, regardless of whether these are true or not. Upon arrival, immigrants enter the existing racial/ethnic hierarchy of the US. In most cases, this racial system does not completely overlap with that of their countries of origin. Thus, in order to further clarify this discussion, we introduce some key concepts related to race and ethnicity. Then we discuss the implications for the educational outcomes of immigrants. In this chapter, we ask the reader to think about how paths of migration, parental resources, and race and ethnicity matter for immigrant children's educational outcomes. How do these factors influence which children are able to succeed in America's educational institutions? Does the way in which children in immigrant families fit into US society matter and, if so, in what ways?

Racial Formations in the US

In their seminal work, Michael Omi and Howard Winant (1994) referred to *racial formations* where societal-level decisions about racial categories and hierarchies are reinforced through micro-level interactions that individuals experience on a daily basis. Their theory focuses both on the fluidity of racial categories, and also on the overarching importance of race over ethnicity or national origin. They contend that, in the United States, perceptions of racial differences continue to matter and shape the everyday experiences of ethnic groups. It is important to remember the differences between race and ethnicity that we mentioned earlier. Ethnicity may be chosen or assigned. It is usually linked to ancestry and geographic region of origin. It is also not necessarily linked to the distribution of power in society. Race, on the other hand, is assigned and intimately linked to how power and resources in a society are distributed. It is rooted in ideas of naturalness and connected to physiological or biological differences between groups (Hartmann and Cornell 2007).

While racial differences across immigrants may shape experiences in the US, resources that families provide also matter. The pattern of educational outcomes of immigrant adults helps to account for the differential educational outcomes of their children. One of the most enduring findings in social science research is the transfer of socioeconomic status from parents to children (e.g. Coleman 1988; Haveman and Wolfe 1995). While there are no guarantees that parents who have completed college will also have children who eventually obtain a four-year degree, on a group level, children whose parents have a college degree are more likely to obtain a college degree than children whose parents did not complete college (Bound et al. 2010; Buchman and DiPrete 2006). In fact, there is no better predictor of an individual's educational outcome than his/her parents' socioeconomic status (Steelman and Powell 1989; Teachman 1987).

Whereas social scientists had traditionally pointed to the family as the main predictor of one's eventual socioeconomic status, most research until the mid-twentieth century was based on limited data. Sophisticated statistical analyses of this relationship began with the Wisconsin School studies in the 1960s. These studies focused on a representative sample of the High School Class of 1957 in Wisconsin (e.g. Hauser 1972; Sewell and Hauser 1972; Sewell et al. 1970). This sample was surveyed in 1957, during their senior year in high school, and then the participants were interviewed again in 1964, 1975, 1994, and 2005. These researchers carefully analyzed data and used state-of-the-art techniques to examine the relationships between the fathers' educational and occupational status and their children's long-term well-being. While these advanced techniques have helped sociologists better estimate the size of these relationships, there is no doubt that parents' educational and occupational outcomes translate to higher socioeconomic attainment for their children (Hallinan

1988). So, social class matters in the United States, and the inter-generational transfer of socioeconomic status from parents to children remains one of the most robust and enduring findings in the social sciences. Hence, it is imperative that when studying the educational outcomes of immigrant youth, we must document the very different family backgrounds from which these youth emerge, as we did in chapter 4.

In chapters 3 and 4, we showed that immigrant groups arrive to the US with very diverse socioeconomic circumstances, and these differences are associated with their race, ethnic, and national-origin backgrounds. In addition, upon their arrival, immigrants are absorbed into the pre-existing racial hierarchy of the US – together, socioeconomic and racial differences are at the center of why groups will take very different paths as they assimilate. Related to the socioeconomic and racial differences, where they settle in the country, what types of neighborhood they live in, or the level of contact with other immigrants are also important in defining their paths to assimilation.

Immigrants from Nigeria provide one example of how immigrants are absorbed into the American racial hierarchy. Most Nigerian immigrants arrive with high average levels of education, but as soon as they arrive, they are seen as African Americans, who are stereotyped to be low-achieving minorities. What might this mean for Nigerian immigrants? Teachers may have lower expectations of their school performance compared to the newcomer German student in the same class, they may not be listened to as respectfully as other students and, in short, they may not receive the same quality of education as non-black immigrants. Despite the resilience that immigrants demonstrate against discrimination, these stereotypes have been shown to have negative consequences on some of their educational outcomes (Owens and Lynch 2012).

Similarly, while the statistics in chapter 4 clearly show that the average Argentinian adult is well educated, they may be associated with the larger pan-ethnic Hispanic group, who are seen as minorities with low levels of education. As with the example of the Nigerian immigrants, for Argentinians, their classification as a minority also affects them in many ways, such as teachers expecting less of these students. However, for white Argentinians, who may be grouped with other whites, this may also confer a benefit in terms of how they are treated by others – the black Nigerian student would not have this opportunity. These two examples represent cases in which the US racial hierarchical system may be detrimental and discriminatory towards these immigrants. However, we can also think of the opposite situation. Cambodian refugees have relatively low levels of educational outcomes, but because they are from Asia (and seen as Asian American), they are lumped along with other relatively affluent Asian immigrants and seen also as a "model minority." Thus, teachers may have heightened expectations of these students.

In the remainder of this chapter, we first discuss the importance of understanding the ways race, class, and immigration intersect. Then, we review the demographic shift among the school-aged population in terms of minority and immigrant status over the past three decades. Next, we focus on educational outcomes first in elementary school-aged children and then at the secondary and post-secondary levels. Within these sections, we look at outcomes such as test scores, grades, educational aspirations, high-school completion, college enrollment, and college completion. We pay specific attention to variation by the racial and ethnic identification of the main immigrant groups in the US. As we present data on educational outcomes, we review different explanations for the racial and immigrant gap in educational achievement. Finally, we carefully examine the debates surrounding the ways that immigrant and minority groups' educational achievement is described in the US and the ways in which it relates to how immigrants are perceived to "fit in" to US society.

Race versus Class

Scholars have long focused on the disparities in educational outcomes of minority youth. When US-based studies from the 1960s through 1980s focused on blacks and whites, the story was simply about the lower educational achievement of blacks versus whites – with very few discussions of immigrants and other racial groups

(Kao and Thompson 2003). Comparable to research on adult outcomes, such as occupational status and income, the primary question that researchers pondered was whether racial disparities in education stem from continuing racial discrimination or whether they are simply a remnant of past discrimination against blacks. In other words, there is no doubt that slavery and the historical oppression of African Americans led to lower academic and occupational achievement, but were the outcomes of subsequent generations in the 1970s and 1980s simply a result of the transmission of class status rather than contemporary experiences of racial discrimination? Those who argued that racial differences in educational outcomes were not solely due to class differences between groups, but may actually have to do with racial classification, suggested that racial differences in educational outcomes persist not necessarily because of institutional racism (e.g. teachers and employers having different – lower – expectations for these groups than for whites) but that they may have more to do with pathology in black families that hinders youths' academic achievement. Sometimes, social scientists argued that slavery may have weakened family ties and worked to devalue marriage which then led to problematic families and parenting (cf. Furstenberg 2007, who argues against this notion). Other researchers proposed that generations of poverty led to the formation of norms that served well for coping with poverty but worked against upward socioeconomic mobility. We will say more about these ideas later, but for now, we can refer to this notion as the "Culture of Poverty," a phrase coined by anthropologist Oscar Lewis (1959; 1966a; 1966b) in the 1950s. More simply, however, sociologists informally organize these explanations for racial disparities along the lines of "race versus class." Perhaps the straightforward title of an important sociological text by William Julius Wilson says it best – *The Declining Significance of Race* (1980).

Quantitative sociologists attempted to answer this question by using statistical analyses on representative samples of adults or students (depending on their research foci). Simply put, the logic behind these studies was something like this: if one wanted to evaluate whether blacks were discriminated against in the job market, one could statistically hold constant (control for) differences in other characteristics such as education, occupational class, and so forth. If the statistical model showed that blacks were no different from whites after controlling for variables that were seen as independent of race, then this would be evidence that any observable differences between blacks and whites was not due to race but rather these other characteristics. If the model showed that the coefficient for black remained statistically significant, it would point to the fact that the other characteristics did not account for racial differences and perhaps something else was the cause of these differences.

While this general approach is straightforward and logical (and generally describes what researchers do in their articles and books), there are many problems that plague all of these studies. While we cannot discuss these ideas fully here, suffice it to say that there are a few essential issues that arise. First is simply the idea that the measures available in a data set do not fully capture the elements of the characteristics one is trying to measure. The logic behind a basic idea such as class may progress along these lines:

- How do we measure class?
  - Do we use educational attainment (e.g. years of education)?
    - Perhaps simply having years of education is not enough.
    - If we added degree completion, maybe that would be better.
    - However, that does not capture differences in the prestige of schools.
  - Maybe it is income.
    - Do we use family income or individual income?
    - But wait, larger families need more money to live on to maintain a similar class status as a smaller family.
    - Is the difference linear?
    - It costs more to live in Manhattan, New York, than in Erie, Pennsylvania, so we need to control for region of residence.
  - Perhaps wealth (net worth) is a better measure.
    - How do we measure this? Should we use home

ownership or the value of the home? Perhaps we should use other resources (cars owned; stocks and mutual funds, etc.).

- Maybe it really is about occupational prestige.
  - For instance, there may be more relative educational value of having parents who are college professors who may earn less money than parents who are not college educated but are entrepreneurs and earn more money.
- If race is such a pervasive defining characteristic by which American society is segregated, are there really class measures that are not in some way related to race?
  - For example, if neighborhoods matter (for schools, etc.) and US residential segregation by race and class are high and interrelated, how can we estimate the relationship between race and neighborhood effects on outcomes?

One can imagine that this conversation (either within the mind of a single social scientist or between different researchers) can go on indefinitely. However, if a particular notion (such as parents' class, however it is measured) is correlated with an outcome (such as a student's test scores) in many studies using many different measures of these concepts, social science researchers have more faith in the relationship between these two characteristics.

Qualitative studies are plagued with a multitude of problems as well. Simply put, they rely on small unrepresentative samples. One cannot evaluate whether the findings from observations or interviews with 10 or 20 or 50 people can actually illuminate what is true of the entire population one is interested in studying. If we (the authors of this book) hosted a dinner party for our friends in Philadelphia and asked them about their educational background, children's schooling, and so forth, we would find that everyone has at least a Master's degree (but more likely a PhD) and that they all live in the Philadelphia Metropolitan Area. Most of them do not have children, or had children in their thirties. All of them send their children to schools with high average test scores (several may take their children to private schools), and, given our own racial and ethnic backgrounds, most of them would be Asian American, white, and/or international scholars. They live their lives in Philadelphia, Pennsylvania – would their experiences be applicable to individuals in New York City, Chicago, San Francisco, or Des Moines? Needless to say, it would be ridiculous to argue that this group represents a slice of the average person or household in the US. Most adults in the US do not have graduate degrees nor are the majority of Americans either Asian and/or from abroad. However, everyday conversations and newspaper articles arguably stem from individual experiences, and generalizing from these anecdotes can be wildly misleading when thinking about the overall population.

Evaluating social science work on the presence and causes of racial and immigrant disparities in educational outcomes is extremely difficult. Part of the challenge is in separating explanations that are associated with social background like parents' education, family income and wealth, and parents' occupations from explanations that focus on students' race. Do Chinese American youth primarily benefit from having well-educated parents? Perhaps their educational success is due to positive stereotypes about their supposed educational prowess. Or perhaps these stereotypes come from actual observations of their educational outcomes. Maybe both (or even more) explanations have some merit. Below, we review some of the empirical findings on differences in test scores, grades, educational aspirations, and enrollment in college and finally college attainment rates. In the context of these findings, we explore some of the prevalent explanations of these differences, paying particular attention to the gap in achievement for immigrant versus native-born students. But let us start by presenting data on how many children we are talking about. What proportion of school-aged children are immigrants and/or minorities?

Growth of the Minority and Immigrant Population among School-Aged Children

Before we review patterns of educational stratification among youth, it is important to go through some of the recent demographic

Educational Achievement and Outcomes of Children

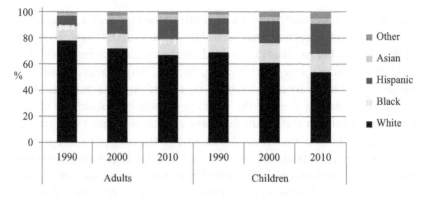

Figure 5.1   Racial and ethnic composition of US population, adults and children (1990–2010)

Source: Adapted from figure 2 of Frey (2011)

changes in the school-aged population. William Frey (2011), in a report for the Brookings Institution, used the 2010 Census to demonstrate some of the dramatic shifts in the youth population. Figure 5.1, which is adapted from table 2 in Frey's report, shows the shift in the racial composition of the US population from 1990 to 2010 overall, as well as separately for adults and children. We can see that among adults, 79% of the total US population was white in 1990, and by 2010 it was 67%. For children, however, 69% of the total US population was white in 1990, and by 2010 this percentage had fallen to 54%.

According to Frey (2011), the 2010 Census shows that only 54% of the school-aged population is white. Also, white children already represent less than 50% of children in ten states (Hawaii, New Mexico, California, Texas, Arizona, Florida, Georgia, Maryland, Mississippi, and Nevada). While the Census Bureau projected in 2000 that by 2025 almost half of 15–19-year-olds in the United States will be from a minority group (Malone et al. 2003), we are actually on pace to reach that milestone much sooner. In 35 of the school districts of the largest metropolitan areas in the United States (including New York, Los Angeles, Chicago, and Phoenix), racial minority children are now the majority. Again, because minorities are a younger population than whites, racial changes in the population will first appear among the youngest members of society. Moreover, a significant proportion of minority youth come from immigrant families. As we stated in chapter 1, about 23% of children aged 0–18 in 2007–8 had at least one immigrant parent. This represents tremendous growth from 1990, when 13% of all children were from immigrant families and even compared to 2000, when 19% of all children were from immigrant families (Mather 2009).

The overlap between immigrant status and minority status is especially crucial in studying Asian and Latino youth because approximately 60% of Hispanic and almost 80% of Asian youth come from immigrant families (see table 1.1 in chapter 1). Moreover, given the rise of Hispanic immigration to the US, the share of children who are Hispanic has dramatically increased over the past several decades. This is especially true for six states: California, New York, Texas, Florida, New Jersey, and Illinois, which together account for two-thirds of newly arrived immigrants.

According to a 2009 Population Reference Bureau Report, there are 16 million Hispanic children currently residing in the US and they account for 22% of all school-aged children (Mather and Kent 2009). This reflects a 200% increase from 1990 when there were only 8 million school-aged Hispanic children. At the same time, the numbers of white non-Hispanic children actually fell from 44 million in 1990 to 42 million in 2008. It is also important to note that Hispanics have a younger age profile than whites or blacks – this means that the proportion of children who are Hispanic is greater than the proportion of adults aged 65 and older, for instance, who are Hispanic.

In contrast to Asians and Hispanics, most African Americans do not come from immigrant families. Among the African American population overall, only about 8% are foreign-born in 2005 (Kent 2007). Still, this figure represents tremendous growth from 1960, when only 1% of the black population was foreign-born, or even compared to 1980, when 3% were foreign-born (Kent 2007). In a Population Reference Bureau publication, Kent (2007) reports that 1 million black children were foreign-born or had immigrant parents in 2005. In contrast to the numbers for Asians, Latinos, and blacks, only 3.5% of the white non-Hispanic population was foreign-born, according to figures from the 2000 US Census (Malone et al. 2003).

There is no doubt that the number and share of minority and immigrant youth has been increasing and will continue to increase. The educational outcomes of these youth will, to a great extent, become the educational profile of youth in America. It is obvious that this transformation has already occurred in many cities and states across the US. In fact, every state in the union has seen an increase in recent decades in the number of foreign-born individuals, so that even non-traditional gateway states (that is, states that have not historically served as the initial destination for immigrants) like Iowa or North Carolina now have substantial numbers of immigrants.

Early Childhood Outcomes

Studies that focus on immigrant primary school-aged youth are fairly recent. Many of these children, even if they were born outside the US, immigrated at such young ages that they may not have had experiences of schooling elsewhere, or maybe they did not have to learn a new language. Perhaps many do not even remember the transition of moving from one society to another. Recall from chapter 1 that these children, often known as the 1.5 or 1.75 generation, reside somewhere between the first generation (those born outside the US who immigrate as adults) and the second generation (those born in the US with immigrant parents). Certainly, individuals who migrate to the US as adolescents experience the transition from one country to another, but it is clear that their lives are notably different from those who migrate as working-age adults and those who migrate as very young children. Hence, for very young children, researchers simply examine immigrant versus non-immigrant households.

The few studies that exist looking at the educational achievements of these young children come from the National Center on Education Statistics, which collected data on a nationally representative sample of kindergarteners in the 1998–9 school year. The Early Childhood Longitudinal Study-Kindergarten Cohort (ECLS-K) has allowed researchers to examine a plethora of outcomes among young children more generally. Data came from about 17,500 students in approximately 3,500 classrooms in 1,280 schools. The data include questionnaires from parents and teachers. Because minority and immigrant households were over-sampled (meaning data were collected from more of these families than would occur given their share in the US population), the data allow researchers to examine questions for minority and immigrant youth. Finally, the data are longitudinal, meaning that data have been collected from the same children, teachers, and parents at several points in time over the primary school years.

This survey has been used to examine the achievement of young children by race and by immigrant status. For example, results from this survey have demonstrated that educational achievement differences between whites, blacks, Hispanics, and Asians are evident (and follow the same pattern in adolescence and adulthood) in kindergarten (Turney and Kao 2009). This research extends earlier work with data that were not nationally representative, which finds that the gap in educational achievement between white and black children is present at the onset of entry to school (e.g. Alexander et al. 2002).

Glick and Bates (2010) use data from the ECLS-K to look at differences in children's educational outcomes by race, ethnicity, and immigration status. They find that, with the exception of children of Chinese foreign-born mothers, children of white native-born parents have the highest math scores at kindergarten. However, beyond that, children from immigrant families have wildly varying math achievement depending on their ethnic background. Note that math scores in kindergarten are simple measures of whether children can count from 1 to 20 and so forth, and not traditional written tests. When they add measures of parental education and income to their statistical models, this accounts for some, but not all, of the differences by race, ethnicity, and national origin.

In their models, as in other research, household characteristics, such as parental education, income, and living in a two-parent household, are shown to affect the initial set of math skills children have in kindergarten, but also the growth in those skills over time. By fifth grade, the gaps along immigrant and national-origin lines widen. Children of Chinese foreign-born parents not only had the highest scores at kindergarten but also experience the greatest growth by fifth grade and maintain their high scores. Black and Hispanic children who earned lower scores than whites in kindergarten experience lower rates of growth so that they not only continue to underperform the white and Chinese children but fall further behind (Glick and Bates 2010).

While it makes sense for us to think about educational trajectories from early childhood to adulthood, the bulk of studies of immigrant youth focuses on adolescent outcomes. Further, these data come from surveys that collect information on both youths' and their parents' birthplaces (so that their generational status could be determined). We summarize research on adolescents below. It is important to note that most of the theoretical paradigms and hypotheses that shape recent work on early childhood outcomes among immigrant youth come from these studies of adolescents.

Schooling Outcomes during Adolescence

While research from the 1990s on immigrant adolescents suggests that they achieve higher educational outcomes than their native-born counterparts, it is fair to say that more recent work from the past ten years portrays a more complex picture of the educational performance of children in immigrant families. The seemingly positive educational outcomes of immigrant youth are sometimes referred to as the "immigrant paradox." As we discussed in chapter 2, traditional assimilation theory suggests that as immigrants assimilate, their educational achievements and attainments should become greater. However, the "paradox" is that these newcomer children have higher levels of attainment and achievement, despite not yet being "assimilated."

Most educational research finds clear differences by race and immigrant status in studies when examining grades and test scores as outcomes. For example, in the 1990s, Kao and Tienda (1995) found, using a nationally representative sample of eighth graders in 1988, that Asian American students reported having the highest grades, followed by whites, blacks, and Hispanics. In terms of test scores, the Asian advantage was much more modest. Racial differences in both test scores and grades persisted even when parental socioeconomic background was accounted for, with the exception of Hispanics who were no longer different from whites after parents' background was considered.

In addition to differences across broad racial categories, Kao and Tienda (1995) also found evidence of an immigrant advantage within racial groups once differences in parents' backgrounds were taken into account. They noted that this may be due to *immigrant optimism* because immigrant parents were less likely to interpret experiences of racism and unequal treatment as due to their status as new arrivals, hence may be more likely to blame their language barriers (Kao and Tienda 1995). When language barriers disappear for their children, whom they presume will speak accentless English, immigrant parents may believe that their US-born children may be treated like white native-born Americans. In other words, they may be less likely to believe that racial differences are the primary source of any discriminatory experiences they may face. Hence, they may also be more likely to believe that their children will enjoy the full benefits of educational attainment in the labor market. It is important to emphasize that this view does not suggest that minority immigrant parents or their children will not face discrimination, but simply that immigrant parents may be more likely to attribute it to their status as foreigners rather than to their status as racial minorities. This is similar to the work of Ogbu, which we described in chapter 2, except that Ogbu attributed this phenomenon to an entire ethnic group, while Kao and Tienda argued that this was limited to immigrant parents just after their arrival. Immigrant students may use a different "frame of reference" (their non-migrant peers, rather than native-born whites) to evaluate their chances of success.

Gaps in test scores between children from immigrant families and those who are not are documented less frequently than are differences by race. Recent findings suggest that while the magnitude of the gaps by race may fluctuate from year to year, the patterns of

Asian advantage and black and Hispanic disadvantage persist. For example, the results from the National Assessment of Educational Progress (henceforth, NAEP) show that among fourth graders in 2007, white students averaged 231 points in the reading scale scores compared to 232 for Asian Americans, 203 for blacks, and 205 for Hispanics (NCES 2008a). In mathematics, whites scored an average of 248 points compared to 253 for Asians, 227 for Hispanics, and 222 for blacks (NCES 2008b). The racial and ethnic differences are similar for eighth graders in 2007 where whites scored an average of 272 points on the reading scale compared to 271 for Asians, 245 for blacks, and 247 for Hispanics (NCES 2008a). In mathematics, whites scored an average of 291 points compared to 297 for Asians, 265 for Hispanics, and 260 for blacks (NCES 2008b).

These differences are also evident when looking at SAT test scores. For example in the 2005–6 academic year, average scores for the SAT-critical reading tests were 527 for whites, 510 for Asians, 458 for Hispanics, and 434 for blacks. In the SAT-mathematics tests, Asians scored an average of 578 compared to 536 for whites, 463 for Hispanics, and 429 for blacks (NCES 2007). When we examine Advanced Placement (AP) courses taken in 2005, 24.6% of Asians, 10.1% of whites, 5.0% of Hispanics, and 2.9% of blacks had taken AP calculus. The pattern persists for courses taken in AP chemistry, physics, and biology.

One factor that many researchers have argued is key to immigrant adolescents' educational success is high educational aspirations and expectations (e.g. Qian and Blair 1999). During adolescence, youth begin to have the tools to develop ideas about their goals and aspirations for their eventual educational and occupational attainment. From the sociological research on status attainment, we know that educational aspirations for college are correlated with eventual college completion. In other words, the odds of successfully earning a Bachelor's degree are related to the desire, or aspiration, to earn a college degree. Sustained plans for educational attainment also matter for predicting the future outcomes. These are often reflected in a student's educational expectations, which reflect students' assessments of their chances of attaining a college degree in light of their circumstances. We know that many more students begin college than complete it, and high-school plans are a significant predictor of whether they are able to earn a college degree.

While the relationship between educational aspirations, expectations, and eventual attainment is well established, what is less clear is the mechanism through which aspirations and expectations affect or are related to attainment. It may be that children begin taking courses in high school that prepare them for college because of their aspirations. Or perhaps these aspirations and expectations also reflect the fact that all of their friends are planning to go to college, making these plans a seemingly natural and predictable outcome. Parents who are college-educated are more likely to have aspirations for their children to complete college and expectations that they will do so. This in turn affects children's own plans for college.

Traditional status attainment researchers argue that prior plans provide the *psychological motivation* for working towards educational goals (Jencks et al. 1983). However, others have argued that educational aspirations reported in a survey of high-school students (and in particular high-school seniors) are simply a report of something that has already occurred (Alexander and Cook 1979) – in other words, they have already applied and been accepted to a university so "aspirations" in this case is simply a report of what has already happened. So, while some argue that aspirations and expectations matter strongly for educational attainment, others suggest that they reflect plans that have already been made or dominant social norms that have little to do with a student's actual eventual educational attainment.

Recent research shows that the expectation to graduate from college can now be thought of as a social norm, as compared to decades past when many high-school students did not plan to attend college. In 2002, students' plans to go to college were nearly universal. Recent statistics of high-school sophomores find that only 8% thought they would only graduate from high school or drop out of high school. In contrast, approximately four out of five students expected to at least receive a Bachelor's degree (specifically 46% expected to only graduate from a four-year college or university, 20% aspired to a Master's degree, and 16% planned to receive an advanced or doctoral degree such as a PhD or MD) (NCES 2002; Kao and Turney 2010). College graduation is far from commonplace, though, suggesting that there is now a weak link between educational expectations and eventual attainment.

Despite this strong norm of college degree attainment, there are still race and ethnic differences in enrollment in college. For 2004, the NCES reported that 60% of Asians, 42% of whites, 32% of blacks, and 25% of Hispanics aged 18–24 were enrolled in colleges and universities (NCES 2007). NCES does not offer data by immigrant status, but the statistics we presented in chapter 4 suggest that the differences between immigrants and native-born individuals within racial and ethnic groups are much more modest than those between racial and ethnic groups as a whole. These patterns tell a consistent story of the over-performance of Asian American youth and the under-performance of black and Hispanic youth relative to whites.

Initial differences by race grow between enrollment and eventual attainment. This reflects a very large gap between those who expect to go to college and even enroll, and those who actually complete college. Because higher education has expanded over the twentieth and twenty-first centuries, younger cohorts in the United States are on average better educated than their older cohort counterparts. However, even among young adults aged 25–29 in 2005, only 28% have attained at least a four-year Bachelor's degree (NCES 2007). It is hard to argue that the discrepancy between the 72% who expect to obtain a Bachelor's degree and the 28% who attain one is not substantial. Evidence suggests that this may result from a delay in the transition to college right after high school. Postponing college attendance until a year or more after high-school graduation is associated with a lower likelihood that youth will earn a four-year degree.

College Enrollment and Completion

In terms of college enrollment and completion, recent studies suggest that some immigrant groups outperform their native-born same-ethnic counterparts. Using the National Longitudinal Study of Adolescent Health, Keller and Tillman (2008) find that first and second generation youth (who were in seventh to twelfth grades in 1994–5) were more likely to attend college than their third generation counterparts. This gap, however, was not consistent across all ethnic groups. Specifically, for whites, blacks, Chinese, and "Other" Asians, college attendance is highest for immigrant youth and decreases with generational status. For Cubans, however, college attendance increased with subsequent generations (Keller and Tillman 2008).

Massey et al. (2007) found that in a representative sample of freshmen in highly selective universities, 27% of all blacks were children of immigrant parents (remember that only 8% of the black population are foreign-born). This figure is much higher than the overall representation of immigrants among African Americans – suggesting that immigrant blacks have better academic outcomes than native-born blacks. This empirical finding supports the notion of *immigrant optimism* that other researchers had already identified for high-school students.

Even among minority youth who attend college, there are significant differences in their achievement levels. In their study of youth in prestigious universities, Massey and his colleagues (2003a) also found that black and Latino students were more likely to fail a course during the first semester of their freshman year compared to whites and Asian students. Moreover, Latino and blacks had much lower GPAs than their white and Asian counterparts in their first semester of college. From this and other research, we know that black and Hispanic students are more likely to drop out of college. Of course, this may represent the cumulative disadvantage that blacks and Hispanics face in attending poorer schools and simply being less academically prepared than their white and Asian counterparts. There are also significant race differences in college majors, which may help to account for some of the income disparities (Ma 2009). However, they do not describe differences in college achievement by immigrant group status. We also describe how these patterns exist for language-minority youth in the following chapter.

Gender and Educational Outcomes

Currently in the US, girls in schools tend to have more educational success than do boys, though they do not necessarily score higher on achievement tests. They do get better grades in general (Duckworth and Seligman 2006) and are more likely to enroll in and graduate from college (Buchman and DiPrete 2006). Gender differences in educational outcomes may be manifested differently among different ethnic and national-origin immigrant groups, however. One possibility is that gender differences between boys and girls are even more extreme. Nancy Lopez (2003b) describes how the academic achievement and aspirations of second-generation Dominican, West Indian, and Haitian high-school girls and boys differ. Boys tend to lower their aspirations, do poorly in school, and drop out more often than girls as they perceive themselves as targeted because of the way they look and the way they dress. Teachers perceive these boys as "trouble-makers," or worse, as dangerous, potential criminals. Because they are treated this way, boys view success in schooling as difficult to achieve given the stereotypes of them that exist. In contrast, although girls also experience discrimination based on perceptions of them as being sexually permissive, they are less likely to be harassed by teachers, police, and other authority figures. Because girls perceive (often correctly) that they may have to support their current and future families without the help of a partner, they work hard in school. They perceive that success in school will allow them a stable career that will enable them to support their own families.

Another gender difference that Lopez (2003a) describes is how girls and boys are treated by their families. The girls in Lopez's study were subject to more control from parents, particularly mothers, than were boys. Boys spent more time outside playing games or "hanging out," while girls had responsibilities toward their families. This description is similar to Zhou and Bankston's (1998) depiction of gender differences in Vietnamese families. The behavior of girls in Vietnamese families is more tightly controlled than that of boys, and, similar to the case for Dominican, West Indian, and Haitian children in immigrant families, they typically exhibit even higher achievement than do boys. Unlike the boys in Lopez's (2003a) study, though, Vietnamese boys do not experience the same disengagement with school, as they are not subject to the same types of stereotypes or enhanced surveillance. Vietnamese boys in immigrant families, particularly those who identify with their ethnic heritage and community, also achieve educational success.

Not all gender differences in immigrant communities favor girls, however. Stacey Lee (2005) finds that the rigid traditional gender roles in Hmong communities often conflict with the academic responsibilities of girls. Men are expected to provide economically for families in Laos while women care for families, and that belief exists to varying degrees in Hmong families and communities in the US. Hmong girls, particularly those of the first generation, are expected to marry early and they find that their responsibilities to their husbands, children, and sometimes even to their husbands' families (Hmong women traditionally live with their husband's family) conflict with their schoolwork. Hmong girls drop out of high school at higher rates than boys and native-born girls to take care of families. Lee (2005) finds that these norms are changing among later-generation Hmong, but they do still persist in noticeable differences in dropout rates between Hmong boys and girls. So, while immigrant girls often follow the pattern of the native-born in having higher school achievement than boys, though for different reasons, there is still variation in how gender affects academic performance across immigrant ethnic and national-origin groups.

The Role of Immigrant Families

It is clear that immigrant parents encounter a schooling system that is foreign to them when they arrive to the United States. Many immigrant parents find it difficult to understand and engage with schools and teachers. Part of these difficulties stem from a language barrier that prevents them from communicating with teachers and schools. It is difficult to overestimate the importance of language in affecting parent–school relationships, and we explore this more closely in chapter 6.

However, immigrant parents also face very different cultural expectations of teachers and schools. In most other countries, students are expected to learn primarily through their teachers and at school. There is little expectation that parents have to play a time-intensive role in helping children with their homework or attending parent–teacher conferences. Learning occurs at school, with little participation from parents. In the United States, teachers expect parents to be active partners in the schooling of their children. Countless scholars, such as Annette Lareau, have convincingly documented the difficulty lower socioeconomic status parents have in meeting the expectations of teachers. Simply put, they believe education should primarily lie in the teacher's domain at school (Lareau 2000). Teachers interpret the lower levels of parental participation of working-class youth as a sign that their parents are less interested in educational goals and view their families in a negative light. This may be even more prevalent among immigrant parents, whose limited English skills may make them feel less prepared and qualified to manage their children's academic careers. It also makes the actual communication with teachers more difficult.

Despite these challenges to participating in schooling among minority and immigrant parents, the benefits to educational outcomes of parent involvement are unclear. In fact, parental participation does not have great power in explaining the racial and ethnic differences in educational performance. Simply put, while white and Asian youth enjoy higher achievement levels, white parents are among the most active participants but Asian and Hispanic parents are less active in participating in school. In recent surveys, African American parents have higher levels of participation than their Asian and Hispanic counterparts, yet their children have the lowest levels of academic performance. In fact, most models of how parent–child or parent–school interactions affect schooling outcomes do not seem to work for Asian (and perhaps more specifically Asian immigrant) households (Kao 1995; Kao and Thompson 2003).

It is likely that many models of parent–school interaction that were developed using studies of white families simply do not work for other groups. This may be especially true in the case of immigrant families. Asian American and Hispanic families face similar language and cultural barriers. Their lack of communication with teachers can be interpreted as a lack of interest in educational endeavors. Still, Asian American youth have higher educational outcomes than Hispanics and these differences cannot be attributed simply to their parental socioeconomic status or parent-teacher communication.

This leads some scholars to argue that culture is the key to understanding racial and immigrant differences. While there is no doubt that there are important cultural norms among immigrant families of different national-origin backgrounds, it is not clear to us how cultural differences actually explain immigrant variation in academic outcomes. If "Asian values," as some have argued, really do stress educational performance, then one would expect Asians in all countries to excel. Moreover, it is difficult to argue that there is something unique to all Asians that is shared by so many disparate national-origin groups who do not always identify with one another. China and India are each large heterogeneous countries with very different ethnic and religious groups. What they do have in common is a shared immigrant experience and common treatment by native-born Americans, but it is unclear how that equates to any type of innate cultural norm. It is important for us to keep in mind how historical relations between the US and other countries have defined the racial landscape of the United States.

Nonetheless, these are obvious and influential explanations that describe how cultural norms (and which norms among certain groups) are compatible with American systems of socioeconomic mobility. While most scholars attempt to avoid vilifying traits associated with certain ethnic groups, others often interpret these findings to suggest that some minority groups do not have the right values to succeed in their education. In other words, some groups are seen as naturally hard-working or have cultural values that are compatible with educational success, while other groups are seen as not having the right values that promote socioeconomic success. These perspectives are sometimes termed *cultural deficit* models (e.g. Deutsch and Associates 1967).

A Closer Look at the Popular Portrayals of Minority Group Educational Outcomes

Are Asian Americans Really Model Minorities?

Due to the more advantaged circumstances of Asian American parents and the exemplary school performance of Asian American youth, researchers, the popular press, and even presidents like Ronald Reagan have heralded Asian Americans as the "model minority." In a seminal 1966 *New York Times Magazine* essay, sociologist William Petersen wrote of the success of Japanese Americans despite the long history of discrimination toward them (Petersen 1966). Petersen found it remarkable that just 20 years after Japanese Americans (most of whom were US citizens) were forced into concentration camps, they emerged from the experience of losing everything to enjoying relative economic success. He states, "By any criterion of good citizenship that we choose, the Japanese Americans are better than any other group in our society, including native-born whites" (Petersen 1966). A few years later, in 1971, *Newsweek* stated that Asian Americans were "outwhiting the whites." Mike Wallace stated on a *60 Minutes* episode on Asian Americans, "They must be doing something right. Let's bottle it" (Kao 1995).

On February 23, 1984, President Ronald Reagan spoke to Asian and Pacific American leaders and stated, "Asian and Pacific Americans have helped preserve that dream by living up to the bedrock values that make us a good and a worthy people . . . It's no wonder that the median income of Asian and Pacific American families is much higher than the total American average (Reagan in Woolley and Peters 2010a). The quote by President Reagan is an oft-cited one by Asian American academics because it shows the extent to which this image of Asian Americans had become accepted among all Americans (see Kao 1995 and Lee 1996 for examples). In President George Bush's 1990 remarks when signing the Asian/Pacific American Heritage Month Proclamation, he said "These 7 million Americans show us an example of how strong families can instill an abiding respect for the law, tenacity in the endeavor of life and work, and most of all, excellence in education" (Bush in Woolley and Peters 2010b). In fact, in our brief review of Presidential Addresses from the 1960s to the present that mention Asians, Hispanics, African Americans, or immigrants, it is clear that there is a bias towards viewing Asian Americans as successful (especially in terms of educational outcomes), while emphasizing the need to expand educational opportunities for blacks or Hispanics.

Some scholars have also supported the image of Asian Americans as model minorities and sought to account for their high academic performance. In a 1990 article, Schneider and Lee (1990) argued that Asian Americans had extraordinarily close ties to their parents, and that Asian parents valued academic success over success in other domains. This is in contrast to white parents, who may be supportive of their children's success in art, athletics, or other areas. Caplan, Choy, and Whitmore (1992) also found that close family ties were the key to educational success even among families without financial resources or much human capital. They addressed the puzzle of high educational achievement among a low socioeconomic status group, Southeast Asian refugee children. They found that these strong family ties manifested themselves in practices such as older siblings tutoring younger siblings and that these practices reinforced the importance of educational outcomes. Similarly, Zhou and Bankston (1998) studied Vietnamese children in Louisiana. Here, the youth are not only from less advantaged family backgrounds but also attend schools with other poor children. Still, they found high academic performance, and similarly argued that strong family ties, as well as robust family–community integration, were responsible for high academic achievement. They also argued that Vietnamese children who were less Americanized and identified more with their Vietnamese heritage (by using the language, for example) had better academic outcomes.

While this image is consistent with the high average educational outcomes of Asian American youth and adults, other scholars warn against this stereotype. These scholars (many of whom are themselves Asian Americans) argue that the pan-ethnic group

"Asian American" encompasses so many diverse groups such that the image of success glosses over great disparities. As we saw in the previous chapter, Asian American national-origin groups include the richest (South Asians) and the poorest (Hmong) – hence there are also divergent educational outcomes.

Differences in educational pathways can also vary within ethnic groups according to the class resources of families. Vivian Louie (2004) interviewed Chinese American college students and their parents in the New York City area. She found that while being Chinese American resulted in a common cultural script that parents sacrificed everything by immigrating to the United States, and that the primary goal was to improve their children's educational outcomes, class differences made the actualization of this abstract aspiration vary greatly in practice. Working-class Chinese Americans (many of whom resided in Chinatown) were more likely to have older siblings who did not attend college or had participated in criminal activities. Moreover, these youth were expected to work throughout their college years and lived at home. One respondent even reported that she chose Hunter College because it was on a subway line (Louie 2004). Their experiences greatly contrast the experience of choosing a university for the middle- and upper-class Chinese Americans. They could afford to visit a number of prestigious institutions and carefully decide where to go, regardless of costs or distance.

In addition to the ways that the "model minority" image masks important differences between and within ethnic groups, researchers critique it because it suggests that Asian Americans have "made it" in the US. These researchers point out that high academic achievement does not necessarily guarantee assimilation in all aspects of life. Authors such as Mia Tuan (1998) and Stacey Lee (1996) argue that while Asian Americans are heralded as the "model minority," they are never viewed as authentically American. Mia Tuan describes them as "forever foreign" because even third or fourth generation Asian Americans are constantly asked about where they are really from or where they learned to speak English so well. Stacey Lee (1996) notes that the absence of Asian Americans in educational discourse stems from their being seen as unassimilable. Filipina American writer Jessica Hagedorn (1993) states:

> In our perceived American character, we are completely nonthreatening. We don't complain. We endure humiliation. We are almost inhuman in our patience. We never get angry. (Hagedorn 1993: xxii–xxiii in Lee 1996)

Finally, there are many scholars who dislike the term "model minority" because it is used implicitly to critique other minority groups, who do not have such successful educational outcomes. Lee (1996) argues that the perceived silence of Asian Americans is a hegemonic device used to critique other minorities (especially African Americans) for their outspoken complaints about racial injustice. Often the implication of the "model minority" stereotype is that being a minority does not necessarily put one at a disadvantage. If Latinos and blacks had the "right" values that promoted educational success then they, too, could achieve as Asians Americans have done. It is to the perceptions of the educational outcomes of these two groups that we now turn.

Latino Students: Strong Family Values Lead to Weak Educational Outcomes

Public attention to the educational outcomes of Latino students in the United States is almost a polar opposite to that of Asian American students. Policy-makers and scholars alike worry about the lower academic achievement and attainment of many Hispanic youth. As Hispanic youth become a larger proportion of the school-aged population in the United States, their academic outcomes will increasingly affect the overall educational profile of American youth. This sentiment can be seen in President George Bush's comments during his signing of the National Hispanic Heritage Month Proclamation and the Educational Excellence for Hispanic Americans Executive Order on September 24, 1990. He stated:

Tragically, too many Hispanic Americans are not getting the kind of first-rate education they need and they deserve. And that must change. And we must work together. And we must start now ... Today, though, less than two-thirds of Hispanic young adults earn a high-school diploma. We must find new strategies to boost graduation and literacy rates, strategies that really do get the job done, strategies that really work. We must figure out how to help these young people, how to equip them with the tools to enter a nation and a world where technology advances so rapidly that literacy and analytical and technical skills are not luxuries but essentials. We must help education to help Hispanic children enter the 21st century prepared to take their rightful place at the American table of opportunity. (Bush in Woolley and Peters 2010c)

Scholars have largely focused on socioeconomic differences between Latinos and whites to account for the lower educational outcomes of Latino youth. In many empirical studies, controlling for differences in parental socioeconomic status accounts for the Latino–white disparity in educational outcomes. Simply put, many Latinos do not do well in school because they come from poor and disadvantaged families. However, prior to modern statistical analyses that enabled researchers to systematically examine the effects of parental background characteristics on educational outcomes, many authors argued that Hispanic, or more specifically Mexican families did not value education as much as other ethnic groups. For instance, Economist Thomas Sowell wrote that, "The goals and values of Mexican Americans have never centered on education" (Sowell 1981: 266). In fact, Oscar Lewis's influential formulation of the notion *culture of poverty* came from his study of families in Mexico (*Five Families: Mexican Case Studies in the Culture of Poverty*, 1959) and later of Puerto Ricans in New York and Puerto Rico (*La Vida: A Puerto Rican Family in the Culture of Poverty*, 1966a). The strong values for family and the necessity of caring for family members have been pointed to as reasons why Hispanics do not focus more on educational achievement.

More recently, though, scholars have begun to examine how schools may further marginalize Latino populations. For example, Angela Valenzuela (1999) argued that for a group of students in

Houston, schools worked to discourage distinct cultural attributes by limiting ties to their home language and culture. She called this "subtractive schooling." Public schools in the United States have historically worked to "Americanize" and homogenize all immigrant youth, and English-only policies apply not only to Latinos but to other students as well. What is important, perhaps, is not simply the attempt to Americanize Latino youth but that the school in her study actively worked to devalue Mexican American family life. Hence, students felt that their teachers did not care about them as individuals. Scholars seeking to understand and improve the educational outcomes of Latino children have focused more on how families and schools work together (or do not work together) to influence children's outcomes.

African Immigrant Students: Reproducing the Enduring Black–White Achievement Gap?

Researchers have paid relatively little attention to African immigrants. As we discuss above, one of the reasons for the lack of studies on this group is that, compared to Hispanics and Asians, Africans contribute to a much smaller proportion of the immigrant population in the US. However, studies agree on the advantage that many African immigrants have in their education upon arrival to the US compared to other immigrants. The parental selectivity of this group seems higher than that for Hispanics or Asians. Thus, in general, Africans' educational achievement tends to be higher than that of non-immigrant blacks, both in high school (Kent 2007) and college (Massey et al. 2007). Among both the first and second generation, black Africans also seem to perform better than first and second generation blacks from other origins – such as Haitians (Rong and Brown 2001). As we discuss above, this is not completely surprising as Africans are among the most highly educated immigrant groups in the US (see also chapter 4 and Kaba 2007).

Despite the advantage of black immigrants over black natives, race remains an important mediator of the schooling differences of these children and this becomes more evident among the second and third generation. African immigrants' racial classification as "black" most certainly accounts for their lack of improved socio-economic outcomes as they assimilate (Thomas 2012).

Most of the research on the black–white educational achievement gap (such as the theories on stereotype threat and oppositional culture presented in chapter 2) has been done using African American students who are native-born. Therefore, it is not clear how black immigrant youth would respond to negative images of African Americans. Would they believe that negative stereotypes about blacks applied to them? One recent study by Deaux and her colleagues (Deaux et al. 2007) found that first and second generation West Indian students performed equally under conditions of stereotype threat neutrality. However, when conditions of stereotype threat were introduced, second generation West Indians performed worse than first generation West Indians (and more like African Americans). Their findings suggest that while new immigrants can more successfully see themselves as part of a distinct group, subsequent generations of black West Indian youth become assimilated into the racial hierarchy in the United States. Their racial status becomes more important than their immigrant status in their performance on educational tests, at least in an experimental setting. This suggests that how race is defined in the US has long-term effects on educational achievement, and that these racial categories will shape the educational outcomes of future generations from immigrant families. Whether the findings on West Indians can be extrapolated to African immigrants is still to be studied.

A few studies that directly examine immigrant African youth also attempt to explain the higher performance of African students compared to non-immigrant blacks. Some commentators have pointed to the "unique" cultural traits that black immigrants have which help them excel more than non-immigrant blacks (Rimer and Arenson 2004), but further research in this area is greatly needed.

A Note on African Immigrants

Although they do not constitute the majority of immigrants from Africa, a portion of Africans are white (or Asian) and the discussion above does not completely apply to them. As some have demonstrated, the educational experiences of white Africans are different from those of black Africans. For example, Thomas (2012) discusses differences in the educational outcomes of black and white African immigrants. According to his study, which uses data from the 2000 US Census, white African immigrants come from families with higher incomes and educational attainment than those from black African families. White African immigrants in the US are also more likely to remain enrolled in school when compared to their black African counterparts, and this difference grows larger over the second and third generation. In general, evidence supports that pre- and post-migration experiences situate white African families in a better position to succeed in the US. For instance, white Africans arrive to the US with higher socioeconomic positions than those of black Africans and they do not encounter the same structural barriers associated with racial minority status as they assimilate into US society.

Conclusion

Racial and ethnic minority and immigrant students achieve very different levels of educational performance and attainment. While many white and Asian American students enjoy relatively higher levels of academic success, a significant number of African American and Latino students do less well at school. These patterns can be found using multiple indicators of performance (e.g. standardized test scores, grades) and attainment (aspirations, enrollment in college, and college completion). Moreover, these differences are apparent at entry to kindergarten and persist to university level (even for youth who manage to get to this point).

Overall, it is crucial that we keep in mind the complex ways in which immigrant status, national origin, class, and race and ethnicity work together. Individuals and families come from very different environments and countries. They bring with them a wide range of educational and economic resources that give them very different starting points in the US. A family with a father or mother who was a physician in China, India, or Russia, who has to take a job as a medical assistant in the US, is still advantaged by simply having a college-educated parent in a white-collar occupation. Compare this family with one in which a mother or father finished fourth grade and worked as an unskilled laborer in his or her country of origin and now works as a janitor. While the first family has experienced significant downward socioeconomic mobility and the second family has not, it is clear that the first family still enjoys a higher occupational status and income. Members of the second family may in fact believe their lives are much better in the US than before, both in terms of occupational prestige and income.

However, all of these individuals faced great disruption in their lives. They had to leave family and friends behind and enter a foreign environment where, for many, the English language was a great obstacle to becoming integrated to the United States. Many work and sacrifice with the hope that their children will learn English, enjoy greater educational opportunities in the US and experience socioeconomic mobility.

We believe that the part of this story that is most often neglected is how immigrants are absorbed into the racial landscape of the United States. Immigrants from Africa come with extremely high levels of education, but they are placed with African Americans who are still viewed negatively by most Americans (Kluegel 1990) and suffer from lower socioeconomic status. Chileans also have very high levels of education, yet are also grouped under the Hispanic panethnic umbrella and identified as members of a lower-status minority group. Cambodians enter the US with low levels of education, yet they are taken as Asian Americans, who are identified as the model minority. Teachers may be more likely to expect these children to be studious and good at math. This may be reflected in their assessment and in their expectations for them. Immigrant differences in educational achievement are substantial. Their causes cannot be attributed to a single source. In research on differences in educational outcomes, there is still considerably more attention paid to race and ethnicity than to immigrant status; however, for many students, these two theoretically distinct characteristics coexist in reality. Despite this, researchers do not pay sufficient attention to the interaction between national origin, immigrant status, and race and ethnicity. As we have stressed in this chapter and the previous ones, we need to examine the interaction between individual resources, group position, and how immigrants are assimilated into the racial hierarchy in the United States in order to get a better understanding of their educational outcomes.

In the next chapter, we look at one aspect of immigrants' daily experiences that separates them from many native-born students: their language use and proficiency. We focus on the effects of language proficiency and use on educational outcomes.

6

Language and Educational Success

In previous chapters, we presented evidence suggesting that under the same socioeconomic circumstances, immigrant students' educational outcomes may be higher than those of their native counterparts. As we also discussed, both immigrant children and their parents are more likely to report higher personal and parental aspirations than native families. Immigrant students are also more likely to take advanced math and science courses, and to take Advanced Placement (AP) tests in preparation for college (Ruiz-de-Velasco and Fix 2000). Immigrant students, in general, are more likely to graduate from high school and from college than their native-born counterparts (Ruiz-de-Velasco and Fix 2000). However, as we have also discussed, immigrants do not experience "equal conditions" upon their arrival to the US. Even among those who have lived in the US for a number of years, their daily lives can vary greatly, relative to the native-born population. One of the most defining characteristics of new arrivals to the United States, relative to the native-born population, is their English proficiency and their use of languages other than English at home, and, as we will show in this chapter, this greatly influences educational success (Singh and Hernandez-Gantes 1996).

The benefits of learning English to immigrants in the US are obvious. Achieving English proficiency allows them to successfully navigate life in the US. For instance, English proficiency is key in performing everyday tasks such as chatting with neighbors, reading labels in the supermarket or the pharmacy, or paying bills. Moreover, it is crucial for individuals as they engage in more complex activities such as reading a newspaper or deciphering a legal document. In terms of language and educational outcomes, immigrants who learn English well obtain higher levels of education and tend to have higher-paying jobs than immigrants with limited English language skills (Bleakley and Chin 2004; Carnevale et al. 2001). Speaking English proficiently is one marker of assimilation. However, there may be additional benefits to being proficient in both English and one's (parents') mother tongue. Being proficient in one's parents' mother tongue can help tie youth to parents and to the ethnic community, which in turn promotes the transfer of social capital from these sources to youths. For example, Bankston and Zhou (1995) find that youth who are bilingual tend to do better in school.

In this chapter, we present data on the language diversity among the population living in the US as well as data on the use of other languages at home and English proficiency among the three immigrant and ethnic minority groups studied in this volume (Asians, Hispanics, and Africans). We discuss the extent to which English is more quickly acquired by some immigrant groups than others, and the possible explanations for these differences. Then, we present the specific ways in which English proficiency is related to educational success among the immigrant population. How do English proficiency and/or being bilingual enable students to succeed educationally and to "fit in" in the US?

Immigrants and English Language Learners

Let us start by addressing two popular ideas about English language use and immigrants: (1) most English language learners are immigrants; and (2) there are many more English language learners in the US now than in the past. One may reasonably believe that all English language learners are newly arrived immigrants, or at least first generation individuals (that is, people who migrated to the US but were born in countries where English was not spoken). This is actually somewhat of a myth. Up to 80% of English language learners in US schools were born in the US. In other words, they are US citizens (Gándara and Hopkins 2010). This does not suggest, however, that immigration is not related to English language proficiency. In most cases, English language learners are individuals born in immigrant families who live in linguistically isolated conditions. These children live in segregated neighborhoods with families from a similar ethnic background, so these children can go through early childhood with little exposure to English or at least Standard American English, and few opportunities to learn and practice English. Moreover, the limited English they may be exposed to is more likely to be a vernacular English and is not conducive to higher educational achievement in school. Teachers will grade homework that uses Standard American English grammar more positively than assignments that use an informal or vernacular English. Children who use Standard English may be considered smarter (Klesmer 1994). Teachers may have higher expectations for these children and therefore they may obatain access to more educational opportunities.

The intensity of debates by political pundits and the controversy that surrounds bilingual education, as well as the promotion of "English-only" laws and policies, suggests that there are more non-English speakers now than in the past. In fact, while the *total number* of people who do not speak English well is greater than in the past (about 10 million) because the US population is much bigger, the *proportion* of English language learners is less than what the country has seen in the past. Think, for instance, about the first European settlers to the US. They faced a Native American population from hundreds of different tribes, each with their own language. Slaves from Africa also brought with them their native tongues. Moreover, remember that European colonials were not just from England, but there were also Spanish, French, German, Swedish, and Dutch arrivals. For example, between 1890 and 1910, those who could not speak English accounted for about 4% of the total US population (Gibson and Lennon 1999; Labov 1998; Stevens 1999; Watkins 1994). In 2006, they only accounted for 1.5% of the population (Kominski et al. 2008). To recap, the total number of people unable to speak English has grown, but so has the total of the population living in the US. Hence, while the total number of people who do not speak English has grown from the turn of the twentieth century to the present, the proportion of the US population who do not speak English is much more modest than it was 100 years ago (Fix and Passel 1994).

Next, it is important to note that not all newcomers need to learn English. Although immigrants from English-speaking countries account for a relatively small proportion of recent immigrants, those migrating from Canada or Britain, for example, do not face a language barrier. As we discussed in previous chapters, Hispanics (especially Mexicans) and Asians make up the majority of new arrivals to the US, and most of these immigrants arrive from non-English-speaking countries (though English is commonly spoken in India, Singapore, and other Asian countries, especially among the well-educated individuals who are also most likely to migrate). Thus, it is reasonable to expect that the majority of new immigrants arrive without the necessary English language abilities. For this group, researchers need to understand why it is important that they learn English and what the consequences of not learning English are for educational attainment.

The Language Debate

The US is a country where many languages are spoken. In other words, it is a polyglot nation. There is no official language in the United States (although a number of states have adopted English as their official language). According to the 2000 US Census, there were about 47 million people who spoke a language other than English at home. The languages reported total to over 300 different ones.

The list of the top 20 languages spoken at home in the US according to the 2000 US Census appears in table 6.1. As can be seen from this table, over 80% of individuals speak English at home, and only Spanish is spoken among a sizeable proportion of the population (nearly 11%). However, this still leaves room for about 20 million individuals who speak a non-English or non-Spanish language at home. Among the most commonly spoken foreign languages in US

Table 6.1 Top 20 languages spoken at home in the US

	Language	Number of speakers	Percent of all languages	Share among non-English languages
1	English	215,423,555	82.11	NA
2	Spanish	28,100,725	10.71	59.85
3	French	1,606,790	0.61	3.42
4	Chinese	1,499,635	0.57	3.19
5	German	1,382,615	0.53	2.94
6	Tagalog	1,224,240	0.47	2.61
7	Vietnamese	1,009,625	0.38	2.15
8	Italian	1,008,370	0.38	2.15
9	Korean	894,065	0.34	1.90
10	Russian	706,240	0.27	1.50
11	Polish	667,415	0.25	1.42
12	Arabic	614,580	0.23	1.31
13	Portuguese	563,835	0.21	1.20
14	Japanese	477,995	0.18	1.02
15	French Creole	453,370	0.17	0.96
16	Greek	365,435	0.14	0.78
17	Hindi	317,055	0.12	0.68
18	Persian	312,085	0.12	0.66
19	Urdu	262,900	0.10	0.56
20	Cantonese	259,750	0.10	0.55
	Others	5,224,474	1.99	11.13

Population 5 years and over.

Source: US Census Bureau (2006), Census 2000 Special Tabulation 224

homes, over 1.5 million people speak French at home, another 1.75 million speak Chinese (Mandarin, Cantonese, or another dialect) with their families and 1.4 million speak German. Asian languages make up over 12% of the non-English languages spoken in the US, which represents over 6 million people.

While some see the benefits to having so many languages spoken in the US, others lament the diminished role of English. In fact, language diversity has been a topic of discussion and concern throughout American history. Marc Shell (1993) argues that discussions about the relative prominence of English compared to other languages began from the time of the earliest European settlers and continued through World War I. At the time the *Federalist Papers* were written, only one-quarter of the total white population was English-origin. In *The Second Federalist Paper* (1787), John Jay famously states:

> With equal pleasure I have as often taken notice that Providence has been pleased to give this one connected country to one united people – a people descended from the same ancestors, speaking the same language, professing the same religion, attached to the same principles of government, very similar in their manners and customs, and who, by their joint counsels, arms, and efforts, fighting side by side throughout a long and bloody war, have nobly established general liberty and independence.

Even some of our forefathers who had formerly supported multilingualism eventually defended a vision of a monolingual English-speaking America. Ben Franklin printed not only in English, but tried to print the first German-language newspaper in 1732 (The *Philadelphische Zeitung*) (Shell 1993). The German-language paper failed, and later Franklin promoted the use of English only. He lamented the fact that Pennsylvania "will in a few Years become a German colony; Instead of their Learning our Language, we must learn theirs, or live as in a foreign Country" (Franklin 1750, in Shell 1993: 109). He more broadly claimed that all foreign nationals would eventually "drown and stifle the English" (Franklin 1784, in Shell 1993), and argued for more immigration from England to counteract such potential loss of English as the dominant language (Shell 1993).

English was not the only language that was considered as the "national language" of the US. The Louisiana Purchase in 1803 made French a leading contender, while the Treaty of Guadalupe Hidalgo in 1848 (that marked the end of the Mexican–American War) also resulted in a large number of new Americans who spoke Spanish. Other proposed solutions to the "problem" of having a multilingual America included using an ancient language, like Hebrew or Greek, as the single official language of the United States. German continued to be seen as a legitimate second language in the United States. The start of World War I, however, eliminated German as a potential second language to English. English, in the end, seemed to win out.

In 1918, President Theodore Roosevelt famously stated (Roosevelt 1918): "We have room for but one language in this country, and that is the English language, for we intend to see that the crucible turns our people out as Americans, of American nationality, and not as dwellers in a polyglot boarding house." Although this quote is almost a century old, it reflects an ideology that has been shared by many in American history and remains a source of debate today. The sentiment expressed in the quote is not only that everyone must learn English, but also that all aspects of daily life must be conducted in English. The use of other languages is seen as a threat to the well-being of America, and non-English speakers are not perceived to be real Americans.

The overwhelming push toward "English Only" is alive and endorsed by many. For example, by 2010, 30 states had passed laws that explicitly state that English is their official language. The arguments emphasize the idea that English has to be protected so the US does not become a *Tower of Babel* or a "polyglot boarding house." In other words, there is a belief that immigrants do not adopt English as their primary language unless they are obligated to do so, and this goal is only achievable with laws that dictate English as the official language. These laws suggest that immigrants must learn English to become truly "assimilated" Americans who are loyal to the United States and only then are they able to achieve the "American Dream."

Research has not supported the claim that immigrants *resist* learning English, however. While it may take time, immigrants and their offspring eventually learn English (Portes and Hao 1998). Learning a language does not happen overnight, however. Immigrants from non-English-speaking countries who arrived during the 1800s and early 1900s did not suddenly become English speakers upon arrival to the US, but learned English over time and over generations. Most native-born individuals of European descent who are fluent in English had grandparents, great grandparents, or great-great grandparents who did not speak English fluently when they migrated to the US. The accounts of how many years the first generation took to learn English are quickly forgotten.

In contrast to the position that immigrants and their offspring are unwilling to speak English, researchers have demonstrated that ancestral language was lost very quickly for the children and grandchildren of these European immigrants. However, it rarely happened among the first generation; rather, it took between two and three generations. In her book *Ethnic Options*, Mary Waters describes how this process occurred for European immigrants using the accounts provided by descendants of European immigrants who arrived during the 1800s and early 1900s. According to Waters, the first generation tended to maintain communication with their children (the second generation) in their ancestral language, which became a "home language" for the second generation. The second generation only spoke their non-English languages with their parents and some relatives. The second generation rarely maintained the ancestral language with their own children (third generation or the grandchildren of immigrants), except for perhaps a few simple phrases or words they had heard from their grandparents; that is, the third generation was unable to speak the language, but many remembered being able to understand it when they were young (Waters 1990).

Are the language acquisition and language-use patterns of today's immigrants much different from those of the immigrants of the past? Do they primarily apply to immigrants from Europe? Or, are these patterns similar for Hispanic and Asian immigrants today? There is ample evidence that contemporary patterns of English acquisition by immigrants and their offspring are not as different from those in previous centuries as some may claim. Contemporary immigrants learn English rather quickly, even within the first generation. For example, among Hispanic immigrants who have been in the US for less than two years, only 14% speak English very well, but this number rises to 43% for those who have been in this country for 26 or more years, indicating that even if they do not abandon their ancestral language, many first generation immigrants become English proficient given enough time (Hakimzadeh and Cohn 2007). Additionally, whereas only

23% of first generation Hispanics speak English very well, this number dramatically rises to 88% in the second generation, and to 94% among third and higher generations (Hakimzadeh and Cohn 2007). English proficiency among foreign-born Africans is higher than for Hispanics and Asians, with about two-thirds of African immigrants reporting being proficient in English. However, even fluent Africans report having problems being understood by native-born Americans (Kent 2007; Shabaya 2006). These data suggest that today, as in the past, the adoption of English is widespread, certainly by the second generation. Sociologists have also demonstrated that the adoption of English and the preference to speak only English does not depend on one's education or occupation (Alba et al. 2002; Portes and Fernández-Kelly 2008; Portes and Rumbaut 2006; Rumbaut 1994).

Most evidence, past and present, suggests that linguistic assimilation does invariably happen over time. What is less clear is the extent to which linguistic assimilation precedes other types of assimilation (Portes and Hao 1998). Recall that, according to traditional assimilation theory (Gordon 1964), assimilation was expected to occur in a "straight line," with immigrants acquiring US customs while simultaneously abandoning their own. This implies that immigrants abandon their native language and overwhelmingly adopt English as their main language of communication. Current theorists do not completely agree with this unidirectional and inevitable outcome for all contemporary immigrants. Under segmented assimilation, some argue that immigrants selectively acculturate and that there are advantages for these immigrants to retain certain aspects of elements from their culture of origin. Retention of their mother tongue may be one of those traits that indicate that immigrants are exercising "selective acculturation" (Portes and Rumbaut 2001; Portes and Zhou 1993).

Under "selective acculturation," learning English does not imply that one must abandon one's native language. While descendants of European immigrants did eventually abandon their native tongues in favor of English, for current immigrants, the relationship between their mother tongues and English may be more complex than in the past. The pattern of language use among the fourth generation of the post-1965 immigrant groups remains to be seen. Among contemporary immigrants, language of origin may remain present over more generations; however, this does not necessarily suggest that English is not spoken. In the next section, we examine the languages that are spoken at home in the US and the language proficiency of both the general and the foreign-born population of the US.

English at Home and English Proficiency among the US Population

Tables 6.2, 6.3, and 6.4 in this chapter present information on English language in the US by using the same format as in chapter 4. We present detailed data on ethnic groups as well as for the foreign-born population. At the top of table 6.2, you can also observe the percentages of the whole US population, as well as by race/ethnicity, aged 5 and older who speak non-English languages at home and who are not proficient in English. Table 6.2 presents these percentages for each of the specific Asian ethnic and foreign-born groups. Table 6.3 displays the same information but for Hispanic ethnic and immigrant groups, while table 6.4 does so for African ancestry and immigrant groups.

The data for this section and the next come from the American Community Survey 2008, a survey of a nationally representative sample of individuals in the US. Among the entire US population aged 5 or older, about 20% speak a language other than English at home, but only less than 9% lack English proficiency. Among whites, the numbers are much lower than other groups, about 6% and 2% respectively. For blacks, about 7% do not speak English at home, and 2% are not English proficient. Among Hispanics and Asians, roughly 76% speak another language at home, and 37% are not proficient in English.

The top part of tables 6.2, 6.3, and 6.4 present data for Asian, Hispanic, and African ethnic groups. Clearly, when we examine only the large pan-ethnic groups, we miss some important ethnic group differences. For example, if we focus on the ethnic groups among Asians, in table 6.2 we observe that only 46% of Japanese

Table 6.2 Percentage of US population 5 years and older who speak other languages at home and speak English less than "very well": Asian ethnic groups and foreign-born

	% other language at home	% speak English less than "very well"
US population	19.7	8.6
White alone (non-Hispanic)	5.8	1.7
Black alone (non-Hispanic)	6.7	2.3
Hispanic (any race)	76.3	37.3
Asian ethnic groups	76.7	36.1
Chinese	82.3	46.9
Filipino	67.6	22.8
Asian Indian	79.5	22.7
Vietnamese	86.9	52.5
Korean	78.2	46.9
Japanese	46.2	25.2
Cambodian	85.5	48.3
Hmong	92.5	44.3
Laotian	85.3	45.7
Pakistani	88.2	28.6
Thai	78.4	43.9
Bangladeshi	91.4	43.8
Other specified Asian	88.0	51.6
Asian foreign-born	89.1	46.7
China	91.7	60.6
Philippines	85.7	30.4
India	90.5	28.1
Vietnam	93.8	67.4
Korea	84.6	57.0
Japan	80.6	49.7
Cambodia	92.9	67.4
Laos	93.7	65.3
Pakistan	92.3	35.3
Thailand	85.1	47.8
Bangladesh	94.3	50.4
Indonesia	83.6	40.5

Source: American Community Survey 2008 (US Census Bureau 2009) 1-year estimates

people speak a language different from English at home and that 25% of them are less than proficient in English. This contrasts with other Asian groups, such as the Hmong, with over 92% of Hmong using a non-English language at home and about 44% reporting not being English proficient. These differences are a result of the groups' very different immigration histories. Most Japanese Americans in the US migrated in the late 1800s or early 1900s or are descendants of these early migrants – hence most of the Japanese Americans are at least second or third generation. Among the Hmong population, all of whom migrated after the wars in Indochina, almost no one is beyond the second generation.

The top half of table 6.3 shows the variation among the Hispanic national-origin groups in their language spoken at home and their English proficiency. Over 90% of Dominicani, Guatemalans Hondurans, and Salvadoreans report speaking a non-English language (presumably Spanish) at home, while only 34% of Spaniards report doing so. Even 66% of Puerto Ricans speak a non-English language at home, which is much lower than the other Hispanic groups (except for Spaniards), but still constitutes a majority of them, which may be surprising given their native-born status. Examining this a different way, we note that only 8% of Spaniards say they speak English "less than very well," compared to 61% of Guatemalans and Hondurans.

Table 6.4 presents the same information for African ancestry groups as reported by the American Community Survey. Among individuals of sub-Saharan African ancestry, over a third (35.8%) use a non-English language at home, but the differences by ancestry group are important. For example, only 19% of those of African descent use a non-English language at home, but 80% of Ethiopians and 76% of Ghanaians do. Despite the high levels of non-English use at home, we observe that most people of sub-Saharan descent have a good command of English. Only less than 6% of African and 9% of Nigerians speak English "less than very well," however people of Ethiopian, Cape Verdean, and Ghanaian descent have higher rates of speaking English "less than very well," with 36%, 23%, and 19% doing so, respectively.

These tables demonstrate that there is large variation among the

Table 6.3 Percentage of US population 5 years and older who speak other languages at home and speak English less than "very well": Hispanic and foreign-born ethnic groups

	% other language at home	% speak English less than "very well"
US population	19.7	8.6
White alone (non-Hispanic)	5.8	1.7
Black alone (non-Hispanic)	6.7	2.3
Asian alone (non-Hispanic)	77.0	36.3
Hispanic ethnic groups	76.3	37.3
Mexican	76.2	38.4
Puerto Rican	66.4	19.7
Cuban	83.4	41.7
Dominican	91.5	46.3
Costa Rican	77.6	35.5
Guatemalan	91.1	60.9
Honduran	91.8	60.9
Nicaraguan	88.1	44.4
Panamanian	63.5	18.8
Salvadorean	92.8	56.2
Argentinian	83.9	31.4
Bolivian	86.8	34.4
Chilean	78.6	31.1
Colombian	87.4	42.8
Ecuadorean	91.6	51.2
Peruvian	86.7	45.1
Venezuelan	88.8	33.9
Spaniard	33.6	7.7
All other Hispanic	51.6	14.1
Hispanic foreign-born	89.8	64.4
Cuba	95.2	61.6
Dominican Republic	96.7	65.8
Mexico	97.0	73.9
Costa Rica	92.0	51.3
El Salvador	96.0	72.3
Guatemala	95.0	74.0
Honduras	95.9	73.5
Nicaragua	95.5	61.8
Panama	81.1	28.7
Argentina	91.1	38.5

Table 6.3 (continued)

	% other language at home	% speak English less than "very well"
Bolivia	94.6	43.9
Brazil	90.5	47.0
Chile	90.0	42.3
Colombia	93.5	55.7
Ecuador	96.5	64.8
Peru	94.5	55.3
Venezuela	94.1	38.7

Source: American Community Survey 2008 (US Census Bureau 2009) 1-year estimates

ancestry groups in the proportion of individuals who do not speak English at home and their English fluency. Most importantly, we observe that it is not always the case that a higher percentage of non-English language at home is correlated with high proportions of people who do not speak English well. In other words, we cannot assume that those individuals who speak a non-English language at home are not English proficient. It may be that some individuals, particularly those in the second or third immigrant generation, know English well, but choose to speak another language at home. In the next section, we focus on language spoken at home and English proficiency among immigrants specifically.

English at Home and English Proficiency among the Foreign-Born

In this section we focus on the bottom panels of tables 6.2, 6.3, and 6.4, which present the same data on language just discussed, but on the foreign-born population. Again, we present data on "no English spoken at home" and "percentage that speak English less than very well." As we can see from table 6.2, among foreign-born Asians, between 80% and 95% of immigrants do not speak English at home. However, no more than two-thirds of any national-origin group reports that they lack English proficiency.

Table 6.4 Percentage of US population 5 years and older who speak other languages at home and speak English less than "very well": African ancestry groups and foreign-born

	% other language at home	% speak English less than "very well"
US population	19.7	8.6
White alone (non-Hispanic)	5.8	1.7
Black alone (non-Hispanic)	6.7	2.3
Hispanic (any race)	76.3	37.3
Asian alone (non-Hispanic)	77.0	36.3
Sub-Saharan Africa	35.8	11.9
African	19.2	5.7
Cape Verdean	53.4	23.3
Ethiopian	79.8	36.0
Ghanaian	76.5	18.6
Nigerian	56.7	9.0
African foreign-born	76.8	28.2
Ethiopia	90.0	43.3
Kenya	80.4	17.9
Somalia	83.9	58.2
Egypt	84.2	33.9
South Africa	35.8	5.5
Ghana	80.2	18.2
Liberia	31.1	10.2
Nigeria	73.9	12.4
Other African countries	71.9	27.3

Source: American Community Survey 2008 (US Census Bureau 2009) 1-year estimates

The sharpest differences between national-origin groups are in English proficiency, not so much whether the group members speak English at home. Non-English use at home is widespread among the foreign-born population, but their English command presents a lot more variation. Among Asians, for example, whereas over 90% of foreign-born Indian, Vietnamese, and Cambodian immigrants do not speak English at home, only 28% of Indians lack English proficiency, but over 67% of Vietnamese and Cambodian immigrants responded not being proficient in English.

Similarly, in table 6.3 we can see that most foreign-born Hispanics also speak another language at home. For these immigrants, as for Asians, maintaining their mother tongue does not necessarily mean they are not English proficient. For example, less than 30% of those from Panama are not proficient in English, but over 70% of those from Mexico, El Salvador, Guatemala, and Honduras lack English proficiency.

Finally, the bottom panel of table 6.4 shows that among foreign-born Africans, generally over two-thirds of individuals speak a non-English language at home. There are two exceptions, however: one is Liberia, where English is the official language, and the second is South Africa, where English is one of 11 official languages, but considered the lingua franca. Only about 30% of the foreign-born population from these countries speaks a language other than English at home. The proportion of non-English proficient foreign-born individuals is much smaller among African immigrants than among Hispanics and Asians, most likely because English is a vernacular language in many of their countries of origin.

From these tables we can draw four conclusions. First, most immigrants speak a language other than English at home. Second, speaking a non-English language at home does not necessarily mean that an individual lacks proficiency in English. Third, only about half of immigrants report speaking English "less than very well." Finally, among the foreign-born, English proficiency varies by region and country of origin, with Hispanic-origin immigrants least likely to be English proficient.

While these tables suggest that individuals who speak another language at home do not necessarily lack English proficiency, they do not tell us anything about how using another language at home or not speaking English fluently affects children's educational outcomes. We turn to this question in the next section.

English Proficiency and School Outcomes

English language proficiency is extremely important in understanding variation in school outcomes given that almost all school instruction in the US is in English. In the next three sections, we present the relationships between language proficiency and the three main educational outcomes we discuss in this volume: achievement, aspirations, and attainment. We look at the research concerning those who are bilingual, in addition to research on students who lack English proficiency. The terms used to classify individuals who are not proficient in English have changed over time, and while not all of them are completely equivalent, they are very similar (Grissom 2004). The most common terms are: Language Minorities (LM), considered students from "homes in which a second language is spoken"; Limited English Proficient (LEP), referring to those students "who would derive little benefit from school instruction conducted only in English" (NCES 1992: v); English Language Learners (ELL), and English as a Second Language (ESL) students. In this chapter, we use English Language Learners to refer to any of these terms.

Achievement

Simply put, students who lack English proficiency have lower achievement levels than their English-proficient classmates. Most research demonstrates that they score lower on standardized tests and have lower grades in school. Educational achievement refers to outcomes such as grades, test scores, grade retention (the frequency that students had to repeat a grade), and the courses that students take. Whereas the lower achievement of non-English proficient students is not surprising when one thinks of reading or writing, English Language Learner (ELL) students lag in all areas subject to standardized tests, including science, mathematics, US history, geography, and others.

In table 6.5, we report standardized scores in science, math, and reading, comparing ELL and non-ELL students (all without disabilities) for all available years reported by the National Assessment of Educational Progress (NAEP). NAEP, the official institution which administers these tests, did not start including most English Language Learners until 1995; for this reason, data presented in these charts only go as far back as 1996. Science, reading, and

Table 6.5 NAEP scores for math, reading and science (years available)

Year	4th Grade ELL	4th Grade NO ELL	8th Grade ELL	8th Grade NO ELL	12th Grade ELL	12th Grade NO ELL
Math						
1996			226	274	267	304
2000	200	226	235	278	272	303
2002	202	230				
2003	215	239	245	283		
2005	218	242	247	285		
2007	219	244	249	287		
2009	220	244	247	289		
Reading						
2000	170	220				
2002	184	224	228	269	247	290
2003	189	224	227	269		
2005	189	225	228	268	251	291
2007	191	227	226	268		
Science						
1996	100	151	93	152	108	152
2000	104	152	104	153	107	149
2005	122	156	110	154	111	151

Note: The NAEP mathematics and reading scales range from 0 to 500. The NAEP science scale ranges from 0 to 300

Source: US Department of Education, Institute of Education Sciences, National Center for Education Statistics, National Assessment of Educational Progress (NAEP)

math scores increased over time for everyone, including ELL and non-ELL students. There is also a slight narrowing over time of the differences in math and science scores between these two groups of students. However, the gap is substantial and does not show any signs of disappearing soon. Further, while we see a slight narrowing of the gap between ELL and non-ELL students for science and math, the gap in reading scores persists over time. Some reports find that in the last ten years the gap between ELL and non-ELL students has actually widened (Plucker et al. 2010).

In recent years, school policy-makers and practitioners have taken these school achievement differences seriously, and have made some accommodations for ELL students. Accommodations include extra time on exams, the use of a dictionary, or other types of language assistance. However, despite the widespread use of these allowances (37 of the 49 states with tests offer some type of accommodation for ELL students), there is still considerable variation in the type of accommodations available to ELL students and in their effectiveness in improving test-taking (Wolf et al. 2009). Most studies, in fact, find only limited support for the effectiveness of these accommodations. For example, Abedi and colleagues compared ELL and non-ELL students' scores from a NAEP science assessment on 20 science items to assess the potential benefits to adding some accommodations (dictionaries and glossaries) for ELL students (Abedi et al. 2001). According to the study, not all accommodations seem to be effective in helping students. They found that on a standard test (with no accommodations), ELL students earned a score of 8.36 versus 11.71 for non-ELL students. When dictionaries (i.e. accommodations) were provided, the mean score for ELL students was 10.18 compared to 11.37 for non-ELL students. When glossaries (another type of accommodation) were provided, ELL students scored 8.51 versus 11.96 for non-ELL students (Abedi et al. 2001). In short, while dictionaries nearly closed the gap between ELL and non-ELL students in their science scores, glossaries did not reduce the gap between ELL and non-ELL students. This suggests that only particular accommodations may result in improved test scores for ELL students.

There are many reasons why students who lack English proficiency obtain lower grades in school. Language barriers create impediments to understanding academic content, which in turn makes it difficult for them to complete their homework or to understand classroom instruction. Students may not necessarily understand what is required of them and they may not be able to gain this information from peers. English-language ability affects school track placements, so that otherwise talented ELL students are placed in remedial or vocational tracks. Track placement has been extensively studied, and studies generally concur that it has a negative effect on the achievement of those students in the lower tracks (Oakes 1990; Rosenbaum 1976; Wiley et al. 2009). Separating ELL students from classes that have higher achieving students ignores the continuum in language learning that occurs in the school (Freeman 2004). Students who are not exposed to their English-fluent peers may not get the rigorous content they need to achieve academic success.

In addition, for students in high school, organization of classes into subject departments (such as math, science, and social sciences) creates additional barriers to integrating both language and content learning for ELL students. First of all, English as a Second Language (ESL) coursework, which ELL students are required to take, is usually at the expense of normally scheduled classes, like elective and advanced courses (Callahan et al. 2008; Ruiz-de-Velasco and Fix 2000). Academically rigorous classes are important for both access to and completion of college (Callahan and Gándara 2004; Schneider et al. 1998). In addition, because subject area teachers tend to have few incentives to assume responsibility for ELL students' outcomes, ESL teachers are often solely responsible for the education of these students even in content areas (Fry 2005, 2007). Over time, the educational aspirations of ELL youth may fall as they face these numerous challenges.

To make matters more complicated, it is important to note that English proficiency is related to socioeconomic factors such as family poverty, and ELL students tend to be concentrated in marginal schools (Capps et al. 2005; de Cohen et al. 2005; Gándara et al. 2003). While family background and school resources undoubtedly affect the education of any student, the influence of this may be even greater among ELL students. High levels of racial and ethnic segregation and poor urban schools can make it more difficult for disadvantaged immigrants to learn English. This may be especially true of Hispanic students, who are more likely to live in neighborhoods that are racially segregated and poor, and are more likely to come from disadvantaged backgrounds. The more residentially segregated an immigrant group is, the fewer opportunities there are to become fluent in English. With mounting evidence that schools have been rapidly re-segregating (Orfield and Yun 1999), opportunities for students to assimilate and to learn English may become more limited for some groups. Again, Hispanics are especially at risk, given that they are a fast-growing population and are quickly becoming the majority in many school districts across the country. This growing segregation in schools may also help to account for Hispanics' relatively lower levels of educational achievement and attainment (Schmid 2001).

Even within schools, students can be segregated by race or English language status. Many honors programs are exclusively or predominantly white, even in schools that are racially diverse (Ladson-Billings 2004). English learners may be grouped in classrooms with other English learners, thus reducing their opportunities to interact with peers who are native English speakers. The lack of contact reduces the opportunity for newcomer students to gain social capital from native-born peers who can provide useful information, serve as role models, and help immigrant students navigate through school. These links between native-born and immigrant students positively contribute to the educational success of immigrant students (Suárez-Orozco et al. 2008). The effects of linguistic isolation may be far-reaching for some ELL students, as some have suggested that this isolation removes students from the "college-going discourse" that happens in high schools. It also limits the amount of information about post-secondary education that they can gather (Gándara et al. 2001). All of this can limit an ELL student's desire and expectation to attend college. We discuss this next.

Educational Aspirations

In the US, the number of students aspiring to go to college has steadily increased. Specifically, between 1980 and 2002, the proportion of tenth graders who aspired to at least finish a four-year Bachelor's degree almost doubled, from 41% to 79% (Fox et al. 2005). Most importantly for our purposes, these proportions doubled for all students independently of their racial/ethnic background. Asian/Pacific Islanders are the only exception to this rapid growth, as already over 67% of this group expected to attain at least a Bachelor's degree in 1980. By 1990, 70% of Asians had such aspirations, and by 2002, 87% of Asian tenth graders aspired to at least a Bachelor's degree. Unfortunately, educational aspirations and expectations for ELL or foreign-born students are not as consistently reported.

Those reports that do look at aspirations among English Language Learners show that among Asian and Hispanic students, ELL students have lower educational aspirations than English-proficient youth (NCES 1992). English Language Learner Asians were less likely than non-ELL Asian eighth graders to plan to enroll in an academic program while in high school (24% vs. 46%). English Language Learner Asian students were also less confident that they would graduate from high school (60% vs. 83% for non-ELL Asian students). The situation for Hispanic students was even more dire: only 12% of ELL Hispanic students planned to enroll in an academic program while in high school compared to 25% of the English proficient, and about 38% of the ELL Hispanic students did not plan to pursue education beyond high school compared to 14% of the English proficient Hispanic youth (NCES 1992).

Despite these figures that show the lower educational aspirations of ELL students compared to non-ELL students, it would be overly simplistic to assume that ELL students enter the educational system with lower aspirations. In fact, educational aspirations of students and parents do not initially depend on language proficiency (Fuligni 1997; Kao and Tienda 1998). Rather, evidence indicates that lower educational aspirations are the result of a "cooling down process," in which students who do not have the language skills miss out on acquiring the academic skills necessary for college. Qualitative research suggests that ELL students enter the school system with optimistic plans for their future, but their aspirations erode over time as these students face barriers in their schooling (Orellana 2008). Poor academic training, lack of integration in the academic context, lower grades and test scores have cumulative effects that impact their aspirations and chances to further their education.

Attainment

The National Center for Educational Statistics (NCES) periodically publishes statistics on educational outcomes among students in the US. In 2004, they released a monograph on language minorities and their educational and labor market outcomes. This report serves as the main source for the data presented here (NCES 2004). According to the NCES, about 9 in 10 students aged 18–24 who spoke only English at home graduated from high school. However, only 7 in 10 students who spoke a non-English language at home completed high school. Among adults, the differences are large as well. About 51% of those who spoke English very well had completed high school, but only 18% of those who spoke English with difficulty had received a high-school diploma.

According to the same NCES report, there were no important differences between 18- and 24-year-olds who spoke a non-English language at home versus those who only spoke English at home in their enrollment in post-secondary education. Specifically, among those who had completed high school and had enrolled in higher education, 11% of those who spoke only English and 10% of language minorities received a Bachelor's degree or higher. However, differences in educational attainment persisted among some language minority groups. Young adults who spoke Spanish were less likely than those from all other language minority groups to have attained either some college or a Bachelor's degree or more, with only 5% obtaining a Bachelor's degree or higher. This is in contrast to all other language minorities, of whom 17–19% have a Bachelor's degree or higher.

While you have read in previous chapters that first- and second-generation immigrants are significantly more likely to graduate from high school and attend college than their third-plus generation counterparts, even when they come from the same race/ethnic, socioeconomic, and family background, language can be an additional factor determining the educational achievement and attainment of some groups. Many ELL students drop out of high school at higher rates than non-ELL students, and those who graduate from high school may not be ready for college (Kreitzer et al. 1989). Especially among Hispanics, there are differences in the rates at which they enroll in post-secondary education, and their rates of success in these institutions. These young people with language barriers are more likely to enroll in two-year colleges, where admission requirements are fewer, remedial classes are offered, and overall, tuition is cheaper, etc. (Dougherty 1994; Santibáñez et al. 2007). A lack of English language skills, which may have resulted in lower GPA and test scores prior to college, also may make it more difficult for ELL students to graduate from college. Certainly, proficiency in English is not simply a marker of "assimilation," but it also contributes to how well immigrants are able to assimilate in other dimensions of American life, particularly in educational achievement and attainment.

Are There Benefits to Speaking a non-English Language?

While policy-makers and the public-at-large tend to focus on the disadvantages of speaking a language other than English at home, some academic research finds advantages to being bilingual or multilingual. Theories of "segmented assimilation" or "accommodation without acculturation" suggest that maintaining one's native tongue can have benefits. Speaking a native language can better enable communication between parents and children, and can connect students to their ethnic communities. This may strengthen and expand the social capital that is available to these students and may improve students' ability to succeed educationally (Feliciano 2001). Speaking more than one language fluently is less common in the US than it is in other countries, so many Americans admire those who can speak more than one language. However, the benefits of bilingualism have not always been appreciated, and they continue to be questioned to this day (Garcia 2005).

Early psychometricians argued that children in homes where

more than one language was spoken did not master either one, and they tended to learn how to speak later in life. Some went as far as to argue that bilingualism created mental confusion and concluded that bilingual children were genetically inferior (Darcy 1953; Goodenough 1934; Saer 1923; Terman 1919, 1975). It was with the work of Peal and Lambert (1962) that researchers started shifting their stand on the matter. They found a positive relationship between bilingualism and cognitive abilities. Since then, many scholars (e.g. Bankston and Zhou 1995; Garcia 2005; Matute-Bianchi 1991; Nielsen and Lerner 1986; Rumbaut 1995; Rumberger and Larson 1998; Stanton-Salazar and Dornbusch 1995) suggest that bilingualism promotes both academic achievement and higher academic expectations.

While many of these recent authors agree on the positive association between bilingualism and cognitive abilities, they do not agree on the mechanisms that link them. Some emphasize the cognitive benefits of bilingualism, which provide individuals with a mental advantage as they become accustomed to switching between concepts in two languages (Peal and Lambert 1962). Others have emphasized the cultural benefits of bilingualism. For example, bilingual students have access to schools and community networks not available to others who do not speak both languages. Another explanation is that the advantage takes place at the family level – bilingual children can better communicate with parents who speak their native languages, while also accessing the information and resources of English speakers outside of their homes. Some even focus on the expanded ethnic and cultural capital of bilingual children as they are able to access both their parents' and the US cultures (Bankston and Zhou 1995).

Whichever the explanation, most research confirms that bilingualism is beneficial to children's educational outcomes. This benefit may be conditional and short-lived, however. In their study of Asian children, Mouw and Xie (1999) suggest that the benefits of bilingualism are only "temporal," and are only beneficial if a child's parents are not fluent in English. The bilingual child bridges the worlds of their parents and of the US, so the child's bilingual ability helps the family navigate education, as well as other US institutions. If the parents already have moderate English ability, then the child's bilingualism does not lead to better educational outcomes for the child.

There is more research evidence that shows how the benefits of bilingualism may depend on the family and community contexts in which students find themselves. For example, Golash-Boza (2005) argues that bilingual ability is not an advantage in a community where there are not others who speak that language, and that bilingualism has a limited advantage in communities where the resources of those who speak one's native language are limited. She eloquently states that "an immigrant Nigerian who speaks fluent Ibo, Yoruba, and Hausa in addition to perfect, although heavily accented, English will not be admired for his linguistic proficiency in the same way as a European-American who speaks heavily accented French, Spanish, and German" (Golash-Boza 2005, 750). On the other hand, Pong and Hao (2007) found that students who spoke a non-English and non-Spanish language at home had superior school performance compared to their English-speaker counterparts, even though they did not reside in large communities of people who spoke their native languages. Because students did not find large communities with whom they could speak their native languages, they learned English, and could access resources in both English and their non-English languages (Pong and Hao 2007).

Despite the fact that studies do not assume that bilingualism leads to low IQ scores or other measures of cognitive ability, researchers still find mixed evidence that bilingualism has a large effect on educational achievement. These mixed results lead to public ambivalence about, and even hostility to, bilingual education in the US. Public opposition to bilingual education has increased in recent decades, both in states with large immigrant populations and in states where immigrants do not account for a large share of the population. The most notable opposition has found its way into laws in California, Arizona, and Massachusetts. For example, in 1998, California's Proposition 227 was passed with the overwhelming majority of the vote. This initiative largely eliminated bilingual education in the state's public schools. Thus, most English-language learners in Californian public schools are enrolled in English immersion programs (Caldera 2002). Just two years later, in 2000, Arizona voters passed an initiative very similar to that of California, called Proposition 203. In 2002, voters in Massachusetts passed a law that eliminated the oldest bilingual education law in the nation, and replaced it with a "one-year" English immersion instruction. Initiatives like these do not recognize that the ability to speak a non-English language is a valuable resource that should be encouraged in an increasingly global world. Knowledge of two languages may further facilitate the learning of a third language. Benefits to bilingual and multilingual students may also come from closer ties with family and community members that result in more social capital for students. These benefits tend to be drowned out by the public outcry for students to learn English quickly.

Residential Concentration and Language Acquisition

Immigrants enter the US having had a variety of experiences with the English language. Some may speak it fluently because that is a main language spoken in their countries of origin, some may have learned English in classes in schools in their home countries, but have never spoken it, and some may have had very little exposure to the language. Because of variation in exposure to English and for other reasons, immigrants vary greatly in the speed at which they adopt English and become English proficient. Asians and Africans adopt English much faster than Hispanic-origin immigrants. Among the Hispanic population, there is considerable diversity in how long national-origin groups take to become English proficient.

Apart from exposure to English in native countries, there are other reasons why groups vary in the time it takes for their members to become English proficient. A very important one is residential concentration, which not only affects the likelihood of having daily interactions with English speakers, but also is associated with unequal educational opportunities. In other words, while ELL students are about 10% of the school population (de Cohen et al. 2005), they are not equally distributed across schools, neighborhoods, cities, or states. Schools with majority English learners tend to be in urban areas characterized by high concentrations of other minority and economically disadvantaged students, many of whom are also ELL (Gándara and Hopkins 2010). This is the case for many Mexican immigrants, for example. The higher the levels of residential concentration of Mexican immigrants, the fewer opportunities Mexicans have to learn and to practice English. This type of residential segregation is not as common for Asian and African-origin immigrants.

The residential concentration of immigrants has some advantages for recent immigrants in that it may help to cushion the cultural shock that stems from the immigrant experience. However, because recent immigrants are surrounded by co-ethnics who arrived earlier in the US, they may not need to learn English to carry out everyday tasks. In terms of acquiring English skills, residential concentration may have negative consequences for these immigrants. The physical and linguistic segregation that many immigrant students encounter slows English proficiency and does not lead to better educational outcomes in general (Olsen 1997; 2000; Orfield and Yun 1999, Valdés 2001). Thus, even though most immigrants do learn English and most second-generation children prefer English over their parents' native tongue, important differences in English proficiency appear according to immigrant origin. The prospects for those students who do not become proficient in English quickly are not promising. Some have even suggested that ELL students struggle in school at a level that is only rivaled by students in special education (Gándara and Hopkins 2010). Given that they are a sizeable proportion of the school body in some areas of the country, the struggles of ELL youth represent the modal experience of students.

Though racial residential concentration typically has negative effects on the English proficiency of those who live in these communities, racial residential concentration need not have these effects as long as children become English proficient and succeed in schools. In an interesting reversal, Asian Americans who live in residentially concentrated areas may be advantaged and may even represent a threat to white students. Although these accounts are largely anecdotal, a 2005 *Wall Street Journal* article titled "The New White Flight" suggests that white parents are pulling their children out of extremely high-achieving schools in the San Francisco Bay area that have a large proportion of Asian American students because their children cannot compete (Hwang 2005). There were also complaints from white parents that the schools are "too Asian" and too focused on test scores and admission of their graduates to prestigious universities. Cathy Gatley, president of Monta Vista High School's Parent-Teacher Association, and who is white, said that "White kids are thought of as the dumb kids" (Hwang 2005). While the story focused on a high school in California's Silicon Valley, the author also mentioned Thomas S. Wootton High School in Rockville, Maryland, which is nick-named "Won Ton" by some local residents because 35% of its student body is Asian American. CNN also presented a segment recently that showed the changing student composition in many San Francisco Bay area communities from largely white to largely Asian.

Throughout this book, we have talked about how the resources necessary for academic success for children in immigrant families vary by the pathways their parents took to come to the US. Children in immigrant neighborhoods may have vastly different social backgrounds – some with highly educated and some with less educated parents. Families may have access to different amounts of financial capital. Immigrant parents may have high prestige or low prestige occupations. Immigrant families may live in urban neighborhoods with co-ethnic newcomers. They may wind up in predominantly white suburbs. All of these factors vary by immigrants' nationalities of origin. The ways in which children in immigrant families are racially classified in the US also influences their educational outcomes. In this chapter, we showed that English language proficiency and bilingual capability are two more resources that vary amongst immigrants of different national-origin groups, and that have consequences for the educational achievement of children in immigrant families. Those who learn English quickly can "assimilate" in other ways by achieving educationally, which then leads to upwardly mobile occupations. However, there is also evidence that speaking a language other than English (so long as a student speaks English proficiently) can provide access to social capital from parents and from ethnic communities that benefits students educationally. Language use then can be an indicator of "straight-line" assimilation or it can show these "segmented assimilation" processes, both of which may enable educational success.

7

Conclusion

Throughout this volume, we have focused on two essential points. First, we documented what existing research says about the educational outcomes of children in immigrant families. Second, we put these differences in context. We situated educational differences among children in immigrant families according to their different paths of incorporation or assimilation into the US. These paths vary by how families were admitted to the US, where they settled, their fluency in English, and the ways that they are racially classified in the US, among other things. Below, we recap the main arguments put forth in the preceding chapters.

Educational outcomes

In general, children in immigrant families tend to earn better grades, have higher test scores, have higher aspirations, go to college more, and generally attain higher levels of education than children who are not in immigrant families. How we judge the educational "success" of children in immigrant families depends on with whom they are being compared. White children in immigrant families generally perform better than those white children who are not in immigrant families. They also perform better than black and Hispanic children, both those in immigrant families and those who are not in them. Asians in immigrant families generally outperform all other groups, from immigrant and non-immigrant families.

Asians in immigrant families have more educational success than whites in native-born and immigrant families, and they typically achieve more than do Asians who do not live in immigrant families; that is, third-generation Asian Americans. This is not the case for other immigrant minority groups, however. Blacks in immigrant families tend to perform better in schools than do blacks in native-born families, but less well than immigrant and non-immigrant whites and Asians. Some Hispanics are an exception to the pattern that shows immigrant educational advantages compared to the native-born. Among some Hispanics, other studies find that students in immigrant families tend to have test scores and grades below those of their counterparts in the third generation.

However, these general statements mask much variation among immigrants. While Asians in immigrant families tend to see the most success in schools as a group, Hmong youth have high rates of dropping out of high school and low rates of entering college compared to other groups. South Asians tend to have high educational achievement and attainment. Among Hispanics, Mexicans appear to have the most difficulty, along with Guatemalans and Salvadoreans. Argentinians and Cubans attain high educational levels.

Further complicating the description of immigrants' educational outcomes is variation in English proficiency. We discuss this topic in chapter 6. Although speaking another language at home has either small or no effects on the educational outcomes of children in immigrant families, English proficiency appears to have large effects. Those children who do not learn English well have lower test scores (Abedi et al. 2001) and drop out of school at higher rates than English-proficient students. These students take less advanced courses in high school, which may leave them under-prepared for college. This is especially the case for Hispanic students with limited English proficiency.

So, while overall, immigrants appear to outperform their native-born same-race peers, we must be cautious about assuming all immigrants are doing well. Immigrants experience educational success relative to their same-race native peers, but not necessarily when compared to native-born whites. The educational outcomes of some ethnic groups within the larger racial or pan-ethnic classifications of Asian, Hispanic, and black may be higher than others. Some groups, like the Hmong, may find that their struggles to achieve high levels of education are not noticed, as they are grouped together with other high achieving Asian students. Other groups, like African blacks, may find that their high educational achievement and attainment do not shield them from the racial stereotypes and discrimination faced by other groups classified as black in the US. Children in immigrant families struggling to learn English may find it difficult to catch up to peers who speak English fluently. Clearly, being in an immigrant family, in and of itself, does not necessarily confer educational advantages or disadvantages across all groups.

The Context

Another aim of this book was to provide context in which to situate the educational outcomes of children in immigrant families. Here we look at three important factors that shape how children in immigrant families experience education in the US. The first concerns the migration path or history of the immigrant family. In this book, we show how these paths may have changed over time. For example, Chinese immigrants arriving to the US in the 1840s were largely poor migrants recruited to do agricultural work and construct railroads. In 1980, Chinese, South Asian, or Korean immigrants may be coming to the US to work in high-skilled occupations. Or, Vietnamese, Hmong, and Khmer may be immigrating to the US to escape war and persecution in their home countries. The political forces and immigration policies throughout US history, which we reviewed in chapter 3, shaped these varied motivations for migration. We continue to see these policies and laws evolve as state and federal government in the US debate new ways to reinforce our borders and new restrictions to the ability of employers to hire undocumented immigrant labor. We also hear heated discussions about how best to incorporate those who are already in the US, through deportation or amnesty or by allowing for socioeconomic mobility through laws like the DREAM Act (which offer a path toward legal permanent residence for individuals who do not have legal status because their parents brought them in as children). The justification is that no matter what your views are of immigrants and immigration laws, it is difficult to blame those who entered and stayed in the US as children, with or without proper documentation. The profiles of future immigrants and their children, and their ability to achieve in the US educational system, will depend in part on these laws and policies.

US immigration policies influence who is able to come to the US. Immigrants come with varying levels of human capital, different financial resources, and varying abilities to communicate in English. In chapter 4, we documented some of the differences in human capital of adult immigrants. Specifically, here, we look at the educational attainment of the adult immigrant population. Indeed, we find much variation both across and within racial and pan-ethnic groups. In particular, we find that Asian immigrant adults have the highest levels of educational attainment. Immigrants from African countries also have high levels of educational attainment. Hispanics fall below the average educational attainment of these groups overall.

However, there is also much heterogeneity within these racial or pan-ethnic groups. Hmong and Vietnamese Americans have low levels of educational attainment among Asians, and at levels comparable to those of the most disadvantaged Hispanic groups. Among Hispanics, there is a wide range of educational attainment. Groups such as Argentinians and Bolivians have very high levels of educational attainment, while Mexicans, Salvadoreans, and Guatemalans generally have lower levels of educational attainment. Since Mexicans comprise such a large portion of the immigrant population, the average educational attainment of Hispanics as a pan-ethnic group is low compared to the other racial groups.

In addition to the ways migration paths to the US have influenced the human capital of the parents in immigrant families, it is also important to consider how the incorporation of immigrants into the labor force and into their communities (and consequently schools) influences the resources that children in immigrant families need to succeed in schools. The incorporation of immigrants is also influenced by US migration policy. Immigrants who arrive with valued skills in the labor market are able to get visas, and often settle into high-paying occupations. Those who migrate as refugees often have access to government-funded assistance or may be sponsored by church or other social welfare groups. These migrants may be settled into communities with few other migrants, and may take low-wage jobs, but they have access to supports that help with settlement. Still other immigrants, such as those who are undocumented and/or those who migrate to occupy low-wage service positions in the US economy, may be specifically excluded from particular types of employment or social services by specific state immigration policies like those in Arizona, Alabama, and an increasing number of other states. Children of these immigrants may be residentially and linguistically isolated from the native-born in the US and may have lower chances to succeed in schools because of this.

In chapter 4, we also reviewed some of the characteristics of immigrant families that may reflect these differences in incorporation in the US economy and into communities, and that may also be important for children's educational outcomes. Here, we looked at the median incomes and poverty of immigrant families. Typically, Asian immigrant families have the highest median incomes and lowest poverty rates, followed by white, black, and Hispanic immigrant families. Again, there often was a great range within each pan-ethnic or racial group.

Sociologists who study education have long noted that family resources matter for children's educational outcomes (Bankston 2004; Portes 1998). The very different family resources available to children in immigrant families are reflected in their diverse educational outcomes. Those who study racial differences in educational achievement have long pointed to the very high median incomes of Asian Americans as reasons for their educational achievements compared to other groups, while oftentimes, when one controls for family human capital and financial resources, some of the differences in educational achievement between Hispanic immigrants and whites go away.

However, socioeconomic differences do not fully explain inequalities in educational outcomes between groups. In this book, we have paid careful attention to how children in immigrant families are "racialized" in the US; that is, we consider the racial categories in which people perceive immigrant children belong. In our discussions, race does not simply represent or "proxy" for other factors, like socioeconomic status, but how children in immigrant families are racially categorized in the US matters for their educational outcomes and attainment independently.

We discussed at length the "model minority" stereotype of Asian Americans (Kao 1995), which is contrasted with the profiles of Hispanic and black American educational outcomes that portray these groups as "falling behind" and in need of special intervention. While some scholars have remarked that Asian Americans are distinguishable from other minority groups because of cultural norms and values derived from the countries from which they immigrated, others worry that this argument implicitly suggests that Hispanics and blacks could succeed in the US if they only had the right values. Still others point out how the "model minority" stereotype and the stereotypes of low-achieving blacks and Hispanics become self-fulfilling prophecies. Teachers, coaches, guidance counselors, and others may expect Asian students to do well in school because of their positive image. Students may be given more chances to succeed, and may set expectations for themselves that are in line with those of these significant others. Black and Hispanic students may not be expected to excel in schoolwork. These students will be subject to lower expectations and perhaps less challenging work. Such students may be less likely to be directed toward college preparatory and advanced placement classes. And, as do Asian students, these students internalize the expectations that others have of them. Indeed, as Claude Steele and his colleagues (e.g. Steele and Aronson 1995) have found, black students are well aware of the negative stereotypes about their academic performance and may experience anxiety about fulfilling those low expectations when taking tests.

Throughout this book, we have tried to stress that race matters for how children in immigrant families perform, and how their offspring will perform in the future. While being in an immigrant family is a temporary condition, and its effects will likely diminish over generations, being classified in a particular racial category has effects that persist across generations. Being in an immigrant family may most directly influence immigrant children's immediate opportunities for educational and social mobility; for later generations, race will become a more important factor in their future success.

What Does All of This Say about Assimilation?

In chapter 2, we discussed in detail what sociologists have said about how immigrants eventually come to fit into US society. Sociologists of the 1920s through 1960s based their theories about how immigrants would be absorbed into the US on the white Europeans who made up the majority of immigrants prior to 1965 (e.g. Gordon 1964; Park and Burgess 1969 [1921]; Warner and Srole 1945). Observing the experiences of these immigrants, sociologists of this time concluded that immigrants and their offspring would eventually come to resemble the native-born in their educational attainments and labor force positions. These immigrant families would speak English only, adopt the customs and traditions of the US, and intermarry with native-born Americans who were not necessarily of their ethnic group.

Later sociologists, observing the changes in the profile of immigrants to the US after 1965, found these early portrayals of assimilation unsatisfying. These researchers argued that it was not inevitable that immigrants and their offspring would be absorbed into a monolithic mainstream American culture. Not all immigrant families experience upward mobility that leads them to resemble the (white) middle class. Immigrants from Africa, Asia, and Latin America have not followed the same routes to upward mobility as did their white, European predecessors.

Sociologists proposed a new model to capture the more diverse trajectories of assimilation of these recent immigrants. They coined the term *segmented assimilation* to describe three ways that immigrants and their children might become incorporated into the US (e.g. Portes and Zhou 1993; Rumbaut 1997a, 1997b; Zhou and Bankston 1998). Immigrants could assimilate into the middle-class mainstream in a straight line, but they also might experience downward mobility into the urban poor. Finally, an immigrant family could achieve educational success and upward mobility, but the members of the group need not necessarily adopt "American" values and norms to do so. For some groups, particularly those who settle near poor, racially segregated neighborhoods, retaining the values, cultures, traditions, and language of their countries of origin may serve to "buffer" these groups from the influences of their less advantaged neighbors. These groups may succeed educationally and economically in the US precisely because they do not assimilate into their neighboring communities.

These later sociologists took variation in the context of immigration between groups into more serious consideration in their theories. Immigrants settled in very different types of communities – urban and rural, working-class, poor, and middle-class, inner city and suburb. Where immigrants settle has implications for the resources and opportunities available to them. Immigrant families living in disadvantaged inner cities or in poor rural communities have fewer community services and lower-quality schools than do those settling in advantaged middle-class suburbs. Further, these types of neighborhoods differ in the social capital that is available. Children in immigrant families who live in affluent suburbs have access to more information about college, for example. Their peers in school are likely destined for college and they and guidance counselors and teachers are good sources of college information. Highly educated neighbors also provide information and role models. In neighborhoods in which few have attended college, neighbors are not as useful for planning to attend college. Schools in these neighborhoods may have fewer resources to help with planning college, and peers in these schools may be less likely to plan to attend college. These resources, including social capital, affect children's educational outcomes.

Conclusion

The types of occupations or structures of mobility available to immigrants from different groups also matter. Whether immigrant parents are skilled professionals, less-skilled service workers, or agricultural laborers influences whether an immigrant family has the resources, and consequently the opportunities, needed to fit into the American middle class. Highly skilled professionals often have jobs with high earnings, and they can afford private schools, extra tutoring, books, computers, and other educational resources. Immigrant parents who work in the service industry or those who work in agriculture may have lower incomes and be less able to purchase the resources that might further children's educational success. Parents who work many hours for low wages may struggle in many ways that affect their families. For example, it may be difficult to find affordable childcare, transportation may be difficult to manage, and it may be nearly impossible to take time off from work to participate in children's schools or extracurricular activities for parents who have low-wage jobs. The differences between the educational outcomes of children of professional immigrant parents and lower-skilled immigrant parents may accumulate over time. Children of lower-skilled immigrants may over time have fewer educational resources and opportunities, thus, lower achievement than those who have been afforded more by their professional parents.

Finally, sociologists writing about recent immigration have asserted, as do we, that race matters for how children from immigrant families get incorporated into the US. Throughout this book, we have shown variation in parents' and children's characteristics by race, and it is hard not to notice the stark differences between Asians and whites, on the one hand, and blacks and Hispanics, on the other. While there is certainly variation within these racial and pan-ethnic groups, the differences across these main categories are hard to ignore.

Segmented assimilation captures more variation in paths to assimilation and incorporates a more nuanced understanding of how the contexts in which immigrants find themselves matter for these assimilation patterns. Did sociologists finally get it right then? Noguera (2008), writing specifically about the education of

178

children in Hispanic immigrant families, suggests that theorists and researchers have yet to catch up to the realities that many immigrant children face. The assumptions of both more traditional assimilation theories and of the newer segmented assimilation version are that (1) immigrants come to the US to stay, and (2) that immigrants wish to assimilate into an "American" middle class. Neither of these may reflect what is actually occurring in the lives of immigrant children.

Noguera (2008) notes that, particularly for agricultural laborers but even in other types of jobs, children in immigrant families spend only part of the year in the US. Children may be around during harvesting seasons, but return to visit family in their countries of origin during times when there is little work in the US. More privileged children may spend summers in their countries of origin. Some families may even spend a few years in the US after having migrated somewhere before and plan to migrate elsewhere in a few years. These children may not necessarily see the US as home, and paths to assimilation for these families are more complicated.

This frequent movement of some immigrant families may even lead us to question whether all immigrants desire to be part of an "American" middle class. As the world becomes increasingly globalized, the "middle class" is less defined solely by what happens in the US. There is a growing middle class throughout the world. Some may even argue that it is a "global," rather than specific national, middle class that is emerging. If the US is no longer the ideal for those aspiring for socioeconomic mobility, then what are the incentives to assimilate into American society? Immigrants may migrate to achieve socioeconomic mobility, but may perceive that travel is easy, national boundaries are more fluid, and migration spells are temporary. These immigrants may choose to preserve their identities from their countries of origin or they may wish to see themselves as members of a global labor force, or both. Some immigrants may have very little desire to become "American," per se, so long as they are achieving some economic stability or even upward mobility.

Lessons of this Book

One main purpose of this book was to provide a portrait of the educational achievement of children in immigrant families. We showed how a variety of factors may influence this achievement, including immigration context, parental resources, race, and English language ability. However, there are four important aspects of the educational experiences of children in immigrant families we want to stress particularly.

First, there is variation not only between but within immigrant groups. While much of the variation in educational outcomes between children in immigrant families is between larger racial or pan-ethnic groups, we also find big differences within each of these groups. Immigrant contexts, parental resources, and English proficiency vary greatly even within the larger groupings of white, black, Asian, and Hispanic immigrant families. Consequently, the educational outcomes of Asian Indians and Hmong, and Argentinians and Mexicans are very different. As is the case in much of the social world, very few immigrant families actually have the mean or median profile for the group. There is much variation among immigrants, as there is among the native-born in the US.

Second, it is also important to highlight the significance of class resources in the educational outcomes of children in immigrant families and not rely on oversimplified cultural explanations for educational differences. Children in immigrant families are either romanticized or demonized based on their cultures. Immigrants of some groups are presumed to work hard and overcome adversity through sheer optimism that they will succeed. It is important to recognize that those immigrants that the culture valorizes, often white or Asian, often come to the US with considerable class resources compared to other immigrants. These immigrants may be allowed to immigrate because they have valuable technical skills. These skills may enable immigrants to get good, high-paying jobs, which allow them to live in relatively advantaged neighborhoods with good schools. Children in these families may consequently have high educational achievement. Even poor children of refugees have access to some resources to help them settle in the US.

In contrast to the romantic picture of immigrant culture painted by some, the media and popular culture also portray immigrants as undeserving of the better resources in the US. These undeserving immigrants take advantage of the better hospitals and schools of the US compared to those in their home countries. Immigrants are portrayed here as outsiders whose values do not match those of the native-born. And, again, these "undeserving" immigrants have less access to class resources than do those immigrants that are romanticized in popular culture. Immigrants portrayed as undeserving may be in agricultural or service jobs with low wages, living in enclaves with other immigrants, and may be slower to learn English. The children in these families may have less regular access to schooling, and education may be of lower quality than those children of advantaged immigrants. The "cultural values" that are ascribed to immigrants from different places map very closely onto their class resources. Some would argue that these cultural values lead to different class resources, while others suggest that class resources lead to different cultural values or perceptions of these values on the part of native-born US citizens. Whatever the causal direction, sociologists studying children's educational achievement have consistently found evidence that those with less human capital, less financial, and fewer other class-based resources do worse in schools than do those that have more.

Third, as we have emphasized throughout this book, race is not incidental to the educational experiences of children in immigrant families. It does not merely "stand in" or "proxy" for other factors that shape educational outcomes. It, in itself, shapes these experiences. The racial groups into which children fall matter for their current educational achievement and likely for the future achievement of their children. Race may affect both how others perceive children in immigrant families and how children perceive themselves.

Fourth, and finally, we emphasize that language use conditions the educational experiences of children in immigrant families, especially among those who arrive to the US as young adults and later. There is much variation in the English proficiency of children in immigrant families, and how quickly and how well they learn to speak English has consequences for their test scores, grades, and the ability to take challenging college preparation courses. This in turn affects whether those with limited English speaking ability enter college and how well they do once there.

Future Research

Our book documents what we know about the educational achievement of children in immigrant families based on the research that is currently available. However, much more could be done to better understand this special population. As we pointed out in the book, it is not yet common in research to report educational achievement by race and immigrant status. Most published research focuses on differences in educational outcomes by race, but rarely does it report these differences by whether or not students reside in immigrant families. In order to better track the educational trajectories of children in immigrant families, we need to have more regular data on this group.

Research could also pay better attention to the pre-migration characteristics of immigrant families. For example, work by Feliciano (2005) has proposed that how immigrants compare to those from their home countries who do not immigrate has implications for how well children do in school. Innovative research designs could collect information from those who identify as wanting to migrate when in their home countries and then compare those who actually do to those who do not, for example. Perhaps comparable achievement tests could compare children in immigrant families to non-migrant children to get a sense of how "selective" these children may be and how that selectivity might affect their educational outcomes.

We also need to consider more carefully the contexts of incorporation of immigrant families and how they may influence the educational achievement of children in immigrant families. Research looking at differences in educational outcomes between those who live in immigrant families and those who do not should take account of the types of neighborhoods immigrants settle into and the characteristics of the schools they attend. Researchers should pay attention to variation in educational outcomes that may be related to residing in an immigrant enclave. Researchers should also explore whether or not spatial proximity to disadvantaged neighborhoods matters for the educational outcomes of children in immigrant families. Finally, when looking at schools, research should account for the socioeconomic profile of the school, the racial composition, the proportion of English language learners, the proportion of students in the school that are the same race or ethnicity as the student from the immigrant family, and the proportion of other children in immigrant families in the school. Including these characteristics will allow researchers a deeper understanding of the mechanisms that lead to different educational outcomes across children in immigrant families.

Additionally, while some work, particularly ethnographic work that we review in chapter 5, has explored how gender differences within immigrant communities matter for children's educational outcomes, much more could be done. Perhaps statistical models predicting educational achievement and attainment should be separated by gender for some groups.

Further research should also engage with the argument that children in immigrant families have a different repertoire of cultural values to use in the US and these values may either promote or hinder their educational success. Work to date that argues that there are cultural differences between groups is often based on quantitative statistical models that assume that any variation that is unaccounted for after controlling for socioeconomic factors is due to cultural differences. Or, it is based on interview data with educationally "successful" immigrant parents and children without comparison to native-born parents and children, or to other groups of immigrant parents and children. To really explore the argument that cultural differences are a key factor in the educational outcomes of children in immigrant families, deep ethnographic work should explore how values inform the choices that students make. Ethnographic work has been done for some groups (i.e. Chinese Americans), but rarely is this kind of ethnography done across groups to get a sense of the ways in which cultural values and choices vary across very differently situated children in immigrant families (i.e. comparing an Asian American ethnic group to Mexican Americans).

Finally, more longitudinal research that identifies children in immigrant families may help us to more clearly elucidate how children in immigrant families are able to translate their education into socioeconomic mobility. While it is beyond the scope of this book, it is plausible that children in immigrant families may be more motivated to use their educational achievement and attainment to acquire jobs that have a sure route to upward mobility (Sue and Okazaki 1990). Children in immigrant families may choose those jobs that are judged to be based on more "objective" criteria like educational credentials and licensing tests, rather than on political or personal connections. They may also be more likely to choose high-paying and secure jobs based on watching their parents' adjustments and struggles in the US. On the other hand, children in immigrant families may have a harder time converting educational credentials to high-paying jobs. Children in immigrant families may face discrimination or may be limited if they do not speak English fluently or even without an accent.

Generally, researchers find that second-generation and native-born Asian Americans face no disadvantages in the labor market (for a review, see Sakamoto et al. 2009). Earlier research by Hirschman and Wong (1986) that suggests that Asian Americans need more education than whites to succeed in the labor market (the over-education hypothesis) has been shown not to be true for Asian Americans in the 1990s into the 2000s. Studies have shown a labor market disadvantage for first-generation Asian Americans, though that may be due to receiving educational credentials outside the US. US employers may not know how to interpret these credentials and so devalue them compared to educational credentials earned at US institutions (Zeng and Xie 2004).

Still there are signs of a "bamboo ceiling" for Asian Americans. For example, while Asian Americans are well educated, they are not prominent in leadership roles either in corporate America or in academia. For instance, while Asian Americans are estimated to comprise about 8% of faculty in US colleges and universities, they only make up 0.9% of university presidents, according to the American Council of Education's 2006 survey (Gammage 2012). In addition, while Asian Americans are a highly educated group, they make up a disproportionately small number of Fortune 500 CEOs (approximately 10 of 500, or about 2%) in 2012 by the authors' count.

Future Debates about Immigration Policy

As we have pointed out in this book, the United States holds two images of immigrants and their children. The first is the romantic-idealized view of the immigrant, a hard worker who sacrifices much, he is able to overcome adversity, pull himself up by his bootstraps, and achieve the American Dream, if not for himself then for his children. His children reach this dream through their educational success, and the US educational system is the key to his children's upward mobility. The second image held in the US is of the greedy immigrant willing to take advantage of US welfare and other social services. This immigrant has no "right" to be in the US and takes the jobs or services intended for those who do have the "right" to be "Americans." Tax-paying Americans pay for these lazy and at least immoral, if not criminal, immigrants.

These two visions of immigrants and their children underlie the types of policies that we craft to deal with immigration. While the types of general immigration policies and the ways that they are enforced have implications for who is allowed into the US and the circumstances that immigrant families encounter once they arrive, we focus here on how these visions apply particularly to how we deal with immigrant children in schools.

The first vision – that of the immigrant or immigrant's child who is able to use education to achieve upward mobility – informs the drive to make the DREAM Act law. The DREAM Act, or the Development, Relief and Education of Alien Minors Act, sponsored by Senator Orrin Hatch, a Republican, and Senator Dick

Durbin, a Democrat, would provide a six-year-long conditional path to citizenship for illegal immigrants. In order to become citizens, individuals must be of "good moral character" and complete either two years of military service or attain a two-year college degree. While some states have considered allowing undocumented students who reside in their state the chance to pay for in-state tuition at state-affiliated post-secondary institutions, the federal DREAM Act does not mandate this. States determine their own tuition policies regarding illegal immigrants.

The second vision – that of immigrants who wish to take advantage of US services, like schools, at the expense of the US taxpayer – informs other recently enacted state policies. Perhaps the most famous of these was California's Proposition 187, which sought to screen students for citizenship and excluded illegal immigrant children from California's schools. It also sought to make illegal immigrants ineligible for health care and other social services. This was voted into law by a referendum in 1994. States such as Arizona, Colorado, Florida, Georgia, and others followed suit. The law was declared unconstitutional soon after it was passed and, though the ruling was appealed by California Governor Wilson, the subsequent governor, Gray Davis, dropped the appeal, and the law was ended.

There are many ways that the US can treat the children in immigrant families in its schools. In order to consider which ways are best, though, the public has to examine how it views children in immigrant families. Are the children in immigrant families in the US to take advantage of US education and other services? If so, should that be prevented? Are the children of immigrants able to use education to achieve upward mobility, and do they deserve that as much (or some might even say more due to their sacrifices and those of their parents) as those students whose parents are native-born? Are children in immigrant families "innocent bystanders" who should not be seen as the same as their parents, but rather be given the same chances as those who have native-born, citizen parents? Are some children of immigrants (those from legal migrants, whose high level of skills is valued in the US) deserving of educational opportunities while others (whose parents are illegal, who occupy low-skill service work or agricultural jobs) are not? American citizens must sort out how they feel about these questions before beginning to craft coherent policies on the treatment of immigrant children in schools.

The second consideration for the US public should be what the consequences of their decisions about the education of children in immigrant families are. Will turning away illegal immigrant children from schools be better for them and better for our country? What end do policy-makers have in mind? Where do these children go and what will they do? Will this save money in the long run? What if we provide ways for illegal immigrant children to become citizens? How does this benefit the country? Is the benefit of having educated, tax-paying citizens greater than having illegal immigrants in their place or deporting those illegal immigrants we find?

Finally, we need to consider what kinds of services to provide for children in immigrant families. Allowing access to US public elementary and secondary schools and allowing in-state tuition at state colleges and universities for illegal immigrants gives these students access to the same services as those who are citizens, but is this enough to provide opportunities for success? Noguera (2008) contends that children in immigrant families need extra support that schools should be prepared to provide. English language support is one need that many children of recent immigrants may have, but Noguera (2008) also reminds us that we should account for other special circumstances that children in immigrant families may face. These children may move frequently or they may spend part of the year in home countries living with other family members. Children in immigrant families may be separated from one or more of their parents for large parts of the year. Children in immigrant families may need support in getting information about schools, becoming integrated into school communities, and in learning about the US system of higher education and how to apply for college and financial aid. To truly work toward educational success for many children in immigrant families, special services need to be targeted to them.

Throughout this book, we have presented different portrayals of immigrants and their families. In our most hopeful books and movies, the lives of immigrants are inspirational. They overcome great odds to achieve the "American Dream." It is often the children in immigrant families, through their educational successes, who feel responsible to do well in school to justify their parents' sacrifices. Still, when we analyze the data available and research published by researchers, we find that not all immigrant adults and children begin with comparable resources, so that in education there is no single immigrant story that can summarize the experience of all immigrants.

References

Abedi, J., Lord, C., Boscardin, C.K., and Miyoshi, J. (2001) *The Effects of Accommodations on the Assessment of Limited English Proficient (LEP) Students in the National Assessment of Educational Progress (NAEP)* (Los Angeles, CA: University of California, Los Angeles, National Center for Research on Evaluation, Standards, and Student Testing, Center for the Study of Evaluation, Graduate School of Education and Information Studies).

Act of 1893, 52nd Congress, 27 stat. 570.

Adams, J.T. (1931) *The Epic of America* (Boston, MA: Little, Brown, and Company).

Ainsworth-Darnell, J. and Downey, D. (1998) "Assessing Racial/Ethnic Differences in School Performance," *American Sociological Review*, 63, 536–53.

Alba, R.D. (1990) *Ethnic Identity: The Transformation of White America* (New Haven, CT: Yale University Press).

Alba, R., Logan, J., Lutz, A., and Stults, B. (2002) "Only English by the Third Generation? Loss and Preservation of the Mother Tongue among the Grandchildren of Contemporary Immigrants," *Demography*, 39, 467–84.

Alba, R. and Nee, V. (2003) *Remaking the American Mainstream: Assimilation and Contemporary Immigration* (Cambridge, MA: Harvard University Press).

Alexander, K.L. and Cook, M.A. (1979) "The Motivational Relevance of Educational Plans: Questioning the Conventional Wisdom," *Social Psychology Quarterly*, 42, 202–13.

Alexander, K., Entwisle, D., and Dauber, S. (2002) *On the Success of Failure: A Reassessment of the Effects of Retention in the Primary School Grades*, 2nd edn (Cambridge: Cambridge University Press).

American Community Survey (2008a) "Educational Attainment for the Population 25 Years and Over," American Community Survey, US Census Bureau. Available at: http://factfinder2.census.gov/faces/tableservices/jsf/pages/productview.xhtml?pid=ACS_08_1YR_B15003&prodType=table (accessed February 8, 2012).

References

American Community Survey (2008b) "Sex by Educational Attainment for the Population 25 Years and Over (White Alone, Not Hispanic or Latino)," American Community Survey, US Census Bureau. Available at: http://factfinder2.census.gov/faces/tableservices/jsf/pages/productview. xhtml?pid=ACS_08_1YR_B15002H&prodType=table (accessed February 8, 2012).

American Community Survey (2008c) "Sex by Educational Attainment for the Population 25 Years and Over (Black or African American Alone)," American Community Survey, US Census Bureau. Available at: http://factfinder2.census. gov/faces/tableservices/jsf/pages/productview.xhtml?pid=ACS_08_1YR_ B15002B&prodType=table (accessed February 8, 2012).

American Community Survey (2008d) "Sex by Educational Attainment for the Population 25 Years and Over (Hispanic or Latino)," American Community Survey, US Census Bureau. Available at: http://factfinder2.census.gov/ faces/tableservices/jsf/pages/productview.xhtml?pid=ACS_08_1YR_B15002I& prodType=table (accessed February 8, 2012).

American Community Survey (2008e) "Sex by Educational Attainment for the Population 25 Years and Over (Asian Alone)," American Community Survey, US Census Bureau. Available at: http://factfinder2.census.gov/faces/tableservices/ jsf/pages/productview.xhtml?pid=ACS_08_1YR_B15002D&prodType=table (accessed February 8, 2012).

Antiterrorism and Effective Death Penalty Act of 1996, 104th Congress, 110 Stat. 1214.

Aoki, K. (1998) "No Right to Own?: The Early Twentieth-Century 'Alien Land Laws' as a Prelude to Internment," *Boston College Law Review*, 19, 37–72.

Appadurai, A. (1996) *Modernity at Large: Cultural Dimensions of Globalization* (Minneapolis, MN: University of Minnesota Press).

Bankston, III, C.L. (2004) "Social Capital, Cultural Values, Immigration, and Academic Achievement: The Host Country Context and Contradictory Consequences," *Sociology of Education*, 77, 176–9.

Bankston, III, C.L. and Zhou, M. (1995) "Effects of Minority-Language Literacy on the Academic Achievement of Vietnamese Youths in New Orleans," *Sociology of Education*, 68, 1–17.

Bean, F.D. and Stevens, G. (2003) *America's Newcomers and the Dynamics of Diversity* (New York: Russell Sage Foundation).

Behrman, J.R. and Stacey, N. (eds) (1997) *Social Benefits of Education* (Ann Arbor, MI: University of Michigan Press).

Bergad, L.W. and Klein, H.S. (2010) *Hispanics in the United States: A Demographic, Social and Economic History, 1980–2005* (New York: Cambridge University Press).

Bleakley, H. and Chin, A. (2004) "Language Skills and Earnings: Evidence from Childhood Immigrants," *Review of Economics and Statistics*, 86, 481–96.

Borch, C. and Corra, M. (2010) "Differences in Earnings among Black and non-Black African Immigrants in the United States, 1980–2000: A Cross-Sectional and Temporal Analysis," *Sociological Perspectives*, 53 (4): 573–92.

Borjas, G.J. (1987) "Self-Selection and the Earnings of Immigrants," *The American Economic Review*, 77, 531–53.

Boswell, T.E. (1986) "A Split Labor Market Analysis of Discrimination against Chinese Immigrants, 1850–1882," *American Sociological Review*, 51(3), 352–71.

Bound, J., Lovenheim, M.F., and Turner, S. (2010) "Why Have College Completion Rates Declined? An Analysis of Changing Student Preparation and Collegiate Resources," *American Economic Journal: Applied Economics*, 2, 129–57.

Bourdieu, P. (1980) "Le Capital Social," *Actes de la Recherche en Sciences Sociales*, 31, 2–3.

Bowles, S. and Gintis, H. (1977) *Schooling in Capitalist America: Educational Reform and the Contradictions of Economic Life* (New York: Basic Books).

Bowles, S. and Gintis, H. (1986) *Democracy and Capitalism: Property, Community, and the Contradictions of Modern Social Thought* (New York: Basic Books).

Bryk, A., Lee, V.E., and Holland, P.B. (1993) *Catholic Schools and the Common Good* (Cambridge, MA: Harvard University Press).

Buchman, C. and DiPrete, T.A. (2006) "The Growing Female Advantage in College Completion: The Role of Family Background in Academic Achievement," *American Sociological Review*, 71, 515–41.

Burchinal, M., Vandergrift, N., Pianta, R., and Mashburn, A. (2009) "Threshold Analysis of Association between Child Care Quality and Child Outcomes for Low-Income Children in Pre-Kindergarten Programs," *Early Childhood Research Quarterly*, 25, 166–76.

Calavita, K. (2000) "The Paradoxes of Race, Class, Identity, and 'Passing': Enforcing the Chinese Exclusion Acts, 1882–1910," *Law & Social Inquiry*, 25(1), 1–40.

Caldera, R. (2002) *Accountability and Assessment: How do English Learners Fit In? Testimony on the Status of Education for English Learners in California Schools* (Sacramento, CA: Assembly Education Committee).

Callahan, R. and Gándara, P. (2004) "On Nobody's Agenda: Improving English Language Learners' Access to Higher Education," in M. Sadowski (ed.) *Teaching Immigrant and Second-Language Students* (Cambridge, MA: Harvard Education Press).

Callahan, R., Wilkinson, L., and Muller, C. (2008) "School Context and the Effect of ESL Placement on Mexican-Origin Adolescents' Achievement," *Social Science Quarterly*, 89(1), 177–98.

Caplan, N., Choy, M.H., and Whitmore, J.K. (1992) *Children of the Boat People: A Study of Educational Success* (Ann Arbor, MI: University of Michigan Press).

References

Capps, R., Fix, M., Murray, J., Ost, J., Passel, J.S., and Herwantoro, S. (2005) *The New Demography of America's Schools: Immigration and the No Child Left Behind Act* (Washington, DC: Urban Institute).

Carnevale, A.P., Fry, R.A., and Lowell, B.L. (2001) "Understanding, Speaking, Reading, Writing, and Earnings in the Immigrant Labor Market," *The American Economic Review*, 91, 159–63.

Carter, P.L. (2003) " 'Black' Cultural Capital, Status Positioning, and Schooling Conflicts for Low-Income African American Youth," *Social Problems*, 50, 136–55.

Chinese Exclusion Act of 1882, 47th Congress, 22 stat. 58.

Chudacoff, H.P. (2007) *Children at Play: An American History* (New York: New York University Press).

Coleman, J.S. (1988) "Social Capital in the Creation of Human Capital," *American Journal of Sociology*, 94, 95–120.

Colletta, J.P. (1989) *They Came in Ships: A Guide to Finding Your Immigrant Ancestor's Arrival Record* (Orem, UT: Ancestry Publishing).

Comprehensive Immigration Reform Act of 2007, 110th Congress, S. 1348.

Cooney, R.S. (1979) "Intercity Variations in Puerto Rican Female Participation," *Journal of Human Resources*, 14, 222–35.

Cooney, R.S. and Warren, A.C. (1979) "Declining Female Participation among Puerto Rican New Yorkers: A Comparison with Native White Non-Spanish New Yorkers," *Ethnicity*, 6, 281–97.

Coppola, F.F. (1972) *The Godfather* (Paramount Pictures).

Coppola, F.F. (1974) *The Godfather: Part II* (Paramount Pictures).

Cordasco, F. (1973) "The Children of Immigrants in Schools: Historical Analogues of Educational Deprivation," *Journal of Negro Education*, 42(1), 44–53.

Cross, D.R. (1973) "How Historians Have Looked at Immigrants to the United States," *International Migration Review*, 7(1), 4–13.

Current Population Survey (2009) "Educational Attainment in the United States: 2009 – Detailed Tables," US Census Bureau. Available at: http://www.census.gov/hhes/socdemo/education/data/cps/2009/tables.html (accessed December 1, 2010).

Darcy, N.J. (1953) "A Review of the Literature on the Effects of Bilingualism upon the Measurement of Intelligence," *The Journal of Genetic Psychology*, 82, 21–57.

Deaux, K., Bikmen, N., Gilkes, A., Ventuneac, A., Joseph, Y., Payne, Y.A., and Steele, C.M. (2007) "Becoming American: Stereotype Threat Effects in Afro-Caribbean Immigrant Groups," *Social Psychology Quarterly*, 70, 384–404.

de Cohen, C.C., Deterding, N., and Clewell, B.C. (2005) *Who's Left Behind? Immigrant Children in High and Low LEP Schools* (Washington, DC: Urban Institute).

References

de Crevecœur, J.H.S.J. (1904 [1782]) *Letters from an American Farmer* (New York: Fox, Duffield, and Company).

Deutsch, M. and Associates (1967) *The Disadvantaged Child* (New York: Basic Books).

Dougherty, K.J. (1994) *The Contradictory College* (Albany, NY: State University of New York Press).

DREAM Act of 2009, 111th Congress, S.729.IS.

Dred Scott v. Sanford (1857) 60 U.S. 393.

Duany, J. (2011) *Blurred Borders: Transnational Migration between the Hispanic Caribbean and the United States* (Chapel Hill, NC: University of North Carolina Press).

Duckworth, A. and Seligman, M. (2006) "Self-discipline Gives Girls the Edge: Gender in Self-discipline, Grades, and Achievement Test Scores," *Journal of Educational Psychology*, 98(1), 198–208.

Duncan, G.J., Ziol-Guest, K.M., and Kalil, A. (2010) "Early-Childhood Poverty and Adult Attainment, Behavior and Health," *Child Development*, 81, 306–25.

Dunne, T., Roberts, M.J., and Samuelson, L. (1989) "Plant Turnover and Gross Employment Flows in the U.S. Manufacturing Sector," *Journal of Labor Economics*, 7(1), 48–71.

Emergency Quota Act of 1921, 67th Congress, 42 Stat. 5.

Farley, R. and Haaga, J. (2000) *The American People: Census 2000* (New York: Russell Sage Foundation).

Feliciano, C. (2001) "The Benefits of Biculturalism: Exposure to Immigrant Culture and Dropping out of School among Asian and Latino Youths," *Social Science Quarterly*, 82, 865–79.

Feliciano, C. (2005) "Educational Selectivity in U.S. Immigration: How Do Immigrants Compare to Those Left Behind?" *Demography*, 42(1), 131–52.

Fix, M. and Passel, J. (1994) *Immigration and Immigrants: Setting the Record Straight* (Washington, DC: The Urban Institute).

Fordham, S. and Ogbu, J.U. (1986) "Black Students' School Success: Coping with the Burden of 'Acting White'," *The Urban Review*, 18, 176–206.

Fox, M.A., Connolly, B.A., and Snyder, T.D. (2005) *Youth Indicators 2005: Trends in the Well-Being of American Youth* (NCES 2005–050) *US Department of Education, National Center for Education Statistics* (Washington, DC: US Government Printing Office).

Franklin, B., letter to William Strahan, 19 Aug. 1784, in L.W. Labaree et al. (eds) *The Papers of Benjamin Franklin*, 29 vols (New Haven, CT: Yale University Press, 1959) p. 1102.

Franklin, B., letter to James Parker, 20 Mar. 1750, in L.W. Labaree et al. (eds) *The Papers of Benjamin Franklin*, 29 vols (New Haven, CT: Yale University Press, 1959) pp. 4–120.

Franzini, L. and Fernandez-Esquer, M.E. (2006) "The Association of Subjective

References

Social Status and Health in Low-Income Mexican-Origin Individuals in Texas," *Social Science & Medicine*, 63(3), 788–804.

Freeman, D. (2004) "Teaching in the Context of English Language Learners: What Do We Need to Know?" in M. Sadowski (ed.) *Teaching Immigrant and Second-Language Students* (Cambridge, MA: Harvard Education Press).

Frey, W. (2011) "America's Diverse Future: Initial Glimpses at the U.S. Child Population from the 2010 Census. Report for the Metropolitan Policy Program at the Brookings Institution," The Brookings Institution. Available at: http://www.brookings.edu/~/media/Files/rc/papers/2011/0406_census_diversity _frey/0406_census_diversity_frey.pdf (accessed April 26, 2011).

Fry, R. (2005) *The Higher Dropout Rate of Foreign-Born Teens* (Washington, DC: Pew Hispanic Center). Available at: http://pewhispanic.org/ (accessed March 8, 2010).

Fry, R. (2007) *How Far Behind in Math and Reading are English Language Learners?* (Washington, DC: Pew Hispanic Center). Available at: http:// pewhispanic.org/ (accessed March 8, 2010).

Fuligni, A.J. (1997) "The Academic Achievement of Adolescents from Immigrant Families: The Role of Family Background, Attitudes, and Behavior," *Child Development*, 8(2), 351–63.

Furstenberg, F.F. (2007) "The Making of the Black Family: Race and Class in Qualitative Studies in the Twentieth Century," *Annual Review of Sociology*, 33, 429–48.

Galindo, R. (2011) "The Nativistic Legacy of the Americanization Era in the Education of Mexican Immigrant Students," *Educational Studies: A Journal of the American Educational Studies Association*, 47(4), 323–46.

Gammage, J. (2012) "'Ursinus' Fong a Rare Asian American College President," *The Philadelphia Inquirer*, February 3.

Gándara, P. and Hopkins, M. (eds) (2010) *Forbidden Language: English Learners and Restrictive Language Policies* (New York: Teachers College Press).

Gándara, P., Gutiérrez, D., and O'Hara, S. (2001) "Planning for the Future in Rural and Urban High Schools," *Journal of Education for Students Placed At-Risk*, 6, 73–93.

Gándara, P., Rumberger, R., Maxwell-Jolly, J., and Callahan, R. (2003) "English Learners in California Schools: Unequal Resources, Unequal Outcomes," *Educational Policy Analysis Archives*, 11, 1–54.

Gans, H.J. (1962) *The Urban Villagers: Groups and Class in the Life of Italian-Americans* (New York: Free Press of Glencoe).

Garcia, E.E. (2005) *Teaching and Learning in Two Languages: Bilingualism and Schooling in the United States* (New York: Teachers College Press).

Garcia y Griego, M. (1996) "The Importation of Mexican Contract Laborers to the United States 1942–1964," in D.G. Gutierrez (ed.) *Between Two Worlds: Mexican Immigrants in the United States* (Wilmington, DE: Scholarly Resources).

References

Geary Act of 1892, 52nd Congress, 27 stat. 25.

Gentlemen's Agreement of 1907. Text available at: http://www.archives.gov/legislative/guide/senate/chapter-13-immigration.html (accessed July 13, 2012).

Gibson, C.J. and Jung, K. (2006) "Historical Census Statistics on the Foreign-Born Population: Table 1. Nativity of the Population and Place of Birth of the Native Population: 1850 to 2000," US Census Bureau. Available at: http://www.census.gov/population/www/documentation/twps0081/tables/tab01.xls (accessed January 23, 2012).

Gibson, C.J. and Lennon, E. (1999) "Historical Census Statistics on the Foreign-Born Population of the United States," US Census Bureau Population Division Working Paper No. 29. Available at: http://www.census.gov/population/www/documentation/twps0029/twps0029.html (accessed February 9, 2012).

Gibson, M.A. (1988) *Accommodation without Assimilation: Sikh Immigrants in an American High School* (Ithaca, NY: Cornell University Press).

Gibson, M.A. and Carrasco, S. (2009) "The Education of Immigrant Youth: Some Lessons from the US and Spain," *Theory into Practice*, 48, 249–57.

Glick, J.E. and Bates, L. (2010) "Diversity in Academic Achievement: Children of Immigrants in US Schools," in E.L. Grigorenko and R. Takanishi (eds) *Immigration, Diversity and Education* (New York: Routledge Education).

Golash-Boza, T. (2005) "Assessing the Advantages of Bilingualism for Children of Immigrants," *International Migration Review*, 39, 721–53.

Goodenough, F. (1934) *Developmental Psychology: An Introduction to the Study of Human Behavior* (New York: D. Appleton-Century, Inc.).

Gordon, M.M. (1964) *Assimilation in American Life: The Role of Race, Religion, and National Origins* (New York: Oxford University Press).

Granovetter, M. (1974) *Getting a Job: A Study of Contacts and Careers* (Cambridge, MA: Harvard University Press).

Gray, M.J., Rolph, E.S., and Melamid, E. (1996) *Immigration and Higher Education. Institutional Responses to Changing Demographics.* MR-751-AMF. Available at: http://www.rand.org/content/dam/rand/pubs/monograph_reports/2007/MR751.pdf (accessed February 9, 2012).

Grieco, E.M. (2010) "Race and Hispanic Origin of the Foreign-Born Population in the United States: 2007," American Community Survey Reports. Available at: http://www.census.gov/prod/2010pubs/acs-11.pdf (accessed January 16, 2012).

Grieco, E.M. and Trevelyan, E.N. (2010) "Place of Birth of the Foreign-Born Population: 2009," American Community Survey Reports. ACSBR/09-15, US Census Bureau.

Grissom, J.B. (2004) "Reclassification of English Learners," *Education Policy Analysis Archives*, 12. Available at: http://epaa.asu.edu/epaa/v12n36/ (accessed March 2, 2010).

Gryn, T.A. and Larsen, L.J. (2010) "Nativity Status and Citizenship in the United States: 2009," American Community Survey Briefs. US Census Bureau.

References

Available at: http://www.census.gov/prod/2010pubs/acsbr09-16.pdf (accessed January 16, 2012).

Gutierrez, D. (1995) *Walls and Mirrors: Mexican Americans, Mexican Immigrants, and the Politics of Ethnicity* (Berkeley, CA: University of California Press).

Hagedorn, J. (1993) "Introduction: Role of Dead Man Require Very Little Acting," in J. Hagedorn (ed.), *Charlie Chan is Dead: An Anthology of Contemporary Asian American Fiction* (pp. xxi–xxx). (New York, Penguin).

Hakimzadeh, S. and Cohn, D. (2007) *English Usage among Hispanics in the United States.* (Washington, DC: Pew Hispanic Center). Available at: http://www.pewhispanic.org/files/reports/82.pdf (accessed February 9, 2012).

Hallinan, M.T. (1988) "Equality of Educational Opportunity," *Annual Review of Sociology*, 14, 249–68.

Hao, L. and Johnson, R.W. (2000) "Economic, Cultural, and Social Origins of Emotional Well-Being: Comparisons of Immigrants and Natives at Midlife," *Research on Aging*, 22(6), 599–629.

Harris, A.L. (2011). *Kids Don't Want to Fail: Oppositional Culture and the Black-White Achievement Gap* (Cambridge, MA: Harvard University Press).

Hart-Cellar Act of 1965, 89th Congress, 79 stat. 911.

Hartmann, D. and Cornell, S. (2007) *Ethnicity and Race: Making Identities in a Changing World*, 2nd edn (Thousand Oaks, CA: Pine Forge).

Hauser, R.M. (1972) "Disaggregating a Social-Psychological Model of Educational Attainment," *Social Science Research*, 1, 159–88.

Haveman, R. and Wolfe, B. (1995) "The Determinants of Children's Attainments: A Review of Methods and Findings," *Journal of Economic Literature*, 33, 1829–78.

Highman, J. (2002 [1955]) *Strangers in the Land: Patterns of American Nativism, 1860–1925* (New Brunswick, NJ: Rutgers University Press).

Hirschman, C. (1983) "America's Melting Pot Reconsidered," *Annual Review of Sociology*, 9, 397–423.

Hirschman, C. (2005) "Immigration and the American Century," *Demography*, 42, 595–620.

Hirschman, C. and Wong, M.G. (1986) "The Extraordinary Educational Attainment of Asian-Americans: A Search for Historical Evidence and Explanations," *Social Forces*, 65, 1–27.

Hutchinson, E.P. (1958) "Notes on Immigration Statistics of the United States," *Journal of the American Statistical Association*, 53(284), 963–1025.

Hwang, S. (2005) "The New White Flight," *The Wall Street Journal* November 19. Available at: http://online.wsj.com/article/SB113236377590902105.html (accessed February 9, 2012).

Illegal Immigration Reform and Immigrant Responsibility Act of 1996, 104th Congress, 110 stat. 3009-546.

Immigration Act of 1882, 47th Congress, 22 stat. 214.

References

Immigration Act of 1903, 57th Congress, 32 stat. 1213.

Immigration Act of 1917, 64th Congress, 39 stat. 874.

Immigration Act of 1924, 68th Congress, 43 stat. 143.

Immigration Reform and Control Act of 1986, 99th Congress, 100 stat. 3359.

Jasso, G. (1988) "Whom Shall We Welcome? Elite Judgments of the Criteria for the Selection of Immigrants," *American Sociological Review*, 53, 919–32.

Jay, J. (1787). "Federalist #2," *The Federalist Papers*. Available at: http://thomas. loc.gov/home/histdox/fed_02.html (accessed February 9, 2012).

Jencks, C. and Phillips, M. (1998) "The Black-White Test Score Gap: An Introduction," in C. Jencks and M. Phillips (eds) *The Black-White Test Score Gap* (Washington, DC: Brookings Institution Press).

Jencks, C., Crouse, J., and Mueser, P. (1983) "The Wisconsin Model of Status Attainment: A National Replication with Improved Measures of Ability and Aspiration," *Sociology of Education*, 56, 3–19.

Kaba, A.J. (2007) "Educational Attainment, Income Levels, and Africans in the United States: The Paradox of Nigerian Immigrants," *West Africa Review*, 11, 1–27.

Kaestle, C.F. (1978) "Social Change, Discipline, and the Common School in Early Nineteenth-Century America," *The Journal of Interdisciplinary History*, 9(1), 1–17.

Kao, G. (1995) "Asian-Americans as Model Minorities – A Look at Their Academic Performance," *American Journal of Education*, 103(2), 121–59.

Kao, G. (1999) "Psychological Well-Being and Educational Achievement among Immigrant Youth," in D.J. Hernandez (ed.) *Children of Immigrants: Health, Adjustment, and Public Assistance* (Washington, DC: National Academies Press).

Kao, G. (2004) "Social Capital and Its Relevance to Minority and Immigrant Populations," *Sociology of Education*, 77, 172–5.

Kao, G. and Tienda, M. (1995) "Optimism and Achievement – the Educational Performance of Immigrant Youth," *Social Science Quarterly*, 76(1), 1–19.

Kao, G. and Tienda, M. (1998) "Educational Aspirations of Minority Youth," *American Journal of Education*, 106, 349–84.

Kao, G. and Thompson, J. (2003) "Racial and Ethnic Stratification in Educational Achievement and Attainment," *Annual Review of Sociology*, 29, 417–42.

Kao, G. and Turney, K. (2010) "Adolescents and Schooling: Differences by Race, Ethnicity, and Immigrant Status," in D.P. Swanson, M.C. Edwards, and M.B. Spencer (eds) *Adolescence: Development During a Global Era* (Burlington, MA: Academic Press).

Katz, M.B. (1987) *Reconstructing American Education* (Cambridge, MA: Harvard University Press).

Keller, U. and Tillman, K.H. (2008) "Post-Secondary Educational Attainment of Immigrant and Native Youth," *Social Forces*, 87(1), 121–52.

References

Kent, M.M. (2007) "Immigration and America's Black Population," *Population Bulletin*, 62(4).

Kim, J.-K. and Park, D. (2010) "The Determinants of Demand for Private Tutoring in South Korea," *Asia Pacific Education Review*, 11, 411–21.

Klesmer, H. (1994) "Assessment and Teacher Perceptions of ESL Student Achievement," *English Quarterly*, 26, 8–11.

Kluegel, J.R. (1990) "Trends in Whites' Explanations of the Black-White Gap in Socioeconomic Status, 1977–1989," *American Sociological Review*, 55, 512–25.

Kominski, R.A., Shin, H.B., and Marotz, K. (2008) "Language Needs of School-Age Children," Presentation at the Annual Meeting of the Population Association of America. Available at: http://www.census.gov/hhes/socdemo/language/data/acs/Language-Needs-of-School-Age-Children-PAA-2008.xls (accessed February 9, 2012).

Kreitzer, A.E., Madaus, F., and Haney, W. (1989) "Competency Testing and Dropouts," in L. Weis, E. Farrar, and H.G. Petrie (eds) *Dropouts from School: Issues, Dilemmas and Solutions* (Albany, NY: State University of New York Press).

Kwok, P. (2004) "Examination-Oriented Knowledge and Value Transformation in East Asian Cram Schools," *Asia Pacific Education Review*, 5, 64–75.

Labov, T.G. (1998) "English Acquisition by Immigrants to the United States at the Beginning of the Twentieth Century," *American Speech*, 73, 368–98.

Ladson-Billings, G. (2004) "Landing on the Wrong Note: The Price We Paid for *Brown*," *Educational Researcher*, 33, 3–13.

Lahiri, J. (2003) *The Namesake* (New York: Mariner).

Lareau, A. (2000) *Home Advantage: Social Class and Parental Intervention in Elementary Education*, updated edn (Lanham, MD: Rowman and Littlefield).

Lau v. Nichols (1974) 414 U.S. 563.

Lazarus, E. (1883) "The New Colossus," on the Liberty State Park website. Available at: http://www.libertystatepark.com/emma.htm (accessed January 31, 2012).

Lee, J. and Bean, F.D. (2007) "Reinventing the Color Line: Immigration and America's New Racial/Ethnic Divide," *Social Forces*, 86, 561–86.

Lee, S.J. (1996) *Unraveling the "Model Minority Stereotype": Listening to Asian American Youth* (New York: Teachers College).

Lee, S.J. (2005) *Up Against Whiteness: Race, School, and Immigrant Youth* (New York: Teachers College).

Lewis, O. (1959) *Five Families: Mexican Case Studies in the Culture of Poverty* (New York: Basic Books).

Lewis, O. (1966a) *La Vida; A Puerto Rican Family in the Culture of Poverty – San Juan and New York* (New York: Random House).

Lewis, O. (1966b) "The Culture of Poverty," *Scientific American*, 215(4), 19–25.

References

Light, I. and Bonacich, E. (1988) *Immigrant Entrepreneurs: Koreans in Los Angeles, 1965–1982* (Berkeley, CA: University of California Press).

Lleras-Muney, A. (2005). "The Relationship between Education and Adult Mortality in the U.S.," *Review of Economic Studies*, 72(1), 189–221.

Lopez, N. (2003a) *Hopeful Girls, Troubled Boys: Race and Gender Disparity in Urban Education* (New York: Routledge).

Lopez, N. (2003b) "Disentangling Race-Gender Work Experiences: Second Generation Caribbean Young Adults in New York City," in P. Hondagneu-Sotelo (ed.) *Gender and U.S. Immigration: Contemporary Trends* (Berkeley, CA: University of California Press).

Louie, V. (2004) *Compelled to Excel. Immigration, Education, and Opportunity among Chinese Americans* (Stanford, CA: Stanford University Press).

Ma, Y. (2009) "Family SES, Parental Involvement and College Major Choices," *Sociological Perspectives*, 52, 211–34.

Magnuson Act of 1943, 78th Congress, 57 stat. 600.

Malone, N., Baluja, K.F., Costanzo, J.M., and Davis, C.J. (2003) "The Foreign-Born Population: Census 2000 Briefs," US Census Bureau. Available at: http://www.census.gov/prod/2003pubs/c2kbr-34.pdf (accessed February 9, 2012).

Martin, P.L. (1994) "Good Intentions Gone Awry: IRCA and U.S. Agriculture," *Annals of the Academy of Political and Social Science*, 534, 44–57.

Martin, P. and Midgley, E. (2003) *Immigration: Shaping and Reshaping America* (Washington, DC: Population Reference Bureau). Available at: http://www.prb.org/pdf/immigrshapingamerica.pdf (accessed January 31, 2012).

Massey, D.S. (1995) "The New Immigration and Ethnicity in the United States," *Population and Development Review*, 21(3), 631–52.

Massey, D. and Capoferro, C. (2008) "The Geographic Diversification of American Immigration," in D.S. Massey (ed.) *New Faces in New Places: The Changing Geography of American Immigration* (New York: Russell Sage Foundation).

Massey, D.S., Charles, C.Z., Lundy, G.F., and Fischer, M.J. (2003a) *The Source of the River: The Social Origins of Freshmen at America's Selective Colleges and Universities* (Princeton, NJ: Princeton University Press).

Massey, D.S., Durand, J., and Malone, N.J. (2003b) *Beyond Smoke and Mirrors: Mexican Immigration in an Era of Economic Integration* (New York: Russell Sage Foundation).

Massey, D.S., Mooney, M., Torres, K.C., and Charles, C. (2007) "Black Immigrants and Black Natives Attending Selective Colleges and Universities in the United States," *American Journal of Education*, 113, 243–71.

Mather, M. (2009) "Children in Immigrant Families Chart New Path," Population Reference Bureau Reports on America. Available at: http://www.prb.org/pdf09/immigrantchildren.pdf (accessed February 9, 2012).

Mather, M. and Kent, M.M. (2009) "U.S. Latino Children Fare Poorly on Many

References

Social Indicators," Population Reference Bureau. Available at: http://www. prb.org/Articles/2009/latinochildren.aspx (accessed February 9, 2012).

Mattoo, A., Neagu, I.C., and Özden, Ç. (2005) "Brain Waste? Educated Immigrants in the U.S. Labor Market," *Journal of Developmental Economics*, 87(2), 255–69.

Matute-Bianchi, M.E. (1991) "Situational Ethnicity and Patterns of School Performance among Immigrants and Non-Immigrant Mexican-Descent Students," in M. Gibson and J.U. Ogbu (eds) *Minority Status and Schooling: A Comparative Study of Immigrant and Involuntary Minorities* (New York: Garland).

McCarran-Walter Act of 1952, 82nd Congress, 66 stat. 163.

McDonnell, L.M. and Hill, P.T. (1993) *Newcomers in American Schools: Meeting the Educational Needs of Immigrant Youths* (Santa Monica, CA: Rand Corp.).

McHugh, K.E., Miyares, I.M., and Skop, E.H. (1997) "The Magnetism of Miami: Segmented Paths in Cuban Migration," *Geographical Review*, 87, 504–19.

Mendez v. Westminster School District, et al., 64 F. Supp. 544 (S.D. Cal. 1946).

Morawska, E. (2009) *A Sociology of Immigration: (Re)Making Multifaceted America* (New York: Palgrave Macmillan).

Mouw, T. and Xie, Y. (1999) "Bilingualism and the Academic Achievement of Asian Immigrants: Accommodation with or without Assimilation?" *American Sociological Review*, 64(2), 232–52.

Nair, M. (2006) *The Namesake* (Fox Searchlight).

National Center for Education Statistics (NCES) (1992) *Language Characteristics and Academic Achievement: A Look at Asian and Hispanic Eighth Graders in NELS: 88* (NCES Publication no. 920479) (Washington, DC: US Government Printing Office).

National Center for Education Statistics (NCES) (2002) *A Profile of the American High School Sophomore in 2002: Initial Results from the Base Year of the Education Longitudinal Study of 2002* (Washington, DC: US Government Printing Office).

National Center for Education Statistics (NCES) (2004) *Language Minorities and Their Educational and Labor Market Indicators: Recent Trends* (Washington, DC: US Department of Education).

National Center for Education Statistics (NCES) (2005) "Status and Trends in the Education of Racial and Ethnic Minorities – Table 26.2 Number and Percentage of Persons Age 25 to 29 with Bachelor's Degree or Higher, by Race/Ethnicity with Hispanic and Asian Subgroups: 2005," National Center for Education Statistics, Institute of Education Sciences. Available at: http://nces.ed.gov/pubs2007/minoritytrends/tables/table_26_2.asp?referrer=report (accessed February 8, 2012).

National Center for Education Statistics (NCES) (2007) "Status and Trends in the Education of Racial and Ethnic Minorities," US Department of Education.

References

Available at: http://nces.ed.gov/pubs2007/minoritytrends/ (accessed February 9, 2012).

National Center for Education Statistics (NCES) (2008a) "National Assessment of Educational Progress (NAEP), 2000, 2002, 2005, and 2007 Reading Assessments and the NAEP Data Explorer." Available at: http://nces.ed.gov/nationsreportcard/nde/ (accessed January 25, 2008).

National Center for Education Statistics (NCES) (2008b) "National Assessment of Educational Progress (NAEP), 2000, 2002, 2005, and 2007 Mathematics Assessments and the NAEP Data Explorer." Available at: http://nces.ed.gov/nationsreportcard/naepdata/ (accessed February 9, 2012).

Naturalization Act of 1790, 1st Congress, 1 stat. 103.

Nava, G. (1995) *My Family [Mi Familia]* (New Line Cinema).

Nee, V., Sanders, J.M., and Sernau, S. (1994) "Job Transitions in an Immigrant Metropolis: Ethnic Boundaries and the Mixed Economy," *American Sociological Review*, 59, 849–72.

Newsweek (1971) "Success Story: Outwhiting the Whites," *Newsweek*, June 21.

Nielsen, F. and Lerner, S.J. (1986) "Language Skills and School Achievement of Bilingual Hispanics," *Social Science Research*, 15, 209–40.

Noguera, P.A. (2008) *The Trouble with Black Boys, and Other Reflections on Race, Equity, and the Future of Public Education* (San Francisco, CA: Jossey-Bass).

Oakes, J. (1990) *Multiplying Inequalities: The Effects of Race, Social Class, and Tracking on Opportunities to Learn Math and Science* (Santa Monica, CA: RAND).

Ogbu, J.U. (1978) *Minority Education and Caste: The American System in Cross-Cultural Perspective* (San Diego, CA: American Press).

Ogbu, J.U. (1991) "Cultural Diversity and School Experience," in C.E. Walsh (ed.) *Literacy as Praxis: Culture, Language, and Pedagogy* (Norwood, NJ: Ablex).

O'Hare, W. (2004) *Trends in the Well-Being of America's Children* (New York and Washington, DC: Russell Sage Foundation and Population Reference Bureau).

Olneck, M. (2008) "American Public Schooling and European Immigrants in the Early Twentieth Century: A Post-Revisionist Synthesis," in W.J. Reese and J.L. Rury (eds) *Rethinking the History of American Education* (New York: Palgrave Macmillan).

Olsen, L. (1997) *Made in America* (New York: The Free Press).

Olsen, L. (2000) *Made in America: Immigrant students in American schools* (New York: The Free Press).

Omi, M. and Winant, H. (1994) *Racial Formation in the United States: From the 1960s to the 1990s*, 2nd edn (New York: Routledge).

Orellana, M.F. (2008) *Translating Childhoods: Immigrant Youth, Language, and Culture* (Camden, NJ: Rutgers University Press).

References

Orfield, G. and Yun, J.T. (1999) *Resegregation in American Schools* (Cambridge, MA: The Civil Rights Project, Harvard University).

Ortiz, V. (1986) "Changes in the Characteristics of Puerto Rican Migrants from 1955 to 1980," *International Migration Review*, 20(3), 612–28.

Owens, J. and Lynch, S.M. (2012) "Black and Hispanic Immigrants' Resilience against Negative-ability Racial Stereotypes at Selective Colleges and Universities in the United States," *Sociology of Education*, doi: 10.1177/0038040711435856.

Page Act of 1875, 43rd Congress, 18 stat. 477.

Park, R.E. (1914) "Racial Assimilation in Secondary Groups with Particular Reference to the Negro," *American Journal of Sociology*, 19(5), 606–23.

Park, R.E. (1928) "Human Migration and the Marginal Man," *American Journal of Sociology*, 33, 881–93.

Park, R.E. and Burgess, E.W. (1969 [1921]) *Introduction to the Science of Sociology: Including an Index to Basic Sociological Concepts* (Chicago, IL: University of Chicago Press).

Passel, J. (2003) *Further Demographic Information Relating to the DREAM Act* (Washington, DC: Urban Institute). Available at: http://www.nationalimmigrationreform.org/proposed/DREAM/UrbanInstituteDREAM.pdf (accessed January 31, 2012).

Passel, J. and Cohn, D. (2009) "Mexican Immigrants: How Many Come? How Many Leave?," Pew Research Center: Pew Hispanic Center. Available at: http://www.pewhispanic.org/2009/07/22/mexican-immigrants-how-many-come-how-many-leave/ (accessed January 16, 2012).

Peal, E. and Lambert, W.E. (1962) "The Relation of Bilingualism to Intelligence," *Psychological Monographs*, 76, 1–23.

Perez, L. (1992) "Cuban Miami," in G.J. Grenier and A. Stepic (eds) *Miami Now* (Gainesville, FL: University of Florida Press).

Perlmann, J. and Waldinger, R. (1997) "Second Generation Decline?" *International Migration Review*, 31, 893–922.

Personal Responsibility and Work Opportunity Reconciliation Act of 1996, 104th Congress, 110 stat. 2105.

Petersen, W. (1966) "Success Story, Japanese-American Style," *New York Times Magazine*, January 9.

Plucker, J.A., Burroughs, N., and Song, R. (2010) "Mind the (Other) Gap!: The Growing Excellence Gap in K-12 Education," Indiana University, School of Education, Center for Evaluation and Education Policy, Bloomington, IN.

Plyler v. Doe (1982) 457 U.S. 202.

Pong, S.-L. and Hao, L. (2007) "Neighborhood and School Factors in the School Performance of Immigrants' Children," *International Migration Review*, 41, 206–41.

Portes, A. (1987) "The Social Origins of the Cuban Enclave Economy in Miami," *Sociological Perspectives*, 30, 340–72.

References

Portes, A. (1998) "Social Capital: Its Origins and Applications in Modern Sociology," *Annual Review of Sociology*, 24, 1–24.

Portes, A. and Bach, R. (1985) *Latin Journey: Cuban and Mexican Immigrants in the United States* (Berkeley, CA: University of California Press).

Portes, A. and Böröcz, J. (1989) "Contemporary Immigration: Theoretical Perspectives on Its Determinants and Modes of Incorporation," *International Migration Review*, 23, 606–30.

Portes, A. and Fernández-Kelly, P. (2008) "No Margin for Error: Educational and Occupational Achievement among Disadvantaged Children of Immigrants," *The Annals of the American Academy of Political and Social Science*, 620, 12–36.

Portes, A. and Hao, L. (1998) "E Pluribus Unum: Bilingualism and Language Loss in the Second Generation," *Sociology of Education*, 71, 269–94.

Portes, A. and Rumbaut, R.G. (2001) *Legacies: The Story of the Immigrant Second Generation* (Berkeley, CA: University of California Press).

Portes, A. and Rumbaut, R.G. (2006) *Immigrant America: A Portrait* (Berkeley, CA: University of California Press).

Portes, A. and Stepick, A. (1993) *City on the Edge: The Transformation of Miami* (Berkeley, CA: University of California Press).

Portes, A. and Zhou, M. (1993) "The New Second Generation: Segmented Assimilation and Its Variants," *Annals of the American Academy of Political and Social Science*, 530, 74–96.

Qian, Z. and Blair, S.L. (1999) "Racial/Ethnic Differences in Educational Aspirations of High School Seniors," *Sociological Perspectives*, 42, 605–25.

Ravitch, D. (2000 [1974]) *The Great School Wars: A History of the New York City Public Schools* (Baltimore, MD: Johns Hopkins University Press).

Refugee Act of 1980, 96th Congress, 94 stat. 102.

Rimer, S. and Arenson, K.W. (2004) "Top Colleges Take More Blacks, But Which Ones?" *New York Times*, June 24.

Rong, X.L. and Brown, F. (2001) "The Effects of Immigrant Generation and Ethnicity on Educational Attainment among Young African and Caribbean Blacks in the United States," *Harvard Educational Review*, 71(3), 536–65.

Roosevelt, T. (1918) *Speech to State Republican Party Convention* (New York: Saratoga).

Rosegaard, M.H. (2006) *Japanese Education and the Cram School Business: Functions, Challenges and Perspectives of the Juku* (Copenhagen: Nordic Institute of Asian Studies).

Rosenbaum, J.E. (1976) *Making Inequality: The Hidden Curriculum of High School Tracking* (New York: Wiley).

Ruiz, V. (2001) "South by Southwest: Mexican Americans and Segregated Schooling, 1900–1995," *Organization of American Historians Magazine of History*, 15, 23–7.

References

Ruiz-de-Velasco, J. and Fix, M. (2000) *Overlooked and Underserved: Immigrant Students in U.S. Secondary Schools* (Washington, DC: Urban Institute).

Rumbaut, R.G. (1994) "The Crucible Within: Ethnic Identity, Self Esteem, and Segmented Assimilation among Children of Immigrants," *International Migration Review*, 28, 748–94.

Rumbaut, R.G. (1995) "The New Californians: Comparative Research Findings on the Educational Progress of Immigrant Children," in R.G. Rumbaut and W.A. Cornelius (eds) *California's Immigrant Children: Theory, Research, and Implications for Educational Policy* (San Diego, CA: The Center for U.S.- Mexican Studies, University of California).

Rumbaut, R.G. (1997a) "Assimilation and Its Discontents: Between Rhetoric and Reality," *International Migration Review*, 31, 923–60.

Rumbaut, R.G. (1997b) "Paradoxes (and Orthodoxies) of Assimilation," *Sociological Perspectives*, 40, 483–511.

Rumbaut, R.G. (2004) "Ages, Life Stages, and Generational Cohorts: Decomposing the Immigrant First and Second Generations in the United States," *International Migration Review*, 38(3), 1160–205.

Rumberger, R.W. and Larson, K.A. (1998) "Student Mobility and the Increased Risk of High School Dropout," *American Journal of Education*, 107(1), 1–35.

Saer, D.J. (1923) "The Effects of Bilingualism on Intelligence," *British Journal of Psychology*, 14, 25–38.

Sakamoto, A., Goyette, K., and Kim, C. (2009) "Socioeconomic Attainments of Asian Americans," *Annual Review of Sociology*, 35, 255–76.

Santibáñez, L., Gonzalez, G., Morrison, P.A., and Carroll, S.J. (2007) "Methods for Gauging the Target Populations that Community Colleges Serve," *Population Research and Policy Review*, 26, 51–67.

Sassen, S. (1996) *Losing Control? Sovereignty in an Age of Globalization* (New York: Columbia University Press).

Schmid, C.L. (2001) "Educational Achievement, Language-Minority Students, and the New Second Generation," *Sociology of Education*, 74, 71–87.

Schneider, B. and Lee, Y. (1990) "A Model for Academic Success: The School and Home Environment of East Asian Students," *Anthropology & Education Quarterly*, 21, 358–77.

Schneider, B., Swanson, C.B., and Riegle-Crumb, C. (1998) "Opportunities for Learning: Course Sequences and Positional Advantages," *Social Psychology of Education*, 2, 25–53.

Schnittker, J. (2004) "Education and the Changing Shape of the Income Gradient in Health," *Journal of Health and Social Behavior*, 45(3), 286–305.

Scott Act of 1902, 57th Congress, 32 stat. 176.

Secure America and Orderly Immigration Act of 2005, 109th Congress, S. 1033.

Sewell, W.H. and Hauser, R.M. (1972) "Causes and Consequences of Higher Education: Models of the Status Attainment Process," *American Journal of Agricultural Economics*, 54, 851–61.

References

Sewell, W.H., Haller, A.O., and Ohlendorf, G.W. (1970) "The Educational and Early Occupational Status Attainment Process: Replication and Revision," *American Sociological Review*, 35, 1014–27.

Sewell, W.H., Hauser, R.M., and Featherman, D.L. (eds) (1976) *Schooling and Achievement in American Society* (New York: Academic Press).

Shabaya, J. (2006) "English Language Acquisition and Some Pedagogical Issues Affecting the Adaptation of African Immigrant Children," in K. Konadu-Agyemang, B.K. Takyi, and J.A. Arthur (eds) *The New African Diaspora in North America* (New York: Lexington Books).

Shell, M. (1993) "Babel in America: The Politics of Language Diversity," *Critical Inquiry*, 20, 103–27.

Singer, A. (2004) *The Rise of New Immigrant Gateways* (Washington, DC: Brookings Institution).

Singh, K. and Hernandez-Gantes, V.M. (1996) "The Relation of English Language Proficiency to Educational Aspirations of Mexican-American Eighth Graders," *Journal of Early Adolescence*, 16, 253–73.

Smith, M.L. (2002) "Race, Nationality, and Reality: INS Administration of Racial Provisions in U.S. Immigration and Nationality Law Since 1898, Part 2," *Prologue Magazine*, 34(2) (Washington DC: National Archives).

Soltero, C.R. (2006) *Latinos and American Law: Landmark Supreme Court Cases* (Austin, TX: University of Texas Press).

Sowell, T. (1981) *Ethnic America: A History* (New York: Basic Books).

Soysal, Y.N. (1994) *Limits of Citizenship: Migrants and Postnational Membership in Europe* (Chicago, IL: University of Chicago Press).

Stainback, S.B. and Smith, J. (2004) "Inclusive Education: Historical Perspective," in R.A. Villa and J.S. Thousand (eds) *Creating an Inclusive School* (Alexandria, VA: Association for Supervision and Curriculum Development).

Stanton-Salazar, R.D. (2001) *Manufacturing Hope and Despair: The School and Kin Support Networks of U.S.-Mexican Youth* (New York: Teachers College Press).

Stanton-Salazar, R. and Dornbusch, S.M. (1995) "Social Capital and the Reproduction of Inequality: Information Networks among Mexican-Origin High School Students," *Sociology of Education*, 68, 16–35.

Steele, C. and Aronson, J. (1995) "Stereotype Threat and the Intellectual Test Performance of African Americans," *Journal of Personality and Social Psychology*, 69, 797–811.

Steelman, L.C. and Powell, B. (1989) "Acquiring Capital for College: The Constraints of Family Configuration," *American Sociological Review*, 54, 844–55.

Stevens, G. (1999) "A Century of U.S. Censuses and the Language Characteristics of Immigrants," *Demography*, 36, 387–97.

Stevens, M.L., Armstrong, E.A., and Arum, R. (2008) "Sieve, Incubator, Temple, Hub: Empirical and Theoretical Advances in the Sociology of Higher Education," *Annual Review of Sociology*, 34, 127–51.

References

Suárez-Orozco, C., Suárez-Orozco, M., and Todorova, I. (2008) *Learning a New Land: Immigrant Students in American Society* (Cambridge, MA: Harvard University Press).

Sue, S. and Okazaki, S. (1990) "Asian-American Educational Achievements: A Phenomenon in Search of an Explanation," *American Psychologist*, 45(8), 913–20.

Support Our Law Enforcement and Safe Neighborhoods Act, S.B. 1070, 49th Cong., 2010.

Takaki, R. (1993) *A Different Mirror: A History of Multicultural America* (Boston, MA: Little, Brown, and Company).

Teachman, J.D. (1987) "Family Background, Educational Resources, and Educational Attainment," *American Sociological Review*, 52, 548–57.

Terman, L. (1919) *The Intelligence of School Children. How Children Differ in Ability, the Use of Mental Tests in School Grading and the Proper Education of Exceptional Children* (Boston, MA: Houghton, Mifflin & Company).

Terman, L. (1975) *Genius and Stupidity* (New York: Arno Press).

Thomas, K.A.J. (2012) "Race and School Enrollment among the Children of African Immigrants in the United States," *International Migration Review*, 46(1), 37–60.

Tuan, M. (1998) *Forever Foreigners or Honorary Whites? The Asian Ethnic Experience Today* (Piscataway, NJ: Rutgers University Press).

Turney, K. and Kao, G. (2009) "Barriers to School Involvement: Are Immigrant Parents Disadvantaged?" *Journal of Educational Research*, 102, 257–71.

Tyack, D. (1974) *The One Best System: A History of American Urban Education* (Cambridge, MA: Harvard University Press).

Tyson, K., Darity, Jr., W., and Castellino, D. (2005) "It's Not 'A Black Thing': Understanding the Burden of Acting White and Other Dilemmas of High Achievement," *American Sociological Review*, 70(4), 582–605.

Ueda, R. (2007) "Immigration in Global Historical Perspective," in M.C. Waters and R. Ueda (eds) *New Americans: A Guide to Immigration Since 1965* (Cambridge, MA: Harvard University Press).

UNESCO Institute for Statistics (2011) "Education (All Levels) – Mexico," United Nations Educational, Scientific and Cultural Organization. Available at: http://stats.uis.unesco.org/unesco/TableViewer/document.aspx?ReportId=121&IF_Language=eng&BR_Country=4840 (accessed February 8, 2012).

United Nations (1967 [2007]) *Protocol Relating to the Status of Refugees.* Available at: http://www2.ohchr.org/english/law/pdf/protocolrefugees.pdf (accessed February 2, 2012).

Urban Institute (2011) "Urban Institute Children of Immigrants Data Tool. Data drawn from the 2008 American Community Survey," Urban Institute. Available at: http://datatool.urban.org/charts/datatool/pages.cfm (accessed June 24, 2011).

US Census Bureau (1949) Historical Statistics of the United States 1789–1945,

References

US Census Bureau. Available at: http://www2.census.gov/prod2/statcomp/ documents/HistoricalStatisticsoftheUnitedStates1789-1945.pdf (accessed June 20, 2011).

US Census Bureau (1999) *School Enrollment in the US – Social and Economic Characteristics of Students*, Current Population Reports, October.

US Census Bureau (2006) *Census Data Files*. Available at: http://www2.census. gov/census_2000/ (accessed February 9, 2012).

US Census Bureau (2008) American Community Survey, C05002 "Place of Birth by Citizenship Status" and "Year of Entry by Citizenship Status," US Census Bureau. Available at: http://factfinder.census.gov (accessed May 19, 2011).

US Census Bureau (2009) *American Community Survey Data Files, 2008*. Available at: http://www2.census.gov/acs2008_1yr/ (accessed February 9, 2012).

US Census Bureau (2010) "S0501: Selected Characteristics of the Native and Foreign-Born Populations, 2010 American Community Survey 1-Year Estimates," US Census Bureau. Available at: http://factfinder2.census.gov/ faces/tableservices/jsf/pages/productview.xhtml?pid=ACS_10_1YR_S0501& prodType=table (accessed January 23, 2012).

US Census Bureau (2011) "Poverty Definitions," US Census Bureau, Social, Economic, and Housing Statistics Division: Poverty. Available at: http://www. census.gov/hhes/www/poverty/methods/definitions.html (accessed February 8, 2012).

US Department of Homeland Security (2008) *Yearbook of Immigration Statistics*. Tables. Office of Immigration Statistics (Washington, DC: US Department of Homeland Security). Available at: http://www.dhs.gov/files/statistics/publica-tions/LPR07.shtm (accessed January 31, 2012).

USA PATRIOT Act of 2001, 107th Congress, 115 stat. 272.

Valdés, G. (2001) *Learning and Not Learning English: Latino Students in American Schools* (New York: Teachers College Press).

Valenzuela, A. (1999) *Subtractive Schooling: U.S.-Mexican Youth and the Politics of Caring* (Albany, NY: SUNY Press).

Vedder, R.K. and Gallaway, L.E. (1970) "Settlement Patterns of Canadian Emigrants to the United States, 1850–1960," *The Canadian Journal of Economics*, 3(3), 476–86.

Warner, W.L. and Srole, L. (1945) *The Social Systems of American Ethnic Groups* (New Haven, CT: Yale University Press).

Washington, G. (1938 [1783]) "Letter to the Members of the Volunteer Association and Other Inhabitants of the Kingdom of Ireland Who Have Lately Arrived in the City of New York, Dated December 2, 1783," in J.C. Fitzpatrick (ed.) *The Writings of George Washington, Volume XXVII* (Washington, DC: Government Printing Office). Available at: http://etext.virginia.edu/etcbin/ toccer-new2?id=WasFi27.xml&images=images/modeng&data=/texts/english/

References

modeng/parsed&tag=public&part=280&division=div1 (accessed January 31, 2012).

Waters, M.C. (1990) *Ethnic Options: Choosing Identities in America* (Berkeley, CA: University of California Press).

Waters, M.C. (1994) "Ethnic and Racial Identities of Second-Generation Black Immigrants in New York City," *International Migration Review*, 28(4), 795–820.

Waters, M.C. and Jiménez, T.R. (2005) "Assessing Immigrant Assimilation: New Empirical and Theoretical Challenges," *Annual Review of Sociology*, 31, 105–25.

Watkins, S.C. (ed.) (1994) *After Ellis Island: Newcomers and Natives in the 1910 Census* (New York: Russell Sage Foundation).

Wepman, D. (2008) *Immigration* (New York: Facts on File).

White, M.J. and Glick, J.E. (2009) *Achieving Anew: How New Immigrants Do in American Schools, Jobs, and Neighborhoods* (New York: Russell Sage Foundation).

White, T.D., Asfaw, B., DeGusta, D., Gilbert, H., Richards, G.D., Suwa, G., and Howell, F.C. (2003) "Pleistocene Homo Sapiens from Middle Awash, Ethiopia," *Nature*, 423, 742–7.

Wiley, T.G., Lee, J.S., and Rumberger, R.W. (eds) (2009) *The Education of Language Minority Immigrants in the United States* (Buffalo, NY: Multilingual Matters).

Wilson, W.J. (1980) *The Declining Significance of Race* (Chicago, IL: University of Chicago Press).

Wirth, L. (1928) *The Ghetto* (Chicago, IL: University of Chicago Press).

Wolf, M.K., Kim, J., Kao, J.C., and Rivera, N.M. (2009) *Examining the Effectiveness and Validity of Glossary and Read-aloud Accommodations for English Language Learners in a Math Assessment*, National Center for Research on Evaluation, Standards, and Student Testing (CRESST, Report 766) (Los Angeles, CA: University of California).

Wollenberg, C. (1978) *All Deliberate Speed: Segregation and Exclusion in California Schools, 1855–1975* (Berkeley, CA: University of California Press).

Woolley, J.T. and Peters, G. (2010a) "Ronald Reagan: Remarks at a Meeting with Asian and Pacific-American Leaders, February 23, 1984," *The American Presidency Project*, University of California Santa Barbara. Available at: http://www.presidency.ucsb.edu/ws/?pid=39556 (accessed February 9, 2012).

Woolley, J.T. and Peters, G. (2010b) "George Bush: Remarks on Signing the Asian/Pacific American Heritage Month Proclamation, May 7, 1990," *The American Presidency Project*, University of California Santa Barbara. Available at: http://www.presidency.ucsb.edu/ws/?pid=18458 (accessed February 9, 2012).

Woolley, J.T. and Peters, G. (2010c) "George Bush: Remarks on Signing the National Hispanic Heritage Month Proclamation and the Educational

References

Excellence for Hispanic Americans Executive Order, September 24, 1990," *The American Presidency Project*, University of California Santa Barbara. Available at: http://www.presidency.ucsb.edu/ws/?pid=18852 (accessed February 9, 2012).

World Bank (2011a) "Education in India," World Bank. Available at: http://go.worldbank.org/OSFVRGA240 (accessed February 8, 2012).

World Bank (2011b) "Education in Pakistan," World Bank. Available at: http://go.worldbank.org/GT0COFWSS0 (accessed February 8, 2012).

World Bank (2012) "Data – India," World Bank. Available at: http://data.worldbank.org/country/india (accessed February 8, 2012).

Zangwill, I. (1914) *The Melting Pot: Drama in Four Acts* (New York: Macmillan).

Zeng, Z. and Xie, Y. (2004) "Asian Americans' Earnings Disadvantage Reexamined: The Role of Place of Education," *American Journal of Sociology*, 109, 1075–108.

Zhang, W. and Ta, V.M. (2009) "Social Connections, Immigration-Related Factors, and Self-Rated Physical and Mental Health among Asian Americans," *Social Science & Medicine*, 68(12), 2104–12.

Zhou, M. (1992) *New York's Chinatown: The Socioeconomic Potential of an Urban Enclave* (Philadelphia, PA: Temple University Press).

Zhou, M. (1997) "Growing Up American: The Challenge Confronting Immigrant Children and Children of Immigrants," *Annual Review of Sociology*, 23, 63–95.

Zhou, M. and Bankston III, C.L. (1994) "Social Capital and the Adaptation of the Second Generation: the Case of Vietnamese Youth in New Orleans," *International Migration Review*, 28(4), 821–45.

Zhou, M. and Bankston III, C.L. (1998) *Growing Up American: How Vietnamese Children Adapt to Life in the United States* (New York: Russell Sage Foundation).

Zimmerman, W. and Tumlin, K. (1999) *Patchwork Policies: State Assistance for Immigrants under Welfare Reform*. Occasional Paper No. 24 (Washington, DC: Urban Institute). Available at: http://www.urban.org/UploadedPDF/occ24.pdf (accessed January 31, 2012).

Index

Abendi, J. 158
accommodation 29, 32, 162
Adams, James Truslow, *The Epic of America* 25
adolescence, school outcomes during 120–4
adult immigrants 76–105
  characteristics of 76–8
  compared with non-immigrants 77–8
  conditions of reception in the US 82
  differences by race and ethnicity 81–3
  educational attainment 4–5, 12–15, 76, 78, 86–96, 102–3, 107, 173
  educational selectivity 77–8
  selection from countries of origin 76–7, 81–2, 83
  and social capital 83, 84–6
African Americans 4, 6, 137
  and African-origin black immigrants 93, 110, 138
  college enrollment and completion 125
  educational levels 89
  and educational segregation 62
  and parent–school relationships 128
  and racial formations in the US 110
  settlement patterns 73
  and slavery 53–4, 112, 142
  in the US population 117–18
African-origin immigrants 135–7, 138
  and assimilation 33–4, 40, 41, 42, 43
  and the educational achievement gap 135–6
  educational attainment of adults 87, 90, 91, 92, 94–5, 96, 110
  educational outcomes 172
  educational selectivity 77
  English proficiency 141, 148, 149, 151, 154
  household incomes 91, 97, 98
  in the US population 117–18
age at immigration, and educational attainment 13
Ainsworth-Darnell, J. 43
Alba, Richard 36
American Community Survey 23–4
  data on English proficiency 151
  data on socio-economic indicators by ethnic group 87–95
American Dream, the 2, 15, 23, 25–6, 188
  and assimilation 25–6, 27
  and education for immigrant families 16–17
  and English proficiency 146
  and immigration policy 185

Index

Americanization, and education for
  immigrant groups 17–20
Anglo Americans, and the Protestant
  Ethic 45
Antiterrorism and Effective Death
  Penalty Act (1996) 70
AP (Advanced Placement) tests 140
Argentineans
  educational attainment 93, 107,
    110–11, 171, 173
  English proficiency 152
  household incomes and poverty
    levels 100, 102
Arizona, Support Our Law
  Enforcement and Safe
  Neighborhood Act (2010)
  10–12
Arthur, Chester 57
Asian Americans 4, 6, 7
  and assimilation 29, 36, 41, 42,
    43–5, 47, 74
  "bamboo ceiling" for 184–5
  children and bilingualism 164
  children in immigrant families 117,
    125, 137, 170–1
  Chinese immigrants 27
  and class 180–1
  college enrollment and completion
    125
  cram schools for children of
    immigrants 96
  and discrimination 39
  educational attainment of adults
    15, 87, 91–2, 93, 94–5, 102–3,
    107, 173
  educational selectivity 77
  ELL students and educational
    aspirations 161
  English proficiency 141, 143, 147,
    149, 150, 152, 154, 166
  ethnic classification of 102
  generational status of 10, 11, 12
  history of 64, 65, 66, 67
  household incomes and poverty
    rates 88, 97, 97–100, 101,
    174
  household size 101
  and immigration policies 58–60

as the "model minority" 43–5,
    103, 130–3, 138, 175
  national origin and ethnic
    differences 103–4
  national-origin groups 107–8
  and parent–school relationships
    128, 129
  residential concentration 167–8
  schooling and ethnic identities 20
  schooling outcomes during
    adolescence 122
  settlement patterns 73–4
  socio-economic indicators among
    87, 88
  stereotypes of 83
  and the "yellow peril" 74
  see also Indian Americans; South
    Asian immigrants
Asian languages 144
Asiatic Barred Zone (Immigration Act
    1917) 59–60, 61
assimilation 2–5, 25–50, 74–5,
    176–79
  and the American Dream 2, 25–6,
    27
  and Asian Americans 29, 36, 41,
    42, 43–5, 47, 74
  Chicago School and traditional
    theories of 28–37, 176
  and children in immigrant families
    105
  dimensions of 35
  and educational attainment 21, 23,
    26, 27, 39
  and English proficiency 5, 26, 141,
    146, 163, 168–69
  and the history of immigration 52,
    61, 62–3
  and the "immigrant paradox" 120
  and immigration policies 61–3
  and marriage 3, 34, 35–6, 38, 176
  and the "melting pot" 26–7, 32–3,
    37
  multiculturalism and the salad bowl
    analogy 37–8
  power and cultural ecology 38–45
  segmented 45, 46–50, 79–80, 86,
    163, 169, 177, 178–79

Index

assimilation *(cont.)*
  views on "unassimilable"
    immigrants 3–4, 74
asylum-seekers 1, 68, 70
Austrian immigrants 58

"bamboo ceiling" and Asian
  Americans 184–5
Bangladeshi households
  incomes and poverty rates 98, 100
Bankston, C.L. 48, 126, 131, 141
Bates, L. 119
Bayless, Rick 30
Bell, Alexander Graham 4
bilingualism 24, 141
  benefits of 163–6
black ethnic groups
  college enrollment and completion
    125
  educational attainment 21, 95–6,
    121–2
  generational status of 10, 11, 12
  immigrant families 170, 171
  low expectations of 175
  race and class 111–13
  reception in the US 82
  and segmented assimilation 47–8
  see also African Americans;
    African-origin immigrants
Bolivians
  educational attainment of adults
    93–4, 107, 173
  English proficiency 152, 153
  household incomes 100, 101
border security 70, 71, 72
Brazilians and English proficiency
  153
British immigrants 56–7, 64, 143
Buffet, Warren 25
Burgess, Ernest
  theories of assimilation 28–32, 33
Bush, George 130–1, 133–4

California 41
  Alien Land Law (1913) 59
  bilingual education in 165–6
  Proposition 187 69–70, 186
  Proposition 227 165–6

residential concentration and
    educational attainment 168
  settlement patterns in 73–4
Cambodians 45
  educational attainment of adults
    91, 93
  English proficiency 154
  household incomes and poverty
    levels 98, 99–100
  and racial formations in the US
    111
Canadians 27, 58, 64, 92, 143
Cape Verdeans 95, 151, 154
Caplan, N. 131
Caribbean immigrants 64, 96
Carnegie, Andrew 25
caste systems 32
Catholic Irish immigrants 56
Census data
  on English proficiency 149–54
  and immigration policies 63
  languages spoken in the US 143–4
  racial composition of the US
    population 116–17
Chicago School of Sociology
  assimilation theories 28–37, 85
children
  native-born
    educational attainments of 13,
      121
    generational status of by race/
      ethnicity 10, 12
  racial and ethnic diversity,
    immigrant and native youths
    9–12
  schooling and the socialization of
    17–20
children in immigrant families
    106–39, 170–6, 180–2
  age of arrival in the US 9
  and the American Dream 2
  assimilation of 105
  benefits of education for 16–17
  college enrollment and completion
    124–7
  college graduates 122–4
  decimal generations 8–9
  early childhood outcomes 118–20

early school leavers 62
educational attainments of 12–13
educational outcomes 104–5,
    106–39, 140, 170–2, 178
    and gender 126–7
educational segregation of 62
future research on 182–4
growth of the school-aged
    population 115–18
illegal immigrants 186–7
immigrant status of 7–9
Latino students and educational
    outcomes 133–5
Limited English Proficient (LEP)
    75
and model minorities 130–3
and parents' educational attainment
    80, 86–7, 106–7
parents of 127–29, 140
Punjabi Sikh children 37–8
and race versus class 111–15
right to public education 69
schooling outcomes during
    adolescence 120–4
and segmented assimilation 179
services to provide for 187
and social capital 84, 104–5
and socioeconomic status 106–7,
    109–10
variations in educational outcomes
    180
see also ELL (English Language
    Learners); young people
Chileans
educational attainment of adults
    93–4, 107
English proficiency 152, 153
household incomes and poverty
    levels 100, 102
China 129
Asian-style cram schools 96
Chinese Americans 4, 7
and assimilation 27, 36, 42
educational attainment of adults
    91, 107
educational outcomes 132
educational success of young people
    115

history of immigration 56, 57–8,
    59, 172
and national-origin groups 108
young children in immigrant
    families 120
Chinese speakers 144
Choy, M.H. 131
citizenship
and Asian immigrants 59, 65
and illegal immigrants 72, 186–7
Civil Rights Act (1964) 69
class
and assimilation 27
and children in immigrant families
    137–8, 180–1
and cultural values 181
and educational attainment 113
and educational inequalities 18
and immigrant assimilation 179
and income 113
and occupational prestige 114
and race 111–15
and wealth 113–14
see also socioeconomic status
Clinton, Bill 25
cognitive abilities, and bilingualism
    163–4, 165
Coleman, James 84
collective identities of voluntary and
    involuntary minorities 42
college education
and assimilation 49, 177
educational aspirations and English
    proficiency 156, 160–2
enrollment and completion 124–7,
    137
college graduates
by ethnic group 88, 89–91, 93, 94,
    95, 104
and ELL students 162, 163
and gender 126
young people in immigrant families
    122–4
Colombians
English proficiency 152, 153
household incomes and poverty
    levels 100
colonialism, and cultural ecology 39

color, and segmented assimilation
47–8
see also race
"common school" idea 61–2
Contact Hypothesis of assimilation
(Park and Burgess) 28–32
accommodation stage 29, 32, 162
assimilation stage 28, 32–7
competition stage 29, 31
contact stage 29, 30–1
Coppola, Francis Ford 76
Costa Ricans
English proficiency 152
incomes and poverty levels 100
countries of origin
adult immigrants and selection from
76–7, 81–3
persons remaining in
compared with immigrants 77,
182
educational attainment 81, 82
return to after immigration 49–50
see also national origins
criminal behavior, exclusion of groups
by 52, 76
criminal immigrants, and terrorism
70, 71
criminal penalties for undocumented
aliens 72
Cubans 65–6
college attendance 125
educational attainment 94, 171
English proficiency 152
household incomes and poverty
levels 100
household size 101
cultural deficit models 129
cultural deprivation models 40
cultural ecology and power 38–45
cultural hybridization 37–8
cultural identity
and assimilation 26–7
and schooling in the US 20
cultural values, and children in
immigrant families 181,
183–4
culture of poverty 40, 112, 134
Czechoslovakian immigrants 53

death rates, and educational
attainment 16
Deaux, K. 136
decimal generations 8–9
Department of Homeland Security
(DHS) 71
DHS (Department of Homeland
Security) 71
discrimination 21, 23
and children in immigrant families
184
gender and educational outcomes
126
and immigrant assimilation 35,
39–40
and Japanese Americans 44, 130
race and class 112–13
and racial formations in the US
110
documented immigrants, and
educational attainment 21–2
Dominican Republic 96, 100, 101
English proficiency 151, 152
gender and educational outcomes
126–7
Downey, D. 43
DREAM Act 2009 (Development,
Relief and Education for Alien
Minors Act 2009) 72, 75, 173
Durbin, Dick 185–6
Dutch immigrants 142

Early Childhood Longitudinal Study–
Kindergarten Cohort (ECLS-K)
119–20
earnings, benefits of education on 16
Eastern European immigrants
Americanization and the school
system 18
educational attainment 15
and immigration history 61–3, 75
settlement patterns 72–3
Ecuadoreans
English proficiency 152, 153
household incomes and poverty
levels 100
educational achievement 2–3, 24
and bilingualism 165–6

Index

of children in immigrant families
118–29, 170–2, 178
and English proficiency 156–60
and immigrants to the US 4–5
educational aspirations
and English proficiency 156, 160–2
educational attainment 2–3, 23
adult immigrants 4–5, 12–15, 76,
78, 86–96, 102–3, 107, 173
and assimilation 21, 23, 26, 27,
39
benefits of 16–17
and ELL students 156, 162–3
of foreign-born versus native-born
adults 78
immigrant differences by race and
ethnicity 81
and race 14, 21, 24, 78, 87–96
schooling outcomes during
adolescence 120–4
and social capital 84–6
and socioeconomic status 14–15,
16–17, 21, 23–4, 86–96,
109–11, 174–5
young children in immigrant
families 118–20
educational segregation
of English Language Learning
students 159–60
of immigrant children 62
Einstein, Albert 4
ELL (English Language Learners)
and educational achievement
156–60, 183
and educational aspirations 156,
160–2
and educational attainment 156,
162–3
and residential concentration
167
El Salvador see Salvadorans
employment opportunities
and assimilation 31, 32, 48, 178
and educational attainment of
immigrants 15
for immigrant families 173–4
and immigration history 57, 58,
64, 67, 75

English proficiency 1, 3, 182
and assimilation 5, 26, 141, 146,
163, 168–69
benefits of 140–1
and bilingualism 24, 141, 163–6
children in immigrant families 2, 9,
75, 121, 138
and generational status of
immigrants 146–7
languages spoken at home 149–54
language use and immigrants
141–3
residential concentration and
language acquisition 166–69
and school outcomes 155–63
and selective acculturation 148–49
Standard and vernacular English
142
in the US population 149–54
see also ELL (English Language
Learners)
English as a Second Language (ESL)
students 156
equal opportunities 18, 23
ESL (English as a Second Language)
156, 159
Ethiopians and language 151
ethnicity
and children in immigrant families
137–8, 138–39
classification of immigrants by 7
and cultural ecology 39
and educational achievement 24
and educational attainment 14, 24,
78, 87–96, 170–2
and educational inequalities 18
ethnic enclaves 74
and household income 96–102,
174
and immigrant assimilation 3, 5,
26–7, 29, 36, 40–5
Contact Hypothesis of 29, 33–4
dimensions of 35
and immigrant characteristics 77
immigrant and native youths
9–12
and immigration history 52, 53,
53–4, 55

ethnicity (*cont.*)
  national origins and ethnic groups
    92, 102–5, 107–8
  and race 5–6, 108–09
  schooling and ethnic identities 20
  and social capital 85–6
  and variations in educational
    outcomes 180
  see also children in immigrant
    families; race
ethnographic research 183–4
European immigrants 6
  assimilation of 41
  history of 53–6, 58, 60–2
expectations, and social capital 84,
    85–6

family reunification 66, 67, 75
Federalist Papers 145
Feliciano, C. 77, 182
female migrants 57, 67
Fermi, Enrico 4
fertility rates, and assimilation 31
Filipino immigrants 67
  assimilation of 41
  household incomes and poverty
    levels 98–9
films
  The Godfather: Part II 76
  My Family (Mi Familia) 79–80,
    104, 106–7
  The Namesake 78–79, 80, 103–4,
    106–7
first-generation immigrants 4, 7
  black Africans 135, 136
  children of 8, 118
  educational attainment of adults
    80, 88–90, 92–3, 94, 107
  English proficiency 146–7, 148,
    154–5
  Hispanics 88, 89, 90, 151–2,
    155
  income levels 101–2
  race/ethnicity of children 10, 11,
    12
  in the US population 115–17
Fix, M. 21
Fordham, S. 42

foreign-born immigrants *see* first-
    generation immigrants
fourth-generation immigrants 8,
    148–49
Franklin, Benjamin 3, 145
French immigrants 35, 142
French speakers in the US 144, 145
Frey, William 116–17
Fujimori, Alberto 92

Gans, Herbert, *The Urban Villagers:
    Groups and Class in the Life of
    Italian-Americans* 34
Gates, Bill 25
Gatley, Cathy 168
gender 3
  and educational outcomes 126–7,
    183
  and immigrant assimilation 5
generational status of immigrants
    7–8, 118
  and assimilation 35
  and English proficiency 146–7
  race/ethnicity of children 10–12
German immigrants 53, 56–7, 64,
    142
German language in the US 144,
    145–6
Ghanaians and language 151, 154
Gibson, Margaret 37–8
Glick, J.E. 119
Golash-Boza, T. 165
Gordon, Milton, *Assimilation in
    American Life* 35, 36
Guadalupe Hidalgo, Treaty of (1848)
    10, 41, 145
Guatemalans
  educational attainment 93–4, 94,
    171
  English proficiency 151, 152, 155
  household incomes and poverty
    levels 100
  household size 101
guest worker program 72

Hagedorn, Jessica 133
Haitians 126–7, 135
Hao, L. 165

Index

Harris, A.L. 43
Hart-Cellar Act (1965) 20, 47, 66–7
Hatch, Orrin 185
Hawaii 73
health benefits of education 16
Highman, J. 62
high school graduates
  by ethnic group 88, 89, 90, 92, 93,
    94, 95, 96
  and college graduates 123–4
  ELL students 162–3
Hispanics
  and assimilation 36–7, 47, 178–79
  children in immigrant families 117,
    125, 137, 170, 171
  college enrollment and completion
    125
  educational attainment of adults
    21, 87, 89, 90–1, 93–5, 107,
    173
  English Language Learning (ELL)
    students 159–60, 161, 163
  English proficiency 141, 143,
    147–8, 149, 150–1, 152–3,
    155, 166, 171
  family values and educational
    aspirations 133–5
  generational status of 10–12
  household incomes and poverty
    rates 88, 89, 90, 97, 98, 99,
    100–2, 174
  in My Family (Mi Familia) 79–80,
    104
  national-origin groups 107
  and parent–school relationships
    128, 129
  and racial formations in the US
    110–11
  schooling outcomes 120, 121, 122,
    124, 175
  settlement patterns 73
  socio-economic indicators among
    87, 88–90, 93–4
  stereotypes of 83, 175
  as "unassimilable" 75
  see also Mexicans
history of immigration (US) 23,
  51–76, 172

beginnings of mass migration
  (1820s–1880s) 55–8
first humans 51
first "new immigrants"
  (1890–1920s) 58–64
"laissez-faire" (pre-1920)
  immigration policies 53–5
"new new immigrants"
  (1930–1964) 64–6
post-1965 8, 20, 66–71
settlement patterns 73–4
terrorism and September 11, 2001
  70, 71–3
Hmong 172
educational attainment of adults
  91, 104
educational outcomes 132, 171,
  172
English proficiency 151
ethnic classification of 102
gender and educational outcomes
  127
household incomes and poverty 98,
  99
household size 101
settlement patterns 73
Hondurans
educational achievement 94
and English proficiency 151, 152,
  155
household incomes 102
households
incomes and ethnic groups 87,
  88–90, 96–102
size of 88, 89, 90–1, 101–2
and young children in immigrant
  families 119–20
human capital of immigrants 49, 67,
  173–4, 174–5
Hungarian immigrants 58, 65
"hyphenated identities" of immigrants
  3

illegal immigration see undocumented
  immigrants
Illegal Immigration Reform and
  Immigrant Responsibility Act
  (IIRIRA) 70

Index

immigrant optimism 125
the immigrant paradox 120
immigrant stories
  Hyunsuk (South Korea) 1, 22
  Juanjo (Guatemala) 1, 22
  see also films
immigration policies 172–3, 174
  (1965–2000) 66–71
  Asian immigrants 58–60
  and assimilation 61–3
  eligibility for naturalization 65
  future debates about 185–9
  and immigrant differences by race
    and ethnicity 81
  "laissez-faire" (pre-1920) 53–5
  quota systems 63, 65, 66
  restrictive 57–8, 58–64, 76
  Southern and Eastern European
    immigrants 61
income
  and class 113
  household incomes and ethnic
    group 87–9, 90–1, 96–102,
    174
  inequalities 78
India 129
  educational attainment of adults in
    81, 82
Indian Americans
  educational attainment of adults
    80, 81, 82, 83, 91, 93,
    103–4
  English proficiency 154
  ethnic classification of 102
  household income and poverty
    levels 99, 100
  in *The Namesake* 78–79, 80,
    103–4, 106–7
information channels, and social
  capital 84–5
insane people, restrictions on
  immigration of 57, 60
INS (Immigration and Naturalization
  Services) 58, 71
institutional racism 112
internet
  and immigrant connections to home
    countries 50

involuntary immigrants, assimilation
  of 40–3
IRCA (1986 Immigration Reform and
  Control Act) 68–9
Irish Americans 4
  and assimilation 36
  education and Americanization
    18
  history of immigration 53, 56
  settlement patterns 72–3
Italian Americans 4, 31, 34
  history of immigration 53, 58, 64
  settlement patterns 72–3

Japan
  Asian-style cram schools 96
Japanese Americans 4, 18
  and American citizenship 58–9
  and assimilation 29, 33–4, 44
  English proficiency 152
  household incomes and poverty
    levels 99, 100
  language spoken at home 149–51
  as model minorities 130
Jay, John 145
Jews 4
job opportunities *see* employment
  opportunities

Kao, G. 120–1
Katz, M.B. 18, 19
Keller, U. 125
Kennedy, John F. 65
Kent, M.M. 117–18
Kissinger, Henry 4
Korean immigrants 99, 172
Korean War 36

labor market *see* employment
  opportunities
Lahiri, Jhumpa 78
  The Namesake 78–79, 80
"laissez-faire" (pre-1920) immigration
  policies 53–5
Lambert, W.E. 164
language and educational success
  140–69, 181–2
  bilingualism 24, 141, 142

"English Only" policies in the US
146
English proficiency of new
immigrants 140
immigrants and English Language
Learners 141–3
the language debate in the US
143–49
languages spoken at home 140,
149–55
non-English speakers in the US
142–3
residential concentration and
language acquisition 166–9
see also English proficiency
Language Minorities (LM) 156
Laotians 45
educational attainment of adults
91, 93
gender and educational outcomes
127
household incomes and poverty 98,
99
Lareau, Annette 128
Latin American immigrants 6, 12
and assimilation 41, 47
educational attainment 15
history of 63–4, 64–5
see also Hispanics; Mexicans
Lazarus, Emma, "The New Colossus"
51–2
Lee, Stacey 20, 127, 132–3
Lee, Y. 131
legislation (US) 23
1820 Act 53
anti-terrorist 70–1
and bilingual education 165–6
California Alien Land Law (1913)
59
California Proposition 187 70, 186
California Proposition 227 165–6
Chinese Exclusion Act (1882) 57–8
Civil Rights Act (1964) 69
Comprehensive Enforcement and
Immigration Reform Act
(2005) 71–2
Comprehensive Immigration
Reform Act (2007) 71

DREAM Act (2009) 72, 75, 173,
185–6
Emergency Quota Act (1921) 63
Geary Act (1892) 58
Gentlemen's Agreement (1907)
59
Hart-Cellar Act (1965) 20, 47,
66–7
Homeland Security Act (2002) 71
Immigration Act (1882) 57
Immigration Act (1893) 57
Immigration Act (1903) 58–9
Immigration Act (1917) 59–60,
61
Immigration Act (1924) 63
Immigration Reform and Control
Act (1986) 68–9
McCarran Walter Act (1952
Immigration and Nationality
Act) 65, 66
Magnuson Act (1943) 58
Naturalization Act (1790) 55
Page Act (1875) 57
PATRIOT Act (2001) 71
Refugee Act (1980) 66, 68
Scott Act (1902) 58
Secure America and Orderly
Immigration Act (2005) 71–2
LEP (Limited English Proficient) 75,
156
Lewis, Oscar 40, 112, 134
Liberia 155
Limited English Proficient (LEP)
children 75, 156
literacy tests for new immigrants
61
LM (Language Minorities) 156
location, and segmented assimilation
47, 48
longitudinal research 184
Lopez, Nancy 126, 127
Louisiana Purchase (1803) 145

majority groups, power and status
of 39
Mann, Horace 61
manufacturing employment, and
immigrant assimilation 48

Index

marriage
  and educational attainment 16
  and immigrant assimilation 3, 34,
    35–6, 38, 176
Marshall, Thurgood 25–6
Massey, D.S. 125
Mathematics
  and English proficiency 156–7,
    159
  and immigrant students 119, 120,
    122, 140
meritocracy 18, 23
Mexican–American War 10, 145
Mexican Revolution 63–4
Mexicans 4, 6
  and assimilation 36–7, 39, 41, 49
  and the *Bracero Program* 65
  and the culture of poverty 40
  educational attainment 14, 80, 81,
    83, 94, 104, 107, 171
  educational selectivity 77
  English proficiency 143, 152, 155,
    167
  family values and educational
    outcomes 134, 135
  generational status of 10–12
  history of 63–4, 64–5, 66, 67
  household incomes and poverty
    levels 100, 101
  in *My Family (Mi Familia)* 79–80
  settlement patterns 73
  undocumented 69
middle class, and immigrant
    assimilation 179
Miles van der Rohe, Ludwig 4
minority groups, assimilation of 39,
    40–1
mobility ladders, absence of 47, 48
model minorities 43–5, 103, 130–3,
    138, 175
Muir, John 4
multiculturalism 37–8
multilingualism in the US 144–6

NAEP (National Assessment of
    Educational Progress)
  and English proficiency 156–8
  ethnicity and reading scores 122

Nair, Mira 78
The Namesake (film and novel)
    78–79, 80, 103–4, 106–7
National Center on Education Studies
  data on early childhood
    educational outcomes 118–19
National Longitudinal Study of
    Adolescent Health 125
national origins
  and children in immigrant families
    137–8
  and educational achievement 24
  and educational attainment 24, 78,
    80, 86–96, 102–3, 107
  and educational backgrounds 83
  and ethnic groups 92, 102–5,
    107–8
  exclusion of groups by 52, 58–60,
    76
  and immigrant assimilation 3, 5
  immigrant differences by 81
  of post-1965 immigrants 67
  quota systems based on 65, 66
Native Americans
  ancestors of 51
  and assimilation 41
  and language use 142
native-born US residents
  children
    educational attainments of 13,
      121
    generational status of by race/
      ethnicity 10, 12
  and educational outcomes of
    immigrants 140
  and immigrant assimilation 27,
    29–30, 31, 34–5, 46, 48, 75
  and Indian Americans 80
  and racial/ethnic background of
    immigrants 82
NCES (National Center for
    Educational Statistics)
  and ELL students 162
neighborhoods
  and assimilation 177
  and educational outcomes of
    immigrant families 183
  race and class 114

network closure 85
"new immigrants" (1890–1920s)
58–64
"new new immigrants" (1930–1964)
64–6
Nicaraguans
English proficiency 152
incomes and poverty levels 100
Nigerian adults
educational attainment 95
and racial formations in the US
110, 111
Noguchi, Hideyo 4
Noguera, P.A. 178–79, 187

obligations, and social capital 84,
85–6
occupational prestige, and class
114
Office of Immigration 58
Ogbu, John 40–3, 121
Okazaki, Sumie 42
Omi, Michael 108
open door policy on immigration
54–5
opponents of immigration 4

Pacific Americans 44–5
Pakistan 81
Pakistani households
incomes and poverty rates 100
Panamanians
English proficiency 152, 155
household incomes and poverty
levels 100
parents in immigrant families
127–29, 140
and assimilation 178
and bilingualism 164–5
educational attainment 80, 86–7,
106–7
and residential concentration 168
Park, Robert
and Burgess, Ernest, theories of
assimilation 28–32, 35
"Human Migration and the
Marginal Man" 33–4
Passel, J. 21

passenger lists, and pre-1820
immigrants 53–4
PATRIOT Act (2001) 71
Peal, E. 164
Pei, I.M. 4
Personal Responsibility and Work
Opportunity Reconciliation
Act (PRWORA) (1996) 70
Peruvians
English proficiency 152, 153
household incomes and poverty
levels 100
Petersen, William 44, 130
Polish immigrants 4
political beliefs, exclusion of groups
by 52, 58, 76
Pong, S.-L. 165
population growth 69
Portes, Alejandro 46, 47, 48
positive selection (of immigrants to
the US)
and educational attainment 82
poverty 78
culture of 40, 112, 134
and downward mobility 177
and English Language Learning
students 159
and immigration history 57
levels of by ethnic group 87, 88,
89, 90–1, 96, 97–102, 174
US Census Bureau definitions of
97
power relations
and cultural ecology 38–45
race and ethnicity 5–6, 108–09
prostitutes, restrictions on
immigration of 57, 60
Protestant Ethic 45
public services and immigration 4
Puerto Ricans 40, 77, 102
English proficiency 151, 152
Punjabi Sikh children
and assimilation 37–8
"push" and "pull" factors in the
history of immigration 57

qualitative studies on race and class
114–15

Index

race
  and assimilation 3, 5, 27, 29–30,
    40–3, 47–8
  and children in immigrant families
    137–8, 138–39
  and class 111–15
  classification of immigrants by 7
  and cultural ecology 39
  and educational achievement 24
  and educational attainment 14, 21,
    24, 78, 87–96
  and educational inequalities 18
  and ethnicity 5–6, 108–09
  exclusion of groups by 52, 76
  and household income 96–102
  and immigrant characteristics 77
  immigrant differences by 81–3,
    174–5, 178
  and immigration history 52, 53,
    55, 57–60, 65
  importance of 176, 181
  and national origin 102–5
  racial diversity in immigrant and
    native youths 9–12
  racial formations in the US
    108–11, 138
  racial segregation laws 25–6
  and schooling outcomes in
    adolescence 120–4
  see also ethnicity
Reading, and English proficiency
  156–7
Reagan, Ronald 44–5, 130
refugees 65–6, 68, 75, 131, 174,
  181
religion, and immigration history 56
residential concentration, and
  language acquisition 166–69
Rockefeller, John D. 25
Roosevelt, Theodore 3, 146
Rumbaut, R.G. 8
rural areas, immigrants in 74, 177
Russian immigrants 53, 58

St John de Crevecoeur, J. Hector,
  Letters from an American
  Farmer 33
salad bowl analogy 37–8

Salvadorans
  educational attainment 94, 171
  English proficiency 151, 152, 155
  household incomes and poverty
    levels 100, 102
Sanchez, José 79
SAT tests 2, 84, 122
Schneider, B. 131
schooling
  adult immigrants 13–14
  Americanization and public schools
    17–20
  Asian-style cram schools 96
  "common school" idea 61–2
  and the "decimal" generations 9
  educational segregation 62, 159–60
  English proficiency and school
    outcomes 155–63
  parent–school relationships and
    immigrant families 127–29
  research on 183
  school outcomes for children in
    immigrant families 118–24
  and socioeconomic success 16–17
  subtractive schooling 135
  track placements 158–59
  and undocumented immigrants 70,
    75, 186–7
  see also educational achievement;
    educational attainment
Science
  and English proficiency 156–7,
    158, 159
  and immigrant students 140
second-generation immigrants 7
  and assimilation 36, 49
  black Africans 135, 136
  children of 8, 118
  English proficiency 147, 154, 167
  race/ethnicity of children 10, 11,
    12
segmented assimilation 45, 46–50,
  79–80, 86, 163, 169, 177,
  178–79
selective acculturation, and English
  proficiency 148–49
self-made men 25
Shell, Marc 144–5

slave systems 32
social capital 83, 84–6, 104, 177
  and English proficiency 141, 169
  and ethnic enclaves 74
  and social norms 84, 85
social services
  and children in immigrant families
    187
  and undocumented immigrants
    69–70, 186
socioeconomic mobility 173
  and assimilation 40, 42–3, 46–9,
    176, 178
  and children in immigrant families
    184
  and education 2, 20, 23
  and immigration history 53
  race and class 112
  and social capital 83, 84–6
socioeconomic status
  of Asian Americans 45
  and children in immigrant families
    106–7, 109–10
  differences between Latinos and
    whites 134
  and educational attainment 14–15,
    16–17, 21, 23–4, 86–96,
    109–11, 174–5
  household incomes 87, 87–9, 90–1,
    96–102
  of immigrant adults 21, 86–102
  and immigration history 52
  of Mexican-origin communities 64
  and model minorities 131
  and parent–school relationships
    128
  of post-1965 immigrants 67
  race and national origin 102–5
  South Asian immigrants 79
Somalis 95
South Africa 39, 155
South Asian immigrants
  educational attainment 81
  and immigration history 60, 172
  as model minorities 131
  in *The Namesake* 78–79, 80
  and social capital 85
  socioeconomic status 79

Southern European immigrants 60–3,
    75
Sowell, Thomas 134
Spanish immigrants 7, 142
  see also Hispanics
Spanish speakers 143, 144,
    152
Srole, Leo *see* Warner, William Lloyd
    and Srole, Leo
Stanton-Salazar, Ricardo 49
Steele, Claude 175
suburban communities, immigrants in
    74, 82
Sue, Stanley 42
Supreme Court of the US
  and educational segregation 62
  on the education of immigrant
    children 69
Swedish immigrants 142

terrorism and September 11, 2001
    70–2
Thai households
  incomes and poverty rates 98,
    100
third generation immigrants 7–8
  Asian Americans 171
  and assimilation 35, 36
  English proficiency 147, 154
  race/ethnicity of children 10, 11,
    12
Thomas, K.A.J. 137
Tienda, M. 120–1
Tillman, K.H. 125
Truman, Harry S. 65
Tuan, Mia 132
Tyack, D. 61–2
Tyson, K. 43

"undeserving" immigrants
  and immigration policies 185
  media and cultural portrayal of
    181
undocumented immigrants 4, 75,
    186–7
  and citizenship 72, 186–7
  and education 69–70, 71, 75
  post-1965 68–9, 69–70

Index

unemployment
  and educational attainment
    16
  and immigration history 57,
    62
  and opponents of immigration 4
United Nations Protocol Relating to
  the Status of Refugees 68
United States
  English and the language debate
    143–49
  English proficiency in the US
    population 149–54
  immigration and citizenship laws
    3, 5
  as the "land of opportunity" 2, 3,
    4, 25
  racial and ethnic composition of the
    US population 115–17
  racial formations 108–11,
    138
  see also history of immigration
    (US); immigration policies;
    legislation (US)
urban areas
  immigrant settlements in 73–4
USCIS (US Citizenship and
  Immigration Service) 58

Valenzuela, Angela 20, 134–5
Vanderbilt, Cornelius 25
Venezuelans
  educational attainment of adults
    93
  English proficiency 152, 153
  household incomes 102
Vietnamese immigrants 172
  and assimilation 45, 48
  children 126–7, 131
  educational attainment of adults
    91
  English proficiency 154
  household incomes and poverty
    levels 99
  settlement patterns 73
  and social capital 85–6
voluntary immigrants
  assimilation of 40–3

Wallace, Mike 44, 130
Warner, William Lloyd and Srole,
  Leo, The Social Systems of
  American Ethnic Groups
  34
Washington, George 54–5
Waters, Mary 36
  Ethnic Options 147
wealth, measurement of 113–14
West Coast settlements, Asian
  immigrants in 73–4
West Indians 126–7, 136
white immigrants
  Africans 6, 137
  and assimilation 27, 41
  and class 180–1
  educational outcomes 170
  and ethnicity 36
  generational status of 10, 11, 12
  pre-1820 53, 54, 55
  reception in the US 82
white population of the USA 116
Whitmore, J.K. 131
Wilson, William Julius, The Declining
  Significance of Race 112
Winant, Howard 108
Wirth, Louis, The Ghetto 34
Wisconsin School studies of
  socioeconomic status 109–10
women migrants 57, 67
World Trade Center
  bombing (1993) 70
  terrorist attacks (2001) 70–1
World War I 36
  and languages in the US 145,
    146
World War II 36
  and Japanese Americans 44
  and Mexican immigrants 64–5
  and refugees 68

xenophobia, and new immigrants 61,
  62

young people
  and assimilation 48, 49
  college enrollment and completion
    124–7

immigrant status of 7–9
language-minority 125
see also children in immigrant
    families

Zangwill, Israel, *The Melting Pot*
    32–3
Zhou, Min 46, 47, 48, 126, 131,
    141